however long the night

ALSO BY AIMEE MOLLOY

*Then They Came for Me: A Family's Story of Love,
Captivity, and Survival* with Maziar Bahari

Jantsen's Gift: A True Story of Grief, Rescue, and Grace with Pam Cope

For God and Country: Faith and Patriotism Under Fire with James Yee

however long the night

MOLLY MELCHING'S JOURNEY TO HELP MILLIONS OF

AFRICAN WOMEN AND GIRLS TRIUMPH

AIMEE MOLLOY

HarperOne
An Imprint of HarperCollins*Publishers*

HarperOne

The names and identifying details of certain individuals have been changed to protect their privacy.

Grateful acknowledgment is given to the following photographers for the use of their work in this publication's photo insert: © Jennie Balde: p. 9 *(top)*; © Myriam Dems: p. 9 *(bottom)*; © Diane Gillespie: p. 3 *(top)*; © Jim Greenbaum: pp. 4, 6 *(middle and bottom)*, 7, 11 *(top)*, 12, 15 *(top)*; © Jessica Brandi Lifland: p. 14 *(bottom)*; © Niina Pitkänen: p. 8 *(bottom)*; © Sydney Skov: p. 8 *(top)*; © Tostan: pp. 10 *(bottom)*, 11 *(bottom)*, 14 *(top)*, 15 *(bottom)*, 16; courtesy of Molly Melching: pp. 1, 2, 3 *(bottom)*, 5, 10 *(top)*, 13; courtesy of the White House: p. 6 *(top)*

HarperCollins website: http://www.harpercollins.com

HarperCollins®, ®, and HarperOne™ are trademarks of HarperCollins Publishers

FIRST EDITION

Designed by Level C

Library of Congress Cataloging-in-Publication Data
Molloy, Aimee.
However long the night: Molly Melching's journey to help millions of African women and girls triumph / Aimee Molloy. — First Edition.
pages cm
ISBN 978–0–06–226575–3 (intl)
1. Female circumcision—Africa—Prevention. 2. Human rights—Africa.
3. Human rights workers—Africa. 4. Tostan (Organization : Senegal)
5. Non-governmental organizations—Africa. 6. Community education—Africa.
7. Melching, Molly. I. Title.
GN645.M578 2013
392.1096—dc23 2012048654

13 14 15 16 17 RRD(H) 10 9 8 7 6 5 4 3 2 1

For Noelle

CONTENTS

BOOK TWO

AUTHOR'S NOTE

I first met Molly Melching in Philadelphia in the summer of 2011. She was in town for a week to attend a conference at the University of Pennsylvania, and we'd planned to have dinner to discuss her work with Tostan, the NGO she'd started in Senegal, West Africa, where she'd been living since 1974. By this time, Molly's work had received considerable recognition. *Forbes* magazine had recently named her one of the most powerful women in the field of women's rights, and *Newsweek* had included her as one of the "150 Women Who Shake the World." A year earlier, in 2010, she was presented with one of the prestigious Skoll Awards for Social Entrepreneurship, and in 2007 Tostan was awarded the Conrad N. Hilton Humanitarian Prize—the largest humanitarian award in the world—for empowering African communities and also in recognition for doing what no other organization before it has done: help bring about the widespread abandonment of the deeply entrenched and harmful tradition of female genital cutting (FGC).

The issue of female genital cutting is not one that many people are necessarily eager to discuss. In Western cultures, the practice is most commonly referred to as "female genital mutilation" and is generally viewed as a heinous act of cruelty born from gender inequality that girls are forced to endure. But the issue is far more complex than this, and to consider it from the point of view of the millions of women in twenty-eight nations where the custom is practiced is to understand a far different reality. The truth is, women who adhere to the tradition do not view it as an act of cruelty, but rather as a necessary act of love. Cutting one's daughter is critical to her future, ensuring that she will be a respected member of her community and preparing her to find a good husband in cultures where marriage is essential for a girl's economic security and social acceptance. To not cut one's daughter would be unthinkable— setting her up for a lifetime of rejection and social isolation.

With a background in writing about issues surrounding human rights violations and the disadvantages of women in developing nations, I was eager to learn about Tostan's work. But I admit that it was not the issue of FGC that drew me to this story. It was Molly herself. How had a woman like her—a sixty-two-year-old single mother from Illinois—managed to devise a strategy to possibly bring an end to a highly entrenched and revered custom that has existed for nearly two thousand years?

It doesn't take long after meeting Molly to understand that not only is she a gifted intellectual, but she is also extremely likable and funny. Our first dinner, meant to last an hour or two, easily stretched to five. Though she is, at times, somewhat reluctant to speak about herself—her ordinary beginnings in Illinois, her personal life—she comes alive when she speaks about her work. We'd barely finished eating before Molly had pushed aside our dishes to draw for me a rough map of Senegal and guide me through Excel spreadsheets and PowerPoint presentations out-lining the extraordinary movement under way in Senegal.

It began in 1997 when a group of thirty-five women from one small vil-lage became the first to stand up and publicly declare an end to the practice of FGC in their community. Since then, nearly five thousand additional communities have followed suit. In each case, village representatives— including women, men, and adolescents—have bravely stood up before their extended families, government representatives, and journalists from around the world to announce they would no longer cut their girls.

"We are now on the verge of something unique and historic—total aban-donment of FGC in Senegal," Molly said to me at this first meeting. "I truly believe we are at a point where, in a few years, Senegal may be able to say that it is a country free from this practice that is violating the human rights of women and girls, causing so much suffering and, at times, even death."

From small, local organizations to large international NGOs, there have been considerable efforts to bring about an end to the practice. While many have had success in increasing international awareness around the issue, none have come close to having Tostan's success at the grassroots level. Currently, Tostan's approach to FGC abandonment—implementing a human-rights-based education program taught in national languages, disseminating information, and holding public declarations to announce an end to the practice—has been integrated into the strategies of numerous organizations, including ten UN agencies and several African governments. The World Health Organization, UNICEF, UNESCO, USAID, and others have recognized Tostan for its ability to bring about social change and mobilize communities to improve their own lives, and in Senegal the government has officially adopted a national action plan that calls for using the human rights approach pioneered by Tostan to totally end FGC by 2015.

How has this relatively small organization achieved such results?

"I have learned many lessons during the decades I've been doing this work," Molly says, "but none as important as this: if you want to help empower people to positively transform their communities and their lives, human rights education is key. For many years, our education program did not include discussions on basic human rights. We were successful, but it was only after introducing human rights learning that an amazing thing happened. I can't explain it. It felt like magic."

Despite the recognition she has personally received for Tostan's accomplishments, Molly is loath to take the credit, and as our dinner came to an end and we prepared to say good-bye, she grew serious. "It's really the women themselves who should be telling you this story. The only way to truly understand what is happening, to experience the magic, you have to come to Senegal."

THREE MONTHS LATER, I landed at the airport in Dakar, Senegal's capital city, for the first of several trips I would take over the course of the next year. Molly had invited me to attend a weeklong staff retreat at a training center just outside the city of Thiès, about an hour east of Dakar. The seminar was designed, in part, to mark the twentieth anniversary of Tostan—to celebrate the fact that the organization, which had its roots in one small village in 1982 with a team of three, had expanded to thousands of Senegalese villages and nine additional African nations and now employed more than thirteen hundred people.

It is not easy to pull Molly's attention away from her work—she has a singular focus that is truly extraordinary—but she always seems willing to carve out time to show people around. It is clear that Molly wants visitors to Senegal to see what she sees there, to understand and appreciate the country beyond the poverty, the crumbling infrastructure, the trash-lined streets, and for a few hours each day, Molly and I spend time exploring the villages surrounding Thiès. She takes me to the village of Saam Njaay, population three hundred, where she lived for three years in a ten-by-ten-foot hut, beginning in 1982. When she arrived, there was no clean running water, and even today—nearly thirty years later—there is still no electricity. Like the other women of the village, Molly helped with the cooking, used a latrine she dug behind her hut, and had to walk a kilometer to get water from the closest well. As we walk through the village, she points out the landmarks: the courtyard where she first developed and implemented the classes that would become the Tostan Community Empowerment Program; the health center she helped the villagers build; the field where, in the cooler air of late afternoon, she led the children and women in the *Jane Fonda Workout,* played from a portable audio cassette player she carried.

Taking in the remoteness of this village, the utter lack of convenience, I am captivated by the question of what would motivate a young American woman (she was thirty-two at the time) to choose to settle somewhere so isolated and unfamiliar. At one point, I voice the thought that has occurred to me several times that day: "I can't believe you did this." Molly just smiles, and as she is greeted by everyone in the village—most people call her Sukkéyna Njaay, the Senegalese name she was given when she first arrived in Senegal in 1974—I see the joy she experiences here, the love she feels for the villagers and they for her, and I begin to sense what she is thinking.

Why would you *not* do this?

The next day she takes me on a tour of Thiès, and it is during these initial hours spent with her that I first get a sense of what I will later come to believe defines her and her work more than anything else: she is fearless. Driving through the pitch-black streets, she makes a wrong turn and we get lost among the unmarked, muddy back alleys, literally having to outmaneuver a herd of swine in the road, but she doesn't bat an eye. The next day, we get pulled over by a stern-looking police officer as part of a routine stop. Molly slows the car, rolls down the window, and charmingly jokes with the man in perfect Wolof, the indigenous language spoken by a majority of Senegal's twelve million residents. I hear the word "Tostan," and within minutes, after a quick handshake from the officer, we are back on our way.

As she drives, she tells me stories of her life and her work—how she once walked barefoot several miles along scorpion- and snake-infested roads on a rainy night after her car broke down; about her first trip in 2005 to Somalia, a war-torn nation where people have been killed for being white; how she has managed on more than one occasion to bring her program to communities so desperate to block her efforts to empower local women they have threatened her with death. She speaks as if these experiences were normal and ordinary, often forgetting what she is saying after pausing to point out the fields of peanut and millet crops or the kad trees from South Africa, which, unlike every other tree in Senegal, gain their leaves in the dry season and lose them in the rainy months. "Oh, look," she says. "There's one of those beautiful turquoise birds! I've forgotten what they're called in Wolof." Often, she fails to notice the speed bumps—mounds of packed dirt obviously laid by hand by industrious and worried local parents. As we bounce roughly over them, nearly hitting our heads on the ceiling, Molly laughs. "Whoops," she says. "Didn't see that one."

At night, we return to the house Molly has built over the course of several years, as is the Senegalese way, in a beach community on the shores of the Atlantic Ocean about two hours from Dakar. It is large and comfortable. The walls are adorned with colorful paintings from local artists and lined with shelves heavy with books, everything from popular fiction to scholarly texts on management and budget writing. From Molly's favorite spot on the verandah, overlooking the ocean, the sound of the waves mixes with the distant call to prayer. In the morning, over a breakfast of coffee and fried eggs, she points out the song of the weaver birds, which have loaded the trees in the front yard with roofed nests made of palm fronds. It is peaceful here, and private— perhaps the one indulgence Molly allows herself, perhaps the last vestige of her Americanism. She tries to come here every weekend, often hosting guests who are visiting Senegal to learn more about Tostan, or staff members she has invited to come and work. Here, she speaks Wolof unless the phone rings or her Skype chimes, prompting her to switch effortlessly to English or French, depending on the caller. She loves language. She is known among friends for her constant puns, or "Melchings," as they are called. (One morning, we awake to find the electricity has gone out, meaning no coffee for breakfast. "No coffee? Why, that's grounds to be upset," she says with a giggle.) She never seems to tire. Even when she claims she is going to lie down for an hour, you get a sense she spends that time on her computer, replying to e-mails or Skyping someone in Mali. When I comment on the number of hours she seems to work, she shakes her head.

"I don't always work," she says. "Sometimes I play a mean game of Boggle."

DURING THE FINAL DAYS of this visit, Molly brings me to the village of Malicounda Bambara. It is simple and inviting, situated off a main road that leads in one direction to Dakar and in the other to the bustling seaside fish markets and tourist hotels of Mbour. We take the back route, along unpaved roads, where the views are vast and breathtaking—hard blue skies hovering above forests of beautiful, ancient baobab trees, their branches thick, wild, and twisted, as if it's the trees' roots that reach upward toward the clouds. According to a popular Wolof saying, the baobab was once a beautiful tree, but it became so vain that God grew angry, prompting him to turn it upside down.

Small well-worn cement homes, organized into compounds where as many as thirty members of a family may live, surround leafy central courtyards where most of the daily activities take place. Along some of the narrow, interior dirt roads filled with drifting goats and chickens, village residents offer bread and vegetables for sale from tables and crude wooden booths. We climb from the car and a crowd of young girls shyly approach, stretching their hands to shake ours, to welcome us to their village.

A group of women has been expecting us, and we are led to a circle of chairs set under the spreading arms of a great neem tree near the village square. After offering us tea poured from a ceramic pot, the women begin to speak. As I spend time with them that day, and the many days that I will return to be with them over the course of the year, as I hear the stories of their lives, I take in the village. While it is beautiful, it does not at first seem to be particularly extraordinary. And there was certainly a time when people here had very little reason to believe that these thirty-five women—many of whom married as teenagers, never attended school, and were accustomed to remaining in the background—might help spawn one of the most significant human rights movements in modern African history.

But sixteen years ago, in this circle of women, at this exact spot, all of that was about to change.

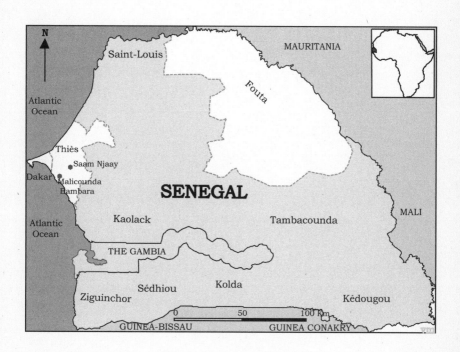

Senegal and the Surrounding Area

BOOK ONE

It's better to find the way out than to stand and scream at the forest.

—WOLOF PROVERB

1

Dogu gi (The Decision)

Malicounda Bambara
August 1996

Kerthio Diawara sat on a stiff plastic chair, pretending to look
through the notebook on her lap and trying her best to avoid eye
contact with the other students. Usually the atmosphere inside the classroom was lively and animated as the participants discussed the theme
of that day's class session—how the body develops, the phases of pregnancy, the importance of pre- and post-natal consultation. But on this
day, the room was filled with an unfamiliar and icy silence as Kerthio
and the other thirty-four women listened uneasily to Ndey, the Tostan
class facilitator, who spoke from her place in the circle.

None of them could believe what Ndey was doing: speaking aloud
about the custom of cutting a girl's genitals to prepare her for marriage—so old and revered a custom, it was known among themselves
simply as "the tradition." Kerthio stole a glance around the room at
the others and saw that most were keeping their eyes to themselves.

Surely they too were nervously trying to make sense of what Ndey was saying, explaining that the tradition could cause a wide range of serious medical problems, such as hemorrhaging, infection, difficulty urinating, stress or shock, and complications during childbirth. While most of the women in the room had known girls or women who had suffered from one or more of these problems, or had suffered them personally, they never would have connected this with the tradition. Rather, everyone believed that problems after the procedure were the work of evil spirits, a punishment for some unknown transgression of the family or cutter. The consequences of talking about the tradition could be quite serious. It could mean mental illness or paralysis. It might even bring death. This is why women never dared to speak about it, and certainly never to anyone who had not been cut.

"What I'm about to read is a statement from the World Health Organization," Ndey said. "*Female Genital Mutilation is an act of violence toward the young girl that will affect her life as an adult.*" She paused. "Would anybody like to share their thoughts about this?"

The room was silent.

"We all know that mothers practice this tradition out of love for their daughters, so that they will be respected and accepted members of their society. Why do you think the World Health Organization would make such a statement?"

Kerthio looked across the room at her mother, Maimouna Traore. A large woman with earlobes stretched long from years of heavy adornment, her age evident in the leathery folds of her face and neck, Maimouna was among the oldest and most respected women in the class. Kerthio could sense the anger in her mother's face, in the way she clenched her jaw and held her shoulders, and she half-expected her to rise from her chair and march out of the classroom. The room remained silent for several minutes. When it seemed the discussion was going nowhere, Ndey announced that the class was over.

Two days later they met again—always three times a week for the three years of the Tostan program—and once again Ndey brought up the subject of the tradition. "We've prepared a theater on the topic," she explained, asking for volunteers to come to the center of the circle. "It's based on a story about a girl named Poolel. Who would like to take part?"

The women typically loved theater. It was an essential part of their culture and used often during their Tostan sessions, but only a woman named Tene Cissoko stepped into the circle to volunteer. With her coaxing, a few others reluctantly followed.

"Be sure to make the theater as vivid as possible," Ndey suggested, taking her seat. "Consider including anything from your own experience with the tradition—songs you sang to your daughters after their procedures or that your mother once sang to you."

The women came alive in their roles. As the story went, the day came for Poolel to undergo the tradition. She was taken to the cutter for her procedure, but afterward something terrible happened. Poolel began to bleed profusely, greatly worrying her mother. When the bleeding worsened, her mother took her to the village health agent. Her efforts to stop the bleeding failed, and it was obvious to her mother that Poolel was in great pain. She was eventually taken to the regional hospital, where the doctors tried to save her life. But it was too late. Poolel died the next day.

"Let's talk about why girls are cut," Ndey said after the women had returned to their seats. "What consequences befall a girl who is not cut?"

Why were girls cut? It was a silly question, like asking why one breathes. Every woman in the room knew that the tradition was among the most momentous events of a girl's life, preparing her to become a woman, to eventually be deemed acceptable for marriage, and, most important of all, to fully belong and have a respected role within her society. For a girl not to be cut—to be a *bilakoro,* a name considered among the worst insults in their culture—was unimaginable. Not only would a *bilakoro* have trouble finding a husband, she would also be rejected and ostracized by the rest of the community, by women especially. Considered impure and unfit to enter the circle of "real women," the food she cooked would not be eaten, the clothes she washed rewashed by others.

Nobody said this aloud, however, and the tense silence in the room was disturbed only by the sound of children playing soccer in a distant courtyard. Ndey began to worry that the women would again decline to speak and she'd have to find another way to fill the remaining hour of class, but then Takko, the village midwife and a mother of three, hesitantly raised her hand.

"I know this is an uncomfortable topic for many of us here," she began, "but all last night I thought very seriously about this. We never talk about the tradition, but maybe it's time." Takko went on to describe the problems in childbirth she'd witnessed in her work as a midwife, and how difficult it was for the doctor to sew up scar tissue, therefore requiring more time for a woman to heal. She had long suspected that women who could not have children may have suffered infections following the cutting, causing their infertility. In Senegal, the majority ethnic group—the Wolof—do not practice the tradition, and during her training as a midwife, Takko had assisted in the births of some of these women. She had noticed they were more elastic and therefore had much easier and less painful deliveries. "What Ndey is telling us is true. This is not a healthy practice."

Takko sat down, her heart racing. She was unsure of how the other women would respond, and she felt the swelling rush of relief when her friend Aminata finally spoke. "As you know, I'm a Toucouleur," Aminata said, referring to the predominant ethnic group from the north of Senegal, "and according to my customs I was cut as an infant and sealed shut afterward." The women knew this was sometimes the type of cutting practiced. After a girl was cut, her legs would be tied together until the wound closed. Aminata's mother had arranged for her to be married at fifteen—at least she thought she was fifteen. Birth registration was a custom of the *tubaabs,* the French who had colonized Senegal beginning in 1890, and in the nation's villages, few people knew their exact age.

"On the night before my wedding, my mother explained I would have to be cut open the next morning in order to consummate the marriage. I panicked and tried to refuse all of it," Aminata said. "Marriage to the man chosen for me, being cut open. But I had no choice. The procedure to open me was agonizing." Afterward, still in pain, she fled her village. "I'd been told that if I wasn't penetrated that night," she timidly told the class, "my wound would again close, but I didn't care. The pain was so severe I couldn't imagine having intimate relations with my new husband." She remained in hiding for a few days until the pain subsided. That man eventually divorced her, and she was married a few years later to another. She ended up having several children, but each time she had great difficulty in childbirth. "My body was so damaged, I could hardly be put back together again," she told the others.

When Aminata finished, another woman stood to speak. And after her, another. One by one, they cautiously shared their experiences of the tradition. Throughout it all, Kerthio sat listening. She too had a story, but it was not one she could disclose. For the last several years, and to that very day, she had kept this experience her most private and guarded secret. One she had once believed she would take to the grave.

TEN YEARS EARLIER, KERTHIO'S daughter, Mariama, had died at three months old. Despite the time that had passed since that day, the aching sorrow Kerthio still felt lingered so deeply and solidly within her, it was as if it originated from somewhere deeper than her bones. Mariama was her first child. Kerthio had been married a year earlier, at the age of sixteen, chosen by her parents to become the second wife of a much older man with a few children already, and she knew she would live the remainder of her life unable to forgive herself for allowing her daughter to die. She'd been told by a local *marabout,* a respected religious leader believed to possess supernatural healing powers, that she needed to buy a special amulet to protect her daughter from evil spirits, but she had, for reasons she would never understand, neglected to get one. She was convinced it was solely because of this neglect that Mariama had died.

Kerthio's second daughter arrived a year later, vibrant and healthy. It was about four years later when Kerthio decided to have the tradition performed on her. She had been planning this day since her daughter was born, and in consultation with Maimouna, they chose an auspicious date. Kerthio mentioned nothing about these plans to her husband. After all, the women's tradition was never spoken about with the men of her village. While a father knew in general terms that the tradition existed and, like the women, often believed it to be a religious obligation under Islam, most men understood very little else—not what the operation entailed, not that it was being planned, and often not even that it had occurred.

On the morning of the chosen day, soon after her husband had left for the fields, Kerthio eagerly awaited the cutter. After she'd arrived and taken her daughter away, Kerthio spent the remainder of the day feeling anxious and distracted as she worked alongside the other women to complete her chores. As late afternoon fell and she stirred the *nebidaay* sauce over the large platter of millet, its steam rising in circles around her face, her head felt crowded with images of what she imagined was happening to her daughter, images born from Kerthio's own experience of having undergone the tradition years earlier.

A clean straw mat would be laid out in the back courtyard, near where the cooking was done, and the tools readied: cloth, a bar of soap, and a razor blade or knife. The cutter's assistant would then go and gather goat dung—it was believed that goat excrement had antiseptic qualities—and stir it into a large, metal tub of water, steeped with special leaves and perfume. She'd boil the liquid until the firewood underneath bloomed crimson with heat and the dung had fully dissolved, and then carry the steaming tub to the ground next to the mat, where Kerthio's daughter waited. Sitting cross-legged at the child's feet, the cutter would grip the razor blade in her hands. Too large for such a delicate job, the blade would be carefully broken in half. The assistant would grip the child's arms, pinning them firmly to the ground, as the cutter lifted the young girl's *pagne,* a traditional wraparound skirt, and spread open her legs. Sure to keep as much pressure as she could on the girl's arms, the assistant would instruct Kerthio's daughter to be brave. *It will all be over with quickly,* she might whisper. *And it will all be worth it.* Kerthio believed these words. Life was filled with hardships and suffering, especially for women. This was her daughter's first opportunity to prove to herself, as well as to the community, that she was courageous, that she could endure the excruciating pain so many women like Kerthio knew so well themselves. Kerthio wondered if the assistant would turn aside her gaze as the cutter took the razor blade and, with a few quick cuts, remove the girl's clitoris and labia.

Kerthio might have imagined it, but she could sense her daughter's screams slicing through the distant, heavy air, scattering the heat and the flies as she was lifted from the mat and placed into the milky dung water, which would quickly turn red with blood. The women would give the water time to clean the wound before lifting the trembling girl back onto the mat and pressing the area with the wet neem leaves they had collected.

Kerthio had expected her daughter to be gone for a few nights, tended to and cared for afterward by the noble elder women who traditionally played this role in the village, but later that same night, as Kerthio swept the dust from the floor of her hut, she heard a soft knock on her door. It was one of the traditional cutter's assistants, and she carried Kerthio's sleeping daughter in her arms.

"Is everything all right?" Kerthio asked, alarmed, scooping her daughter into her arms.

"Something's the matter," the woman said, the nervousness evident in her voice.

"What is it?"

"I'm sure it's nothing, but we thought it best that she return home with you," the woman said. With that, she turned and left.

Kerthio laid her daughter on the bed they shared. The child seemed weak and exhausted, and Kerthio stayed by her side for the next few hours, wiping the sweat that spread like dewdrops on her skin, feeding her sips of tepid water drawn hours earlier from the well. She eventually fell asleep beside her daughter, but later that night she was awakened by the feeling of wetness spreading on the mattress. She thought her daughter had urinated in her sleep, but when she brought the oil lamp closer, she saw the pool of blood.

Her heart racing with worry, she rushed to wake Maimouna, asleep in her hut nearby. "Come," she whispered to her mother. "I need your help." They sat at the girl's side, offering prayers to stop the hemorrhaging. As she watched her daughter grow dizzy and weak from blood loss, her voice become brittle from pain, Kerthio's fear escalated. After losing Mariama, she couldn't bear the thought of losing another child, and the panic she felt threatened to take control of her. She stayed by her daughter's side throughout the night, pausing only to eat a little rice at Maimouna's insistence. By the next morning, the bleeding appeared to subside a little, and Kerthio ran to the nearby hut of one of the village's traditional healers. The man came to Kerthio's room and recited prayers over her daughter. He then instructed Kerthio to offer four yards of material, two candles, and a kilo of kola nuts to an elder woman.

Her daughter slowly recovered, but Kerthio could never forget the child's pain or her own fear that night. Later, a few years after giving birth to another girl, Kerthio knew it was time to have this daughter cut. She was tormented with thoughts that the same thing might happen again. She knew her daughter had been lucky. Some girls in the village experienced serious health problems, some even died. She tried to speak to Maimouna about her anxiety, but her mother became very upset. "Of course you will have her cut. We will not have a *bilakoro* in the family," she said. "If you do not do it, then I will."

Kerthio didn't dare speak of her fears again. *What good would that do?* she wondered. Adhering to the tradition was simply a part of life in her village, part of what it meant to be a good and devoted member of her ethnic group and religion. Even if she had been able to express her misgivings, there was no recourse. After all, every society imposed certain standards on women, born from deeply held beliefs, their origins often long forgotten, and in Kerthio's culture, *this* was the highest standard. It had been this way for centuries and would continue to be this way forever. She didn't have a choice.

Unless.

She deferred the ceremony for one year, and then another. Finally one night, unable to sleep, Kerthio made the decision: she was not going to have her daughter cut. She could not, of course, admit this to anyone. Doing so would guarantee her daughter a lifetime of hardship and rejection. A few months later, Kerthio gathered the courage to lie, announcing to her family and friends that she had had the operation performed quietly. Everyone believed her, of course. After all, what mother would ever *not* cut her daughters?

REMEMBERING THE EXPERIENCE THAT day in the Tostan class, Kerthio shrank in her chair as around her the women continued to speak with an unusual sense of honesty and candor.

"I've heard that women who are not cut are able to enjoy intimate relations with their husbands," Tene was saying. "I've heard sex is sometimes less painful."

As the conversation lingered, a few of the older women in the class grew increasingly discomfited, including Maimouna. "This is our oldest tradition, and it is a religious obligation," she said with obvious annoyance. "It is not right to be discussing it."

Among the other women, Maimouna held a power as forceful as a thunderstorm; an admonishment from her was usually enough to silence a discussion. But the women continued their conversation, during class and beyond. In hushed voices, while waiting in line at the well the next morning, over meals in the evening heat, on quiet walks to the market, they discussed their understanding of the tradition, of why exactly they did it. They'd always been told it was a necessary means of finding a good husband—and it was generally assumed that men expected it—but in reality, it was the future husband's mother who acted as the gatekeeper of the practice. She was the one who insisted a woman be cut when it came time to choose a wife for her son. Men never spoke of it. But even more so, everyone believed it was required under Islam. To not do it, they had been taught, was to defy their ancestors as well as their faith.

But Ndey had said that important religious scholars had attested to the fact that the tradition was not even mentioned in the Koran, and even though the practice is found among Christians, Jews, and Muslims, none of the holy texts of any of these religions prescribes female genital cutting. In fact, the practice is largely thought to predate both Christianity and Islam.

Despite the fact that Ndey was not from their village, they trusted her. She had been a wise, patient, and kind teacher. She'd moved to Malicounda Bambara to facilitate the classes, living in a small room provided to her by one of the families. After this year with them, she had become a treasured part of their community, and the education Ndey brought to the village had led them, they believed, to a true awakening. After all, as far as the women of villages like Malicounda Bambara believed, education was not meant for girls. Of the thirty-five women enrolled in the Tostan class, few had gone to primary school, and those who had did not go far.

But now, through the Tostan program, they had become truly educated. Not only had they learned to read, write, and understand basic math, they'd also come to understand germ transmission, rehydration therapy, and the importance of vaccination. They had been taught leadership and project-management skills and how to conduct feasibility studies for projects in their village, like the soap-making project they'd established, through which many of the women were earning their own income for the first time in their lives.

But most of all, they had come to learn about something they believed might truly transform their lives: the concept of human rights and their own right to human dignity.

WHEN, SEVERAL WEEKS BEFORE the discussion of the tradition, Ndey first led a discussion on human dignity, explaining that all people—men, women, and children—have inherent human rights, the women were puzzled. They had been taught as young girls that their role was to be obedient and submissive, at first to their fathers and then to their husbands. Beyond tending to their children and households, they hadn't any say in how their village or larger community was run. In fact, they had never been invited to village meetings where decisions were made, and even if they had been, they would not have dared to speak. And for many of them, physical violence was simply a normal and expected part of their lives. In fact, there were a few *good* reasons for a man to hit his wife: if she spoke in public, neglected the children, or, most important of all, refused his sexual advances. Should that happen, or should their husbands insult them, they had been taught to be accepting and patient. Before Tostan, they would never have dreamed of questioning these expectations, or their role in the family or society, as that would have been seen as a betrayal of the group and a desire to set oneself apart from others. Which is why in the beginning they didn't believe that Ndey's information—the idea that every person, even women, had equal human rights, including the right to work, health, and education, to voice one's opinion, and, most significantly, the right to be free from all forms of discrimination and violence—could possibly be correct. If these rights did exist, certainly they applied only to men. Again and again, the women in the class asked Ndey to reiterate what she was saying, to make sure they understood: they too had these rights?

Ndey had the facts to support this claim. Over the course of several sessions, she provided evidence that, like men, women were granted many protections under several international human rights instruments. In 1979, she explained, the United Nations General Assembly adopted the Convention on the Elimination of All Forms of Discrimination Against Women, or the CEDAW. This treaty, which had officially gone into effect fifteen years earlier—on September 3, 1981—was the first global document to specifically address the rights of women and was often thought of as the first international bill of rights for women. As the most comprehensive and detailed international agreement to seek the advancement of women, it established rights in areas not previously subject to international standards and assured the protection of women's civil, political, social, economic, and cultural rights.

The CEDAW would become one of the most highly ratified international human rights conventions, having the support of 186 nations, including Senegal, which signed the convention in 1980 and put it into effect in 1985. By accepting the declaration, the government of Senegal agreed to incorporate the principle of equality between men and women and to ensure the elimination of all acts of discrimination against women.

When the women heard this, their confused laughter crackled throughout the room like hot sticks on a cooking fire and the discussion became spirited. After class, the women gathered to further discuss the information. As part of the Tostan education program, they had committed to adopt an *ndey-dikke* (a friend not enrolled in the class) with whom they would share what they learned in each session. This connection was a key element of their Tostan classes, and the women began to talk to their *ndey-dikkes* about what they had learned. Like them, they had a hard time believing this information could be true, and often the response they heard was the same. "Even if what you're saying is true," a friend of Ker-thio said to her one day, "even if we really do have the same guarantee of human rights as men, how do we claim them?"

OVER THE NEXT FEW months, despite the conflict they felt and their lingering fears about doing so, the women of the Tostan class began to seriously question the practice of the tradition. In the first Tostan sessions, they had come to an agreement on their dream for the future of their community—a vision of peace, health, well-being, prosperity, and respect. Was the tradition something that would help them achieve this dream? If not, was it something they should consider ending in their village? Now that they understood the ways in which the practice could harm their daughters, now that they knew of their own rights, and their daughters' rights to live in health and be free from violence, could they claim to be women of peace and still adhere to this custom?

They went first to the village imam. He confirmed what they'd learned in their Tostan class: important religious scholars had attested to the fact that despite what they had always believed, the tradition was not a religious obligation under Islam and was not even mentioned in the Koran. Before long, with this information, it became clear that a bold decision was beginning to form among the group. Every woman of the Tostan class agreed not to cut their daughters that April, the month during which the cutting typically took place in their community.

They then agreed to go further. After all, if any decision was to be made, it had to be made as a village. For only a unified and collective decision would keep a girl from being ostracized as a *bilakoro*.

The campaign to convince every woman of the village, even those not enrolled in the Tostan class, to forego cutting their daughters, was not easy. Over the next few months, the thirty-five women—Kerthio, Aminata, Tene, and before long even Maimouna—went from neighborhood to neighborhood, sharing the information they'd learned. They performed short plays, had long discussions about the knowledge they'd received, and welcomed dialogue. After each meeting, they made the same request: forego all cutting this April. Join us in these efforts and help protect our daughters.

As the month of April 1997 slowly crept by, Kerthio and the other women waited to see what would happen, feeling nervous but hopeful. When the month passed and no preparations were made for the cutting ceremonies, the women of Malicounda Bambara knew that perhaps they were truly on their way to doing what they'd never once believed possible: abandoning the tradition for good.

2

Xabaar bu Mag bi
(Breaking the Silence)

Maimouna Traore spoke first. "As the president of the women's group here in Malicounda Bambara, and on behalf of our entire Tostan class, I'd like to greet you by your first name and your last name."

Molly Melching had always loved this way of addressing people, customary throughout Senegal. Greeting people by their first name acknowledges them as an individual, by their last acknowledges their entire extended family. Maimouna went on to wish peace for the members of Molly's family—her twelve-year-old daughter, Zoé, her sister, Diane, her mother in Arizona, and her father, long since deceased.

Returning Maimouna's greeting in Wolof so perfect it didn't reveal her American upbringing, Molly tried her best to conceal the hesitation she'd been feeling over the last twenty-four hours, since she'd received the news that the women of this village had made a truly remarkable decision: to abandon the centuries-old practice of female genital cutting. The decision, she'd been told, had started to take shape eight months earlier and was the result of extensive discussion and heated debate among the women of the village. Earlier that morning, as Molly slowly steered her creaky Land Cruiser down the bumpy road toward Malicounda Bambara, scaring the goats and chickens aside, she thought back to her decision a year earlier to include a discussion about the risks associated with female genital cutting in a new Tostan series of classes, or module, on women's health. She had been extremely tentative. Having lived in Senegal for twenty years, she had spent much time in villages with traditions similar to those of Malicounda Bambara. She knew it was forbidden for anyone, but especially people from outside the practicing ethnic group, to even *mention* the practice of female genital cutting. As far as she knew, every effort to raise awareness about the practice in Senegal—from health education agents to development workers—had led to few results and had sometimes offended those who practiced it. So to now hear that these women had dared to speak of the tradition's potential harm in front of their entire village and were prepared to speak of it in front of an American woman, to think they may have truly decided to end the practice? It was unfathomable.

After all the proper greetings had been exchanged, Molly attempted to ease into the point of the meeting. "I understand the women of Malicounda Bambara have started a soap-making project to earn income," Molly said.

Maimouna looked perplexed. "Yes, but we don't want to talk about that," she said. "We've invited you here to speak about our decision to end the practice of female genital cutting in our village."

Such directness was unusual, and Molly did her best to hide her surprise. "Can you explain how this has come about?" she asked.

The women of the Tostan class began to speak at once, each of them competing to share the events of the last several months. Finally, Kerthio raised her hand to speak. She explained how overjoyed the women of Malicounda Bambara had been two years earlier when the Tostan program first arrived in their village.

"Each of us has long craved the information we've learned in our classes," she said. "But when Ndey first brought up the tradition, we were speechless, many quite offended. While we feared the consequences of speaking about it aloud, Ndey persisted. Without ever making us feel defensive or ashamed, without ever suggesting we alter or abandon any of our traditions, she explained that the majority of women around the world do not practice female genital cutting, which surprised us."

Many women nodded in agreement.

"Ndey also helped us understand what happens to our bodies when they are cut," Kerthio continued. "Nobody had explained that to us before. In our culture, women are not supposed to look at our bodies. The pictures and diagrams Ndey made available were the first glimpse of a woman's body most of us were ever given. Of course this information made us begin to think differently, to question the practice." She paused. "But nothing would have changed were it not for our new understanding of human rights and a discussion of our responsibilities in relation to those rights. There was no going back after that. It was this knowledge that made us confident in our right to choose for ourselves what happens to our bodies, to preserve our bodies as they are without changes. And we feel confident we can defend this decision if necessary."

When Kerthio finished speaking, others continued. One after another, they shared with Molly their experiences of the last few months, of having to resolve their long-held beliefs about the importance of the tradition and the knowledge they were receiving. Some admitted they had, at times, felt uneasy about its disadvantages and described their slow realization that, as Ndey explained, the pain, hemorrhaging, infection, and problems during childbirth were not the result of bad spirits, as they had thought, but rather of being cut with an unsterile razor blade or knife by an elderly woman with no medical training. They spoke at length about how they had never been approached about the tradition in this way before. The class discussion had been without judgment, focused only on imparting information about human rights and the tradition's potential health consequences. The decision to stop the practice had come solely from the women themselves.

THE NEXT DAY MOLLY called Samir Sobhy, the UNICEF representative based in Dakar. Tostan had been receiving support from the local UNICEF office since 1988, and Molly had developed a great respect for Samir. He was as surprised as she had been to hear what was happening in Malicounda Bambara.

"It's important, Molly, that the women speak publicly about this and share the news of their decision with as many Senegalese as possible," he said. "They need to tell others what they have learned and why they've made this choice." He suggested that they invite journalists to Malicounda Bambara to speak to the women of the Tostan class.

Molly was hesitant. "I don't know, Samir. To stop the practice is one thing, but to speak publicly about it? It's as extraordinary as it is delicate. As you can imagine, this might not be a popular decision. I'm worried that going public will bring them ridicule and harsh criticism from those who continue to practice."

"Molly, if these women were strong enough to make this incredible decision on their own, they are strong enough to defend their position before journalists."

Molly returned to the village to ask the women their opinions on the matter. The class sat in silence for several minutes. "I can leave and give you time to think about this," Molly said. "I know that it is a critical decision, and you should take your time."

Maimouna rose from her chair, her voice fully filling the space around the women. "Where we once had fear we now have courage, because we have been given knowledge," she said. "We know our rights and the rights of all women. We have the right to dignity and the confidence to change customs if they do not bring us that dignity." She paused and reached down to take Molly's hand into her own. "We have left the darkness, and we now live in light. Bring the journalists. We are ready."

A FEW WEEKS LATER, on the morning of July 31, 1997, the thirty-five women of the Tostan class gathered in the public square in Malicounda Bambara. Since before the sun rose, the women had been readying the village for the twenty journalists traveling to see them in just a few more hours. A large cooking fire had been started in the freshly swept courtyard, the water put on to ready the rice. Their *boubous,* the long traditional dresses worn by Senegalese women, were starched so stiffly they barely moved in the early morning breeze. By eleven that morning the aroma of simmering vegetables and fish filled the steamy air, and Kerthio nervously gathered her Tostan classmates for one last rehearsal of the theater they'd prepared. One by one, the women reviewed their roles as well as the information on human rights they'd been studying to better explain, and possibly defend, the brave decision they were about to announce.

Meanwhile, Molly stood anxiously before her closet in her home in Thiès and, with the help of her daughter, Zoé, combed through her own collection of *boubous,* looking for the most fitting choice for the occasion.

"This one?" Zoé asked, pulling out a blue *boubou* with a matching *pagne.*

"Perfect," Molly said, holding it up to her tall frame while Zoé took a stack of Molly's bracelets and slipped them over her wrists.

An hour later, as the bus Molly had arranged for the journalists lumbered down the path toward Malicounda Bambara, Molly slowly let out a long breath, realizing her relief at seeing the women of the Tostan class gathered in waiting, knowing she hadn't simply imagined it all. Despite the fact that she and the women of the Malicounda Bambara Tostan class had been preparing for weeks for this day, Molly couldn't help but question if it would really happen, if something like this were truly possible.

The bus pulled to a stop in the village square. Kerthio led the journalists to special seats under the large neem tree, where they joined several national government representatives who had come to witness the event. When everyone was comfortably seated, the village chief opened the meeting and the village imam said a prayer for all those who had come to visit them. Maimouna then greeted the guests.

"Salaam maaleekum," she began. "We are very happy to receive you today and tell you about a very important decision our Tostan class and members of our community have made, that of ending a tradition of cutting our young girls. It was a decision that was not easy, because our respected ancestors handed this practice down to us all the way from Mali, the country of our origin."

The class then performed the theater they'd prepared, and throughout it Molly could sense the women's nervousness; it wasn't so long ago that many of them wouldn't have felt comfortable even speaking in public, let alone performing in front of a crowd. When they were finished, Kerthio stood to speak.

"We once believed the tradition to be a religious obligation, but we now know it is not," she said. "We once believed it caused no health problems, and we now know it does. As women, we once believed we had no choice but to continue the practice. We now know we have the right to question any practice that brings harm or health problems to our community. We have made the decision to abandon this practice together and are proud of the choice we have made."

When Kerthio finished speaking, Maimouna stood and walked slowly to the center of the circle. With her shoulders held back, her head lifted high, she said the words Molly knew she'd been quietly rehearsing:

"From this day forward, we, the women of Malicounda Bambara, pledge that none of our daughters, and none of our daughters' daughters, will be cut. We stand by our decision, and we've invited you so that we may finally break through the silence, to publicly say no, to choose health and well-being for all of our daughters and granddaughters."

As Maimouna spoke, Molly felt the breath catch in her throat. She looked around the circle of chairs, at the women of the Tostan class gathered under the tree, perfectly aware of the significance of these words and of the fact that these thirty-five women had somehow found the courage to be perhaps the first African women to stand up publicly and break a centuries-old silence.

Around her, the women rose from their chairs and collected in the center of the circle. As they began to dance for their guests, Molly allowed the emotions she felt to wash through her. She was proud that her organization—the fruits of many years of hard work and careful thought, of a deep commitment to the women of Senegal—had played a role in prompting this profoundly brave and historic act. She tried her best to ignore the other emotion she was feeling: worry. She suspected that many of the women's relatives would accuse them of being influenced by Westerners and suspect that they had been paid to make such an announcement. She also knew the risk these women were taking. She knew they might be shunned and insulted, or viewed as unloving, cruel mothers harming their daughters' chances of ever getting married or having a secure future. But their decision was born of the opposite desire: to allow their daughters to live in health, to enrich their lives. She'd always been one to look on the bright side of things, to try to focus on the possible through even the most impossible situations, and Molly chose at that moment to believe that what she was witnessing was not the end of anything. It was just the beginning.

After all, wasn't it possible that this courageous act would be met with respect, that it might even be replicated in the hundreds of other villages of Senegal where Tostan classes were in progress? Couldn't this decision, and the choice to make it public, play a part in shifting the social consciousness of similar communities, possibly renegotiating a centuries-old, harmful, and deeply entrenched cultural practice?

Kerthio came to stand in front of her. Taking Molly's hand, she led her from her chair and into the center of the circle, to join them in dance. As the questions swirled through Molly's head as rapidly as her long, blue *boubou* swirled circles around her sandaled feet, the women of the Tostan class were discreetly watching her with a few questions of their own. How had this exuberant American woman arrived here in their West African village and found a way to instill them with the courage and the confidence they needed to alter the destiny, and guarantee the health, of hundreds—perhaps thousands—of girls and women?

3

Tawféex (Coming into Her Own)

Dakar, 1974

W hat do you mean the exchange program's been called off?" Molly said into the phone a few hours after first landing in Dakar.

It was October 20, 1974, and she was twenty-four years old. She'd just arrived in Senegal's capital city with a suitcase stuffed with jeans and miniskirts, mosquito repellant, novels by African writers, a nearly empty bank account, and the intention of spending six months studying at the University of Dakar as part of a student exchange with the University of Illinois, where she was pursuing a master's degree in expanded French studies. A few months earlier she'd been thrilled to get word that she'd been chosen as one of two students to take part in the exchange program's first year, thrilled about the prospect of spending six months in Africa. She was far less thrilled to be told, just hours after arriving at the Dakar airport, her brain still cloudy with jet lag, that the exchange program had unexpectedly been canceled. The university representative on the other end of the phone argued with her, explaining that they had sent a telegram to her American address notifying her of this development.

"I didn't get a telegram," she said. It would arrive in Illinois the next day.

Unsure of what else to do, Molly called the U.S. Embassy. The woman she spoke to kindly invited her and Steve Canfield, the other American exchange student, to come to her house while they tried to rectify the situation. The woman's home was airy and beautiful, with large rooms filled with comfortable American furniture and a big patio in the back where Molly spent her first few mornings in Africa listening to the birds perched on the flowering trees. While many young Americans might have been bothered by the reality of what they'd sacrificed to come to Africa—a nice apartment, a steady boyfriend, a place in a graduate program, and a respected teaching position—Molly didn't feel one bit troubled. She was too busy enjoying the adventure of it all.

Each day she woke early to take a bus into crowded downtown Dakar or to the rocky shoreline of the Atlantic Ocean on the western edge of the city. Often she would ride one of the many colorfully painted, but somewhat worse for wear, buses called *Alhamdulilaas,* meaning "praise be to God" in Arabic. "Alhamdulilaa if we make it to our destination," a fellow rider explained to Molly, chuckling. Squeezed in alongside students and workers, mothers and their babies, she'd travel to the ministry of education or to the university to see what she might work out. Along the way, she found herself enraptured by the scenes unfolding on the streets around her: the horse-drawn carts competing for space on the crowded roads, the women's vibrantly colored *boubous* blowing in the sand-streaked wind, their hair covered in matching, artfully arranged head wraps. Groups of children drummed on upside-down buckets along the roads as young girls danced dusty circles around them. Late into the evenings, she'd spend hours walking the lively streets of Dakar, getting lost in the life of the city, among the teenage boys playing soccer on makeshift fields in the middle of the road and men huddled over checkerboards on wooden crates set on the sidewalk. She loved spending time in the markets, so exotic to her, filled with tables of old trading beads, plants and herbs for healing, and goat horns and cauri shells used to predict the future or ward off evil. She paused to watch a man walk the narrow footways along the busy streets, his wares balanced on his slender shoulders, crying out that day's offerings to passersby: "*Bale! Bale!* (Brooms! Brooms!)"

Before long, Steve decided to head home to America, back to their program at the University of Illinois, but Molly was determined to remain in Senegal and somehow make it work. Because, while she couldn't aptly describe how or why it had happened, from the moment she'd walked off the plane into the busy and stifling airport, there was something about this place she loved. And over the next few weeks she came to discover that what she was feeling was as wonderful as it was unfamiliar: a deep sense of belonging that made her weak with happiness—the feeling of being at home.

MOLLY WAS BORN IN Houston in 1949, the second of two girls, to Albert Frederick Melching and Anna Vivian Lineberry Melching. Al, as he was called, worked as a traveling salesman, and six months after Molly was born, his job took the family to Higginsville, Missouri, where they stayed until Molly was six, and then on to Danville, a corn-fed town in central Illinois best known, perhaps, as the birthplace of Dick Van Dyke.

Molly's mother, Anna, who preferred to be called Ann, grew up in Madison, Missouri, but every Lineberry in the United States is said to be originally from Galax, Virginia, a Black Mountain town known for its quilts and its annual fiddling contest. It was in 1941 in Kansas City, where Ann was working as a secretary, that she met Al, whose family was from Fort Wayne, Indiana. A salesman with Farmers Insurance Group, Al stood just over six feet four inches tall and had a distinctive warmth and a penchant for making others laugh.

They married a year later. Al was thirty at the time, Ann twenty-nine, and the couple was eager to start a family. But just four weeks into their marriage, Al was drafted into the army to fight in World War II. Though older than most other inductees, he was happy to be called to serve his country; he felt a keen sense of guilt that he'd previously been doing nothing to assist the war effort. He landed on Utah Beach on September 27, 1944, and began a long march across France, eventually making his way through Luxembourg, Germany, and England. Like most American soldiers at the time, Al was not prepared for the extent of death and suffering he'd witness as a member of an infantry unit. "War is hell and I've seen things," he wrote home to Ann while in Europe. "It's hard, but my future is all that counts." Though he rarely spoke about the experience after returning home in 1947, the shock of war and devastation remained with him.

Ann kept her job as a secretary while her husband fought in Europe and remained working until Molly's sister, Diane, was born in 1947. Being a full-time mother and homemaker proved to be hard on Ann. Trapped all day in their small house with nothing to do but care for two young girls, she often felt unhappy and unsettled, given the family's frequent moves in just six years due to Al's work as a salesman—from Utah to Texas and Missouri before Danville, Illinois. This was made worse by the fact that during this time, the 1950s, motherhood was glorified and women were expected to raise perfect children. The social pressure to conform to the image of the happy housewife caused Ann—like many of her generation—to turn inward: she would sometimes sneak into the closet and cry.

She thought often of the career dreams she'd long ago abandoned. One of six children, four of them girls, Ann had been determined as a young girl to graduate from college, despite the fact that growing up female in the 1920s limited the extent of her professional hopes for the future. She enrolled in William Woods College in 1931, at the height of the Depression, but after just one year, her father, Fred, struggling with the responsibility of running a farm, announced he would no longer contribute to his children's education. Ann did everything she could to stay in college, even borrowing a hundred dollars from her brother, but she couldn't make it work. She dropped out of college, enrolled at Huff Secretarial School, and took a job at the Westgate Greenland Oil Company, eventually rising to the position of secretary to the company president.

After becoming a mother and giving up this job, Ann tried her best to stay engaged with the world beyond her children. She studied the stock market each evening, enjoyed listening to classical music, and was a voracious reader. Her husband did not share these interests. While Ann was considered poised and proper and was interested in world events and politics, Al was the adored clown of the family. Called "Sonny" by his family, he was known for his practical jokes and loved to make his young daughters laugh, most often with his clever use of so-called Melching puns. He once left a phone message for his wife: a Mr. Lyon had called. When Ann dialed the number Al had written, she discovered she was calling the city zoo. During services at Trinity Lutheran Church, he would turn to the wrong page in the hymnal and urge his girls to sing loudly for all to hear. One summer, after Ann's sister Thelma swore that Al, who had by this time gone bald, was growing back his hair, he ushered Diane and Molly into the cornfields to collect corn silk, which they all taped onto his bald head like a flaxen wig. That night at the dinner table, when Thelma asked him to kindly remove his hat for dinner, Al revealed his new hair growth to hoots of laughter.

While his daughters loved his antics, his clownish behavior did not often impress his wife. For if there was one thing Ann Melching cared about, it was appearances. Inside their home, things were kept spotless, to the point of merciless obsession. The house felt more like a display room than it did a home. As high school students, Molly and Diane were discouraged from having friends over or from sitting on the expensive beige checkered sofa Ann had purchased from money she'd saved herself; they always had to give at least three days' notice if they did want to invite someone over, so Ann could clean the house thoroughly.

As much as Ann tried to keep control over her house, she also tried to keep control over her daughters. She taught Diane and Molly from a very early age how to properly behave so as to project the right image. She was a stickler for grammar, understanding that to use language incorrectly would be to risk being judged poor. They could never leave the house—even to run to the corner store—without putting in substantial effort to look their best.

Ann's desire to control her daughters was especially difficult for Molly, an effervescent, social, and passionate girl. She had inherited her father's enthusiasm for life, as well as his height—she was five feet ten by her junior year of high school. While Ann may have preferred her to exhibit the type of poise and decorum expected of young ladies, Molly had always felt most comfortable in her own body while active and performing: in theater, on the school newspaper, and (despite not having the best singing voice) in the choir. She was a member of the pompettes, who performed during the boys' sporting events *(So fight, Danville! Fight for Danville High!)*. She was extremely happy and vibrant, and as she would recall later in life, it seemed she spent a lot of time simply trying to find a place where it was acceptable to dance. At home or on the street, she would link arms with her friends or grab Diane and her mother and encourage them to dance along with her. Ann inevitably scolded Molly for this behavior, embarrassed by her daughter's spontaneity. Every time this happened, Molly felt confused. What was the point of taking up space in the world if you weren't going to do it with zest?

As Molly's sister, Diane, remembers, "My mother was overly involved with us, and with Molly especially. I think Molly scared her. Even as a child, Molly was an intellectual, but also very creative. She would spend hours drawing in her room and loved her art classes. Her creativity made her a little messy, a little in her own world, which frustrated my mother and caused a lot of conflict between them. My mother was always trying to get Molly to conform to her way of thinking—to see the importance of being socially accepted, financially secure, and economically mobile."

It was only after Molly became an adult—and especially after her own daughter, Zoé, was born in 1985—that she realized Ann's strictness and control were not a function of spitefulness, as it may have often felt, but an act of love, carefully designed to keep her daughters from experiencing the struggles that had defined her own younger years. Both Al and Ann had lived through incredible hardship: the worst of the Depression, the brutality of war, and, at least for Ann, the sting of humiliation that came with having grown up just on the brink of poverty. Forced to struggle economically her whole life, she continued to make great sacrifices as a mother in hopes of giving her daughters the opportunities she never had. After Diane and Molly started school, Ann took a job as a teacher. By the age of forty, she had wisely invested enough money from her annual salary of just $9,000 to pay for her daughters' college tuition, her own care in the later years of her life, and her eventual funeral.

Molly and Diane would not know of their mother's investments until many years later, after Al and Ann moved to Arizona to be closer to Ann's sisters. Secrecy was not wholly unusual for the Melching family, as much in Al's and Ann's lives were kept private. Neither of them spoke to their daughters about the sacrifices they'd made, the hardships they had endured, or, for that matter, any of the bad things happening in the world—poverty, racism, violence. Instead, Molly would later realize, they did everything they could to keep bad news away from their girls, to build an artificial bubble of cheerfulness and optimism around their family. Perhaps they thought if only their daughters would conform, if only things always played out exactly as they should, no trouble would come. After all, if you can't control the world and make it perfect, if you have to live with all that is irrational and inevitable about life, if you have to endure war, poverty, and depression, you could at least construct the perfect living room.

MOLLY IS THE TYPE of person who perseveres on the things that are important to her, and once she decides to make something happen, there is very little use in trying to stop her. This was true even when she was a child. At the age of eight she was desperate for a dog, an idea her mother wouldn't hear of. When the dog of Molly's good friend Lily gave birth to a litter of puppies, Molly devised a plan.

"Come over to my house next week on the morning of my birthday," she instructed Lily. "And bring one of the puppies with you."

When Lily arrived that morning, Molly feigned surprise, overcome with gratitude at her friend's unexpected thoughtfulness. "You brought me a puppy for my birthday? I'm so happy!" Seeing Ann's annoyed looks, Molly followed her into the kitchen. "We can't turn this down," she whispered. "After all, it's a gift. And Lily went through so much trouble." Molly was able to keep the dog.

It was with this very same persistence that Molly approached the goal she'd set soon after entering Danville High School: she was somehow going to get herself to France. She had enrolled in her first French class in the ninth grade and quickly proved to have a true gift for languages as well as an immense interest in foreign cultures and people. "It's hard to explain now," Molly says, recalling this time in her life, "but even when I was very young, I was fascinated by other cultures, by anything that was different. Most people I grew up around were seeking out that which was familiar. I was always attracted to things that were different."

At fifteen, too young to work legally, she lied about her age in order to get a job as a waitress at the Redwood Inn, a barn-shaped restaurant that offered an all-you-can-eat buffet, to earn money for a trip to France. After several months spending her weekends waiting on farmers and churchgoers, and her weeknights babysitting, she'd saved enough for a plane ticket, and the summer before her senior year in high school—by this time, she was a top student in her French class—she applied to be part of a four-week language-immersion program at the University of Poitiers in Tours, in central France, organized through a nearby high school. The idea that a group of teenagers would travel abroad to Europe for a few weeks was such a novelty to the residents of Danville, the story was written about in the local newspaper.

Accustomed to the routine of life in her small central Illinois town, Molly was immediately charmed by France. In Tours, she lived with a family she grew quite fond of. The mother, unlike her own, loved to cook and prepared large, elaborate meals each evening. In the afternoons after classes, fifteen-year-old Molly would often ride a borrowed bike through the château region. She spent her weekends touring France by bus, seeing the sights of Paris and beyond. "I was so enchanted," she recalls. "Even by little things—how the French could spend three hours over a meal; the sight of farmers in the fields outside of Tours, bending their backs to the earth, alongside their whole family, from grandchildren to spouses." Surrounded by students from across Europe, Molly found a new sense of wholeness in herself, awakening to the fact that as naïve as she might have been to have never considered it before, the world beyond Danville, Illinois, was as interesting as it was immense.

Molly returned to France two years later, this time to spend a year as part of a study-abroad program with the University of Illinois at Urbana-Champaign, where she'd enrolled in 1967 as a French major. While the study-abroad program was strictly and exclusively reserved for juniors, Molly—just a sophomore—applied anyway. She was turned down by the program administrators, who encouraged her to apply the following year when she was eligible. But the more they refused, the more she persisted, and in August 1968, having finally worn them down, Molly boarded a boat in New York City, the only sophomore in a group of thirty students. They went first to Grenoble for two months and then on to the University of Rouen in Normandy to study for a year.

Molly loved life in France as an eighteen-year-old as much as she had when she was fifteen. She immersed herself in the culture, the art, the theater, and her classes in French literature. She discovered Sartre and Camus and began to explore existentialism, and different political philosophies, even attending leftist meetings at the university. In Rouen, she again lived with a family—this time, it was the father who made a mark on her. He had been a prisoner of war during World War II. Fluent in three languages, he had been forced for several years to translate for the Germans. In the evenings, after the empty dinner plates had been cleared from the table, with his hands shaky from too many cigarettes and a past he couldn't forget, he spent hours answering Molly's questions about this painful time in his life. "For the first time, I have some idea of what your life was like fighting the war," Molly later wrote to her father on lined white paper, alone in her bedroom. "As you know, it is very hard for my generation to realize exactly what a world war means and involves. . . . I'm always so proud to say, 'Yes, my father came here to France. He was fighting with you, risking his life so far from home.'"

During every school break, and after classes had finished, Molly traveled. In the summer, she and an American girlfriend left Rouen with just fifty dollars and spent a month hitchhiking through Europe. Depending entirely on hitched rides, they made their way through Germany to Austria, down to Yugoslavia, then Greece, and took a boat to Crete, before heading back to France. Staying in hostels and subsisting on bread, chocolate, and yogurt, they spent most of their money on entrance fees to Europe's museums and out-of-the-way galleries, the ballet, and the opera in Vienna. After that trip, Molly volunteered for a French group working in the Algerian quarters of the city of Caen on the northern coast of France. There she had her first experience with development work and how it can go wrong. With other volunteers, Molly spent weeks painting and renovating a center to be used by young children in the neighborhood. When all was finally finished, she and the other volunteers came to the center to discover that it had been trashed the night before by members of the community. When asked why they'd done this, the community members explained that they hadn't been included in the activity by the leaders and they were suspicious of the motivation and intentions of the group. "This was my first lesson in understanding the best way to really help others," Molly recalls. "People have to be listened to, involved, and engaged from the very beginning."

While in Paris on the weekends, Molly went to the American Cultural Center, where she met Joseph Jarman of the Art Ensemble of Chicago, a modern jazz group very popular with the French. They struck up a conversation, and Jarman, impressed with Molly's fluent French, asked if she'd be interested in working as their translator. She was overjoyed to do so—she knew very little about jazz at the time—and she spent several evenings accompanying Jarman and his band to meetings and to Paris's underground jazz clubs. Inside, the air was thick with smoke and possibility. While she seldom drank alcohol and was interested in neither cigarettes nor drugs, she found the experience exciting and wild, if only because it was so astoundingly different from her life back home. But she sometimes struggled with feeling out of place. Jarman and the other members of the ensemble were at least ten years older than she, and at times she had to work hard to hide the self-consciousness she felt, both because of her age and her lack of worldliness.

This really hit home for her one night while at a club. In the middle of a set, a woman sitting at a table not too far from Molly stood up, walked to the center of the room, and began to dance. The woman may not have been beautiful, at least not traditionally so, but she was tall and graceful, and with the way she moved her arms, the way her body swayed, ensconced in the long flowing fabric of her dress, Molly thought she was the most gorgeous sight in the world. She was mesmerized and wanted nothing more than to watch that woman forever.

And she knew right then: that was how she wanted to live. She wanted to find a place where she too could stand on her own, walk to the center of a room, close her eyes, raise her arms, and, without even a thought that she might look foolish or make a mistake, without an ounce of self-consciousness, dance as freely and beautifully as she wanted.

MOLLY MOVED TO CHICAGO in 1970 to finish her course work at the Circle Campus of the University of Illinois, and after graduating in December she felt torn about where to head with her life. She worked part-time selling clothes at Marshall Field and Company, the well-known department store, before taking a job as a substitute teacher. While she was generally happy, she was never truly able to shake the idea that she was, in so many ways, gravely disappointing her mother. Ann's greatest hope was that her daughters would grow up to be successful and financially secure, whereas Molly was never interested in that. She never concerned herself with money, and although she did hold a deep desire to one day become a mother, she couldn't envision a life behind a white picket fence in the suburbs of Illinois. Whenever Molly returned to Danville to visit her parents, Ann did not attempt to hide her displeasure over the fact that her youngest daughter was wasting her life. Here was a young woman with so much talent and ability—traits Ann feared Molly was at risk of squandering by not pursuing the one thing that could protect her from a life of sacrifice and hardship: the pursuit of economic security.

By the time Molly had entered graduate school at the University of Illinois in 1972 to study French, hoping to one day get a job as a teacher or interpreter, she had given up trying to please Ann. She'd come to feel that her mother's desire to mold her in a certain, specific way was like trying to mold a piece of wet soap in your hands. Try as you might, the soap can't take the pressure; eventually it slips and falls away.

4

Wàcc-bees bi (The Newcomer)

After arriving in Dakar in October 1974, Molly was eventually able to persuade the university to keep the terms of the exchange agreement. She was given a spot in the master's program, a fifty-dollar-a-month stipend, and a room in the women's dorm, which she shared with an undergraduate student for sixteen dollars a month.

"Looking back, I'm not sure how I convinced the university to allow me to stay," she says. "I just kept showing up at the offices saying, 'I can't leave. I'm here. We need to make this work.' I think once they understood how much I'd come to love Senegal, they couldn't help but say yes."

Life at the university was not easy at first. While she'd thought her French would be enough for her to get by with in Senegal, most of the students communicated in Wolof. Originating as a commercial language used for trading purposes among the Wolof people and other ethnic groups, Wolof was the most common national language, spoken by 80 percent of the population. Of course Molly couldn't speak a word of it, and even with the students with whom she could communicate, she found many cultural differences. With her tendency to venture out alone on the weekends to explore the music scene, the beaches, or the different local markets, Molly didn't understand at first why the women in her dorm seemed to regard her so oddly. Many were away from their families and villages for the first time, and while she tried to engage with them as much as possible—asking their opinion on the African literature books she was reading, commenting on their lives as students—they seemed to have very little to say to her. But many asked if they could borrow money, thinking that most Americans were rich. She found this upsetting, partly because of the way it set her apart from the others and partly because she didn't have anything to give. To buy her ticket to Senegal, she'd borrowed $1,000 from a Danville bank, and she had so little money that semester that she subsisted largely on banana-mayonnaise sandwiches she made in her room most nights, on bread she bought from a street vendor next to the women's dormitory.

She also felt that in many ways she had returned to an era she had just recently escaped. As a college student in the late 1960s, she had gone through a period of great personal and political transformation. She'd arrived at the University of Illinois a wholesome, conservative Republican with a strict Christian upbringing—albeit one she'd never fully bought into. In Danville, Molly and her sister, Diane, attended Trinity Lutheran School through the sixth grade, a private religious school. Her family was a regular of the affiliated church, part of the Missouri Synod, a conservative branch of Lutheranism that teaches the strict interpretation of the Bible, espousing the idea that all humankind are sinners who can only gain access to heaven through the acceptance of Jesus Christ as their Savior. Every Sunday, expected to sit primly through the long service held inside the small, rustic, Bavarian-style church, Molly tried her best to fit in. "Everyone was sitting so perfectly stiff, as if they had umbrellas up their bottoms," she recalls. "Though it was never easy for me, I did what I could to mimic them, but it seems like I was always in trouble for something." In high school, having accepted her parents' political beliefs, she campaigned for Barry Goldwater, and when asked by a local newspaper reporter if she liked the longer, duck-tailed hairstyle popular among teenage boys, Molly said she didn't. "I think short hair is neater," she said. "Long hair looks too hoody."

But once she became a student at the university, it didn't take long before she shed her more conservative beliefs and ideals. Intrigued by the social transformations and political activism unfolding around her, she began to attend antiwar protests and marches for civil rights, and witnessed the beginnings of the feminist movement as it took hold, its members calling for equal rights, sexual freedom, and an end to modesty. Molly was enthralled. She grew her hair long and traded in the petticoat skirts and saddle shoes she'd worn in high school for sandals, big hoop earrings, and loose, colorful tops. She hemmed her miniskirts as short as everyone else, and for the first time in her life she began to undress in front of other girls; the modesty her mother had always expected of her felt silly now. After all, why should a woman feel shame about her body?

In Senegal, though, she felt as if she had arrived at a place and time that had missed this progress. The women she met were as she had once been: constrained by expectations and rigid social norms, and generally less free to simply be themselves. Perhaps it could be explained by religion, she thought. Senegal is a predominantly Muslim country—with about 94 percent of the population practicing the religion—and while most Senegalese women do not wear a veil, they do adhere to the tenets of their faith. Perhaps this was why the women did not go out much or express their opinions often, and why Molly's roommate was compelled to finally approach her one day and explain a well-known Wolof proverb that warns that seeing a bare bottom at the beginning of the day brings bad luck all day long.

"The girls in the dorm would appreciate if you'd stop undressing in front of everyone," she said, to Molly's great embarrassment.

Molly did eventually grow close to one woman. Her name was Ndey, and she was from Mauritania, a nation just north of Senegal. They met during a meal in the student cafeteria and began to spend a lot of time together. Ndey came from a village called Sélibaby, in eastern Mauritania, several hours from the border of Senegal. Her family remained in the village, where her father was an ambulance driver and her mother raised her younger siblings. Molly had never met anyone from a place like Sélibaby—a remote African village lacking many modern conveniences—and she peppered Ndey with questions about what it was like to grow up there.

"What do people do for fun?" she'd ask. "Is it hard to live without electricity? What's the food like?"

"You should just come see for yourself," Ndey suggested one afternoon. "Come home with me for Tabaski." One of the most important holidays in Islam, Tabaski commemorates the willingness of Abraham, the biblical patriarch, to sacrifice his son as commanded by God. It is a day of great celebration during which every family slaughters a sheep or goat. Molly couldn't think of a better way to spend a week than traveling to a new country to witness this special holiday with an African family in a remote village.

A few weeks later, on a warm morning in late December 1974, as her family prepared for Christmas back home, Molly followed Ndey and dozens of other students from the university to the Dakar train station to catch the Bamako Express. Carved through some of West Africa's most desolate terrain, the Bamako line opened in 1923 and was once considered one of the most luxurious train journeys through all of Africa, carrying passengers from Dakar to the capital of Mali. This was hardly the case when Molly and Ndey boarded the train that morning. The rundown cars were packed full of passengers heading home for the Tabaski holiday, and Molly and Ndey had to push their way through the crowd to search for seats, squeezing past the men and women strolling the packed aisles selling peanuts and oranges from thin, metal trays. Molly was sure she and Ndey were going to have to stand the entire twelve-hour journey to Kidira, a town in eastern Senegal near the Malian border where they would catch a bush taxi to Sélibaby, but they were fortunate to get two of the last seats in the back of the dining car, crammed beside other passengers sitting with large suitcases and packages balanced on their laps. The engine eventually creaked into action, and before long they had left behind the crowded, bustling streets of Senegal's capital city and entered a long, seemingly endless stretch of dry savannah and eternal scrubland.

The trip was long and slow, and the passengers around her grew restless and bored, often laying their heads on the dining table to rest. But Molly was riveted, loving every minute of the journey—the adventure of taking a twelve-hour trip to a new country, the sights and smells of the train. Outside the window were her first sights of Africa beyond the two months she'd spent in Dakar. For most of the trip, she felt as if they were traveling through a place where only the brush and sand could survive, broken periodically by small collections of desert villages, standing like ancient sculptures in the bush, and surrounded on either side by vast forests of baobab trees hugging the horizon. They passed women in colorful wraparound skirts walking home from a well, large pails of water precariously balanced atop their heads, and men and boys crowded onto horse-drawn carts, heading back from a long day of work in the fields.

It was nearly ten o'clock at night when the train finally screeched to a halt in Kidira. "We have to cross the river here and enter Mali," Ndey explained as they disembarked. "Tomorrow we'll catch a bush taxi from the town center into Mauritania." As they made their way from the station toward the river, Molly expected to catch sight of a bridge they'd be walking across, but none came into view. Instead, they walked down the banks of the river to the water, where a pirogue—a large flat-bottomed canoe—waited. Molly, Ndey, and several other students from the train piled into the boat, and under the soft blue light of the moon, they began the twenty-minute ride across the Senegal River into Mali.

As they landed and began walking through a small town on the other side of the river, a woman from the nearby village approached the six students and invited them to spend the night in her home.

"Is it okay for us to spend the night with a family no one knows?" Molly whispered to Ndey, as she followed the others.

"Of course. This is Africa, Molly! People help each other out when they're in need. You will better understand this the more time you spend here. Who knows? One day we may help out one of her children." The woman led them to her simple home, where she spread sleeping mats on the floor and prepared a dinner of bread and sardines from the local market.

The next morning, after waiting several hours in the hot sun for an available bush taxi to arrive, they finally flagged down a large truck heading in the right direction, its open bed already full of passengers as well as piles of luggage and bags. Ndey, Molly, and the other students hopped onto the back of the truck, and after more than three hours of bumping across the desert on an unmarked dirt path cut through the dry savannah, they arrived in Sélibaby.

The village was beautiful, with small, adobe huts covered in thatched roofs and large verandahs attached in front. With no electricity or running water, Molly felt as if she had traveled back in time, arriving in a world beyond history. She'd felt the same way in Europe at times, standing in the ancient monastery at Mont Saint-Michel or on the steps of the Acropolis in Athens, but nothing compared to what she felt here in Sélibaby. As she and Ndey walked around the village, stopping at every mud-brick house to say hello and wish people a happy Tabaski, Molly could picture what it was like to live two thousand years ago.

She stayed in the village for a week, sleeping on a thin foam mattress in Ndey's room. Molly kept a journal at the time. In it, she wrote: "I knew as the train pulled out of Dakar late Saturday afternoon amidst throngs of people that I should prepare myself for a bit of culture shock. For although Dakar is in Africa, Africa is not always in Dakar." Given

the significant French influence in Dakar, there was easy access to
Western amenities like modern movie theaters and slick cafés selling
French or American food, where expatriates gathered to drink beer
and exchange stories. But during her first few days in Sélibaby, Molly
found that despite the stark differences with Western civilization—and
despite the fact that she could not communicate with the people, as they
too spoke Wolof—here, in what felt like the *real* Africa, she didn't feel
culture shock at all. Rather, she felt more welcomed and at home than
she ever had before, even more at home than she did in her own house
growing up. Everyone was committed to making her feel comfortable,
and the only thing that seemed to matter was that, as a guest, she felt
happy and at ease. Eager to fit in, she rejected her jeans for the long *boubous* she'd bought in Dakar and joined the women in their work, helping
them carry water from the well in the mornings and cook dinner in the
evenings. And just like everyone else, she used the latrine—a crude
hole in the ground surrounded by a fence made of millet stalks to offer
a little privacy. At night, around the cooking fire and oil lamps, Molly
joined Ndey's family, feeling as if she truly belonged.

This year Tabaski fell on December 25th, and Molly woke that morning on her mat in Ndey's room thinking about her family. Ann Melching
loved Christmas. She was very skilled at creating the right atmosphere,
and the Melching home was always beautifully adorned with a large
tree, tasteful lights, and plenty of Christmas decorations. Molly thought
fondly of her family gathering for the holiday, but she was far more eager
to witness the Tabaski celebrations. Everyone rose early. While the men
were at the mosque, the women readied the sheep to be sacrificed after
the special morning prayers. At three in the afternoon, everyone rushed
to put on their best outfits before going from house to house to extend
holiday greetings to each of their neighbors.

A few days after Tabaski, Molly and Ndey were paid a visit by Mamadou, a man they had met on the train. He was from Sélibaby, where his
wife and children still lived while he studied to become a doctor at the

University of Dakar. Tall and lanky, he sank into the pillows laid on the mats on the floor and explained why he had come.

"I needed to leave my house," he said in French. "They're cutting my daughter today."

Molly was confused. "What do you mean they're cutting your daughter?"

Mamadou glanced uncomfortably at Ndey before answering. "It's a tradition we practice here. They cut the girls' genitals—usually the clitoris and the lips."

"Are you serious?"

"I am, yes."

Molly was incredulous. "But why?"

"It's an ancient ritual, necessary for a girl to be respected in the community and find a good husband."

"But isn't it terribly painful and even dangerous for her?" Molly asked.

"It is." He explained that an older woman with no formal medical training performed the procedure using a razor blade.

"But how can you—? You're studying to be a doctor," Molly said.

"I'm against it, but the tradition is stronger than my will," Mamadou said, his eyes fixed on a tree in the distant fields. "It's partly why I came home. I told my wife I didn't want her to do it, but I knew she and my mother would do it anyway. I'd rather be here, close to home when it happens. It can lead to real problems." He looked at Molly with sadness. "I'd rather be here than far from my daughter right now."

For the rest of the day Molly couldn't get the conversation out of her mind. She wanted to ask Ndey about it, but she could tell by her friend's silent reaction during the conversation that Ndey was not open to discussing it, and despite Molly's curiosity, she knew it was far more important she not offend her friend.

EARLY THE NEXT MORNING Molly and Ndey packed their belongings and headed back to the road to take them to the train. Once aboard the Bamako Express, Molly slipped off her sandals and settled into her seat for the long trip back to Dakar. She couldn't help but think more about her conversation with Mamadou. It seemed unbelievable that a mother could do this to an innocent young girl, to her own daughter. How could it be that in the twentieth century such things still occurred? Surely there was something behind this potentially harmful act she just didn't understand.

As Africa's dry savannah rolled past outside, her mind darted back to a childhood experience of her own, one she hadn't given any thought to in many years. It was, of course, in no way comparable to having one's genitals cut, but it was the closest she could come to understanding why a mother would knowingly allow her daughter to go through such pain, and the memory filled her with empathy.

By the time she was three years old, Molly had developed severe buckteeth. When she turned six and started school, she often returned home distraught. "The other kids make fun of my teeth," she complained to her mother. "They call me Bucky Beaver."

Ann took Molly to an orthodontist. "I'm afraid that Molly is causing the problem herself," he said. Molly had developed a habit of aggressively sucking on her bottom lip with her top teeth, causing her front teeth to grow outward. "Until your daughter breaks this habit, her teeth cannot be fixed."

Despite Ann's best efforts, she could not get Molly to stop this behavior. It was a long-held ritual, one that brought her tremendous comfort. At night, lying in bed with her cherished stuffed dog named Pluto, Molly would rub Pluto's soft fur and suck on her lip.

Ann was beside herself with worry. She didn't want Molly to be considered unattractive or be ostracized because of her looks. Not if there was something she could do about it.

The next night Ann snuck into Molly's room while she slept. She quietly took Pluto from where he lay next to Molly's pillow, and she cut away a tiny piece of his worn, gray fur. The next night she did it again, this time taking a snip from his tail. Night after night, as Molly slept, Ann came into Molly's room and cut away a piece of Pluto. It didn't take long for Molly to notice her beloved dog disappearing during the night. She ran to her mother. "What is happening to my Pluto?" she cried out.

"I don't know what you mean," Ann would say, shooing Molly from the room. Each morning Molly would wake, worried that Pluto had further shrunk during the night, and each morning she would find it to be true. Eventually Molly awoke to find that, beside her, all that was left of Pluto was a small piece of his ear. She put the ear away, heartbroken and lonely. But she never did suck on her teeth again. The braces she was given a few months later were extremely painful, giving her headaches and making her gums bleed, and the headgear she had to wear to school just caused her further embarrassment.

She complained to her mother. "Why do I have to have these on my teeth?" she insisted.

"Because they'll make you more attractive, and the kids will stop picking on you," Ann replied. Though she was not an affectionate woman, she placed her hand on Molly's cheek. "Later, when it's time for you to date boys, you'll understand. It might not make sense now, but you'll eventually thank me for what I've done."

5

Teraanga ji (Welcome)

"So, why is a girl like you staying on in a place like this?" Sitting at a table in a Dakar restaurant next to Molly and her sister, Diane, who was visiting her in 1975, this American college student couldn't believe Molly had just said she was going to remain in Senegal. "I came here to live for a while," he said, "but now all I want is to go home. It's the trash and the flies."

"If you look over the flies and into the eyes of the people," Molly replied, "Senegal will grab you by the waist, as it has me; you won't want to let go either."

For a lot of Westerners, this might be hard to imagine, and for that they should be forgiven. The country is certainly beautiful in its way—overwhelmingly so at times. *Teraanga,* meaning hospitality in Wolof, is more than just a word; it's a way of life. And the culture presents an interesting mix of refined French culture and third-world need. But it's arguably not the easiest place to live, especially for anyone accustomed, as Molly was when she arrived in 1974 (at the hottest time of the year, no less, when the threat of malaria is constant), to the modern conveniences of America—hot water, air-conditioning, reliable electricity, paved roads, and fewer flies.

Even after the years she's now spent in Senegal and how well she has come to know the country and its culture, she has a difficult time articulating what it is that initially drew her in so fiercely and immediately. Perhaps it was the simple fact that in Senegal she'd discovered a place where she felt people truly cared about other people, in a way she hadn't experienced before. She also physically fit in. She'd always been the tallest girl in her class, a characteristic that, growing up, made her feel "awkward and gawky," and despite her thinness, her mother had often been quite concerned with Molly's weight, urging her to watch what she ate and to exercise more so that she could be happier and would look better in her clothes. In Senegal, Molly found the opposite to be true. Senegalese women are statuesque—the revered queens of Senegal, the *lingéers,* had all been tall—and large women are considered beautiful, so much so that some of the girls in Molly's dorm at the University of Dakar took pills to help them gain weight. As Diane explains, "Molly was as skinny as a rail in high school and very tall. She was popular and liked, but I don't think she ever felt fully at home in her body there. When she got to Senegal, she was accepted as a tall woman, and that allowed her in so many ways to just be who she was."

Perhaps. As Molly wrote in her journal not long after arriving in Senegal: "I have a great desire to describe Dakar. How easy to laugh and dance and talk here. To live the daily existence in this town . . . I'm a woman in Dakar. A woman."

Or perhaps it was the distance that living in Senegal put between Molly and her parents. The cost of phone calls was far too expensive, and though she frequently wrote letters to her parents, sometimes as often as twice a week, Molly told them very little. She'd write superficially about the African novels she was reading for class, the things she wanted them to send from home, or the translating jobs she eventually took to earn extra money, working for a range of clients—staff from French- and English-speaking NGOs, a blues band visiting from the United States, a fertilizer company. "I've already begun studying my fertilizers," she wrote to her father soon after getting that job, adding a Melching pun of her own. "But it's kind of a shitty job."

What's remarkable about how little she told her parents was how much she actually had to tell. As she settled in to life in Dakar, Molly— the likable, once-awkward girl from Danville, Illinois—quickly became an integral part of the social circle of some of the most well-known and influential artists and intellectuals in Senegal. She was brought into this world through Ousmane Sembène, considered one of Africa's most important and celebrated filmmakers, and his American wife, Carrie Dailey. Ousmane and Carrie, to whom Molly had been introduced through a professor at the University of Illinois, lived in a house that Ousmane had built himself on the Atlantic Ocean, not far from the city center. Carrie had grown up outside of Chicago and had come to Senegal two years earlier as an Indiana University graduate student to interview Ousmane for the Ph.D. thesis she was writing on him and his work. They'd fallen in love and married in 1973.

Standing nearly six feet tall, Carrie was strikingly beautiful. Known for her sharp intelligence and bold style, she would often shave her head and wear beautiful African clothes, and with her confidence and elegance, she could capture the imagination of every person as she walked into a room. She and Molly became quick friends. At the time, Ousmane was occupied with directing his film *Xala,* which many critics would later consider his finest. While he was off writing in his study, Carrie and Molly would take the dinner they'd made together in Carrie's small kitchen to the terrace over-looking the ocean's rocky shoreline—near where Ousmane had inscribed on the house GALLE CEDDO (THE HOME OF A FREE MAN)—or they'd share it Sen-egalese style, from a common bowl set on a colorful African *pagne* spread on the living room floor. In February, when the dusty *harmattan* winds began to blow in from the Sahara desert, turning the sky hazy and the evenings chilly, they'd build a fire in the fireplace, make cookies, and sip tea.

The timing of their friendship was perfect for them both. Ousmane was nearly twenty years older than Carrie, and as an African-American living in an isolated community with a husband who spent most of his time, pipe in mouth, off in his study, Carrie longed for the closeness of a strong female friendship. And in Carrie, Molly found someone in whom she could confide about her experiences in this new culture, the insecurities she felt at the university, and her desire to better fit in. Carrie, who at thirty-two was eight years older than Molly, taught her much about Senegalese culture, showing her the proper way for a woman to sit around the communal dinner bowl and lending her gorgeous, embroidered *boubous* from her closet, telling her to throw away her miniskirts, because a Senegalese reaction to bare thighs on the street was equivalent to an American's reaction to a Senegalese woman walking bare-breasted through a shopping mall.

"The way you dress in America reflects your individuality and how you feel about yourself," Carrie explained. "The way you dress here reflects how you feel about others. Dress as they do, and people will know you respect them."

While the Sembènes never extended formal invitations, it was well known among many members of the world's intelligentsia—European musicians, African writers and filmmakers, and international journalists who came to interview Ousmane—that on Sunday afternoons, the Sembène house was the place to be.

Jean Brière, a Haitian refugee and poet, was a frequent guest at these gatherings, where he was often spotted sitting in a corner writing in a notebook. When he finished, he would stand to interrupt the party, breaking up the conversation and dancing, and loudly announce, "It is time for my poem!"

After he had dramatically recited the ode he had written for the occasion in flourishing academic French, his wife would run screaming from the back of the room to throw her arms around her husband. "Jean, tu es si brilliant! Quel poème extraordinaire!" she would exclaim.

Molly was most impressed with the Africans she encountered and would often have to contain the excitement she felt in finding herself sitting at the heavy wooden table on the Sembènes' patio, which offered spectacular views as the sun set over the ocean, beside the same person whose work she was currently reading in her African studies program: Camara Laye, a well-known Guinean novelist, and Cheikh Hamidou Kane, the Senegalese writer whose novel *L'Aventure Ambigue* (*The Ambiguous Adventure*) gave Molly insight into the dilemma of straddling two cultures—French and African. She got to meet people like Wole Soyinka, a Nigerian playwright and poet who had been very active in Nigeria's struggle for independence from Great Britain and who would go on to win the 1986 Nobel Prize in Literature.

The experience of meeting the Sembènes, of getting involved so quickly after arriving in Senegal with some of Africa's greatest artists, deeply affected Molly. Despite her love of the culture, she had been questioning how she might better assimilate. The misunderstandings she experienced while living in the university dorm—the requests for money from the other students, the persistent feeling of living on the outside and looking in—often left her lonely and confused. "But how can one judge a culture from the outside?" she wrote in her journal at the time. Her biggest question was one she wrote a short time later: "How can an outsider ever really integrate, and do I really want that?"

The answer to this question would come not long after, when she met Cheikh Anta Diop, a man who would forever change her life.

CHEIKH ANTA DIOP'S OFFICE was a radiocarbon laboratory at L'Institut Fondamental de l'Afrique Noir (the Fundamental Institute for Black Africa) at the University of Dakar. Molly met him in May 1975, seven months after arriving in Senegal. By this time, she had begun to learn Wolof; with her love of language and her intense curiosity about the world, the experience of not being able to communicate had proved too frustrating. For two months she studied at a language center in Dakar, learning dialogue, basic vocabulary, and grammar, and then continued to study on her own through books, study guides, and conversations with anyone who would take the time to speak with her and answer her seemingly endless questions of what certain words meant, as well as put the words into context so she could better understand those that had no equivalent in English. She quickly mastered the language. (In 1980, just five years after beginning her study of the language, the U.S. ambassador to Senegal would assert in a letter to a potential funding agency that Molly spoke Wolof as well as native speakers.)

Molly loved the sound and rhythm of the language, but perhaps what drew her in most were the secrets it revealed about this country to which she was becoming so attached. She'd always understood that the culture and values of a people were often hidden deep within their language. In an article Molly once wrote, published in the Danville newspaper when she was a senior in high school, she said, "To understand the heart of a nation is to know and communicate with the people." And now, through this strange and foreign language, she was discovering a way to experience the world and relate to others that was vastly different from her Western worldview. Unlike the familiar American values she'd always been expected to embrace—progress, individual freedom, material wealth and prosperity—she was coming to find that what mattered most among the Senegalese was concern for the group and taking care of one's family and neighbors. Unlike the celebration of privacy in the English language, the word does not exist in Wolof; instead, words for hospitality, peace, unity, and friendship abound.

Despite how far she'd come in speaking and understanding Wolof, she decided on the way to her first meeting with Cheikh Anta Diop that she would not attempt it with this professor. "People were often so surprised that a young American woman would make the effort to learn Wolof that I couldn't get them to speak about anything else," she says. "And on this day, I didn't have time for that." She was simply in search of a book she needed that he had checked out of the library. But when she arrived at Cheikh Anta's office and was called back to see him after a lengthy wait, Molly was immediately taken. In his early fifties, he was tall and athletic—he'd been a renowned boxer during his student days in

France—and in his crisp white lab coat, Cheikh Anta struck an impos-
ing and impressive sight, causing Molly to immediately change her mind.

"Na nga def?" she offered. (How are you?)

"Maa ngi fii rekk," he responded, laughing with delight and offering
the traditional response. (I am here only.)

Molly stayed at his office for three hours. She spoke of her life in
America and her newfound love of Africa, of the literature she was
studying, and of her growing interest in the Wolof language. The next
Sunday, while the Sembènes' guests gathered on the large patio, Molly
mentioned this meeting to Carrie.

"You're kidding me, right?" Carrie said. "Do you know who he is?"

"He's a professor," Molly responded. "I know that he studied in
France before returning to Senegal."

"He's not *just* a professor, Molly. He's arguably one of the most well-
known and influential Africans of our time, and one of the world's most
important thinkers on African history." She went on to explain that nine
years earlier, in 1966, he'd been honored alongside W. E. B. DuBois as
the scholar who had exerted the greatest influence on African thought
in the twentieth century. With a specialty in Egyptology, Cheikh Anta
believed that the struggle for African independence couldn't succeed
without acknowledging the African origins of humanity and civilization,
arguing that the ancient Egyptians were black. "His thinking is controversial but so important," Carrie said. "If I were you, I'd try to spend
more time with him. People would kill for that opportunity."

Molly took Carrie's advice and soon paid Cheikh Anta another visit.
He welcomed her, offering her a seat across from his desk, and before long
these meetings became more frequent. For hours, they would engage in
philosophical discussions about his work in Egyptology, which traced current practices in black African culture back to the ancient Egyptians. This
new perspective provided Molly with an alternative to dominant colonial
narratives, and she saw its power to reshape historical accounts of Africa.

"And now tell me how you spend your time when you're not here," he
asked. She had a lot to tell. Unable to sit still for very long or to decline

any invitation offered to her—whether it be from a famous poet she'd met at Ousmane and Carrie's or a taxi driver she'd struck up a conversation with on her way back from the market—she told Cheikh Anta of her enthrallment with the people and life of Dakar and the observations she was making about Senegalese culture and the Wolof language.

When it came to Wolof, Cheikh Anta insisted Molly speak only the purist form of it. Since Senegal had first come under French control and French was instituted as the official language, many people, especially those in Dakar, had a tendency to mix French and Wolof, diluting the rich Wolof vocabulary.

"Never mix in French words when you're speaking Wolof," he would scold her during their conversations. "Doing so just impoverishes the language. Find the right word."

Molly did everything she could to please Cheikh Anta, having developed a deep admiration for her mentor. Unlike many other men she was meeting, whose first question was to inquire if she was married or had children, Cheikh Anta was interested in her ideas. He treated her not like a student, but a scholar, and he wasn't shy about encouraging her to focus her studies on the importance of African languages for development.

As her semester drew to a close, Molly asked Cheikh Anta if she might remain in Senegal to continue her studies with him. He happily agreed—a decision that left no doubt in her mind that her stay in Senegal would be prolonged indefinitely. The news came as a great disappointment to her parents, her mother especially. As Diane recalls, "My mom couldn't make sense of Molly's choice to live so far away, in such a different culture. She'd call me often to ask the same thing: 'When is your sister coming home?'"

6

Tostan

Molly's transition from the study of French literature to a career in development began to take root during her second year in Africa, largely through her work as a translator—work she was initially drawn to out of a need for income and the chance for new adventures. "I get to travel to Mali," she wrote her parents. "I am so lucky, lucky, lucky!"

Over time, she came to especially love the experience of accompanying visiting development officers to rural villages, where she'd find herself translating not just the language, but also the culture of Senegal. Through these experiences, she soon became very invested in what she observed in the villages, many of which were so remote, the only way to access them was through narrow, improvised paths cut through tall fields of dried grass. She found that most villages lacked even the most basic necessities, such as electricity and clean drinking water, and the opportunities for medical care were abysmal. Most children were not being vaccinated and fell ill from preventable diseases, such as polio, measles, and tetanus. Molly had seen the typical pictures of malnourished African children, bellies extended and swollen. Now such children stood in front of her in these remote communities of southeastern Senegal.

What surprised Molly the most, however, were the interactions she witnessed between development officers and the villagers. "The meetings were very stiff on both sides," she remembers. "There was little true dialogue happening, no deep inquiry into what was working for villagers and what they thought should be changed. I kept waiting for a conversation to happen, but it rarely did."

Rather, it seemed that many development officers arrived with a clear plan of what they wanted to accomplish and the results they desired without ever asking the villagers if they shared these goals. To make matters worse, most development projects did not include a basic education program the communities needed to effectively manage the projects once the so-called experts left. Without the knowledge of how to sustain the projects, they lay dormant, and years later, when representatives of the organizations returned, they would discover rusty vehicles, broken-down millet grinders and pumps, and nonfunctional health centers.

After these trips, Molly would return to her studies and her life in Dakar, but she couldn't easily disregard her experiences in the villages, and certainly not after spending more time at the Sembène home and in Cheikh Anta Diop's office. Alone with Carrie or Cheikh Anta, and during the Sunday afternoon gatherings with intellectuals from across Africa, Molly engaged in intense discussions about the future of Senegal. This was just fourteen years after Senegal had secured its independence from France, and the conversation often centered around life in postcolonial Africa. The 1960s had been a time of great transition for French-speaking West African countries—many had received independence at the same time—and citizens were confronted with the disturbing realities of political turmoil or dictatorship, corruption at all levels of society, and bleak social conditions. The question was often asked: Were the years of colonization truly over? Having been psychologically submitted to French assimilation policies for decades, could these countries conceivably make a decisive break with the colonizers the moment independence was declared?

At the time, Léopold Sédar Senghor was the president of Senegal. The first president elected after independence, Senghor—a Senegalese poet and cultural theorist—was very French in his lifestyle and his approach to politics, and like many concerned Senegalese, both Ousmane and Cheikh Anta were outspoken critics of him. As they saw it, Senghor appeared to be calling for a restoration of African culture, but his own lifestyle was, in fact, highly dictated by Western thought and ideals, leaving the majority of Senegalese who did not speak French feeling marginalized.

Ousmane once told Molly, "Senghor and his political cohorts have turned their backs on the problems of the people in the rural villages of Senegal, on Senegalese values, and worst of all on our mother tongue." For Ousmane and Cheikh Anta, there was one element critical to the economic and cultural development and the "true" independence of Senegal: the promotion of national languages.

The situation was complicated. While French was the official language of the country, less than 20 percent of the population actually communicated fluently in French. Most people spoke Wolof or one of five other major national languages: Pulaar, Serer, Diola, Soninke, and Mandinka. Even so, the nation's formal schools were conducted exclusively in French, and teachers were trained to use French standards and techniques such as rote memorization with little respect for the cultural and social environment of Senegal. It could well be argued that this French system of schooling was hindering the progress of the majority of the people of Senegal. While students spent weeks learning the correct pronunciation of a language they did not use at home, one out of every four children in Senegal was dying before the age of five. And women were particularly far behind when it came to education. Female literacy in the country was just over half that of male literacy—23 percent compared to 44 percent—and the discrepancy was even greater in rural villages.

Ousmane and Cheikh Anta were leading advocates for designating Wolof the official language of Senegal. In a culture where the idea of *masla* (making others happy at all costs) is key, both were unafraid of saying exactly what they thought, no matter how bold or controversial the idea. Although Ousmane had once written exclusively in French, he'd begun to make films in Wolof, so that the people at the village level could understand and hear a different story of their history and culture than that presented by the government. He wrote stories such as "Le Mandat" ("The Money Order"), which was later adapted into a film in Wolof. In it, Ousmane explores the frustration, humiliation, and inadequacy that an ordinary Senegalese man, Ibrahima Dieng, experiences as a citizen in a land where an alien language is imposed on the masses.

"I was becoming aware of how enthusiastically people responded when I spoke and interacted with them in Wolof, helping me to further understand Ousmane's and Cheikh Anta's ideas on the importance of national languages for development," Molly says now. "This really hit home for me when I visited rural communities and saw how efforts to help villagers were failing." She began to question the very nature of how one helps others, understanding that while outside efforts toward progress were done with good intentions, they were rarely producing the hoped-for results. This was partly due to the fact that education was limited to French.

"How can Senegalese children learn anything about science, geography, literature, or the arts if they don't speak French at home and are having difficulty learning a language so different from their own in school?" Molly began to ask everyone she knew. This seemed only to set children up for failure.

These thoughts of development began to occupy a lot of her thinking, and she was always eager to share them with Cheikh Anta. He was not surprised by what she was observing in the field—how a narrow view of education and development, albeit well intentioned, was ultimately proving to be self-defeating.

"As Africans," he explained one afternoon, leaning across his desk, "the people of Senegal have their own world vision, which is oftentimes quite different from the vision of people who grew up in France, the United States, or the rest of the world. A lot of the differences in vision stem from the simple fact that the goals of an African community—particularly in villages—are, at the most basic level, often very different from European goals."

Molly agreed. The best way to bring about change was for community members to initiate the programs their villages needed most and to be made to feel proud of their African heritage and language. "True social change—true development—seems possible only when you work *with* the people," she thought, "when you start with where they are and, with their input, consider what needs to change."

Relaying this idea to Cheikh Anta, he nodded his head in understanding. "For what you describe, there is a perfect Wolof word. Do you know what it is?"

Molly didn't.

"It's a beautiful word, very important in our language. Literally, the word means the hatching of an egg—the breakthrough moment when the chick emerges from the shell. That chick becomes a hen and lays eggs that it nourishes, and so there are more chicks that become hens and the process continues for generations. For me, the word signifies the idea that as people gain new knowledge in a nurturing environment they can then reach out and share it with others, who in turn do the same. Until African villagers themselves are capable of educating others in a language familiar to all, we will never achieve the type of development that is truly African. This is a word you should never forget."

Molly was intrigued. "What is the word?" she asked.

Cheikh Anta paused and smiled. "*Tostan.*"

7

Maasawu (Empathy)

In July 1975, Molly received an invitation to accompany some Senegalese friends to the Casamance region in southern Senegal. There, they were producing a program for a local television station about circumcision rites for one of the Diola ethnic groups. Molly jumped at the chance, eager for the adventure of it. She'd been told that, during these rites, the young men of various ages preparing to be circumcised were honored with an elaborate celebration and a great feast before being sent off into the forest for over a month as part of their initiation into manhood. Because of hard times and a lack of resources, the ceremony had been postponed for nearly twenty years. Thousands of people from across Senegal, as well as relatives from the diaspora, would convene in one village for the event.

It took an entire day to travel to the Casamance, a region that is Dakar's topographic opposite. While most of the west of Senegal was a sandy, baked landscape, the Casamance looked as Molly had always thought Africa would: deep, lush woods; orchards of mango trees; troops of monkeys peering out from the trees; and big baboons sitting right in the middle of the road. Thousands of people were there when their car pulled into the village, and hundreds more continued to arrive throughout the day via horse-drawn cart or bus. A large fire roared in the center of the village, and men shot their guns into the air as *griots* (traditional singers and storytellers) entertained the crowds milling around the grassy field. Cows and sheep were slaughtered and cooked in the mornings; by late afternoon, people were drowsy from the hot afternoon sun and food, their hands sticky with mutton juice. Molly and her friends spent several days in the village, sleeping on mats laid out under the stars and witnessing the celebrations. Through it all, Molly felt as she did so often since she'd arrived in Senegal a year earlier: fortunate to be included in an experience like this, so unusual and unlike anything most outsiders would ever get to witness.

A few days after arriving, as she strolled through the village absorbing the surroundings, the only white person amid the crowd of thousands, she heard music in the distance. Never one to turn down an opportunity to dance, she went to explore, to see if she might join in. But as she got closer, she forgot about the music and instead was captivated by the sight of about twenty teenage girls in the distance. She saw they were dressed in traditional outfits, with beads around their foreheads and their faces painted white. They sat on the ground in a perfect line, each with their legs touching the back of the girl in front of her, like a colorful caterpillar.

Intrigued, Molly approached a woman nearby. "What is this?"

"They're preparing as well," the woman said.

"For what?"

"To be cut."

Molly looked at the woman with confusion.

"The girls will undergo the initiation rites and cutting as well," she explained.

Molly hadn't forgotten her experience in Mauritania and the feelings she'd had then, but as she watched the crowd encourage and dance for the girls throughout the afternoon, bestowing them with good wishes, she began to realize that perhaps she'd misunderstood. This was not a secretive rite, but rather a public recognition of the importance of what the girls were about to experience.

Curious to learn more, Molly began to speak to her friends, and then to some of the women of the village who explained that the girls from this particular ethnic group were preparing for their initiation rites. This initiation is a critical event in the life of many African girls, representing the momentous passage from childhood into womanhood. However, over the years, many ethnic groups in Africa had abandoned these initiation rites, though they still maintained the cutting.

There were three parts to initiation: the cutting itself, during which the girls were forbidden to show signs of suffering, in order to prove their courage; then, education on the girls' new duties as women; and finally, a solemn pledge of silence pertaining to anything they'd undergone or witnessed during the initiation ceremony, in order to preserve the tradition's sanctity.

The girls would live together throughout the one-month initiation process, away from their families, in a hut specifically built for the occasion. After the cutting, which would take place early in their month together, the girls would be tended to and honored. Women from this and surrounding villages would arrive to wash and treat their wounds. Eventually, the girls would be led out to the fields, where they'd burn their old clothes and receive new ones, symbolizing the new life that awaited them. The women would pray over the girls, for good things to come to them—kind husbands and many healthy children—and then the lessons would commence.

Each girl was taught that as a wife and mother she must be patient, polite, obedient, and ready to serve others. She should not talk too much, and never about family secrets, and she must show honor to her parents and relatives, love her husband, and adore her children. She was taught ways in which to show respect: never looking someone in the eyes when speaking, kneeling when greeting or bringing water, speaking softly, and not talking or laughing too much.

The benefits of initiation were considered to be many. After a girl was cut, she would be guarded by benevolent spirits, and ill fortune would be unable to penetrate her protective curtain of politeness and respect. She would know how to tolerate the behavior of others and manage difficult situations. The initiation the girl received would follow her throughout her life and forge her place in society. And most important, when it was all done, she would be ready for marriage.

According to Molly's friend Daouda Ndiaye, a traditional healer and one of the leaders during initiation ceremonies, a common legend shared during certain initiations was the story of the Great Spirit, who came down to speak with the first man and woman on earth. Turning to the woman, the Great Spirit asked what she most desired from life.

"I want to be master, the creator in this world," she declared.

"So be it," replied the Great Spirit. "You will be the master, the creator in this world, but you must be willing to pay for the important role you will play. You will know suffering and you do not have the right to complain, for this is the role you have chosen. Complaining will lead to ill fortune for you and your children." The woman then regretted this choice, but it was too late.

The Great Spirit turned to the man: "What is your desire?"

"I would have been master and creator in this world, but since the woman has already chosen this role, I wish to be master of the woman."

"So be it," the Great Spirit told him. "You will be master of the woman."

According to the myth, this is why women give birth to all the world's leaders. It is also why they suffer and must do so in silence as a sacrifice to humanity. And because their husbands and fathers are their masters, they must honor and obey them. To do otherwise would risk bringing harm to their families.

A few days later, on the trip back to Dakar, Molly reflected on what she had learned and on one part of the initiation process in particular: the vow of silence. As she understood it, girls who participated in the tradition were prohibited from speaking about it. Doing so would only make them appear weak and bring shame to their families. For the rest of their lives it was their responsibility to hold what happened to them in silence, lest they suffer punishment.

Molly watched the dust from the road form circles around the windows of the car as they passed seas of palm-thatched roofs and barefoot women in colorful *boubous* selling fresh milk from plastic bags on the side of the road. Thinking about the idea that for the rest of their lives these girls would endure such silence, she felt the tears begin to well in her eyes.

Because when it came to the idea of suffering in silence, she understood.

SHE WAS JUST SEVENTEEN years old, a few months into her first year at the University of Illinois, when it happened. He was a graduate student at the university, five years older than Molly and a member of a student activist organization on campus. He spoke passionately and intelligently at the antiwar meetings she attended, urging students to more deeply question why, exactly, the United States had gotten involved in Southeast Asia. Molly found him powerful and fascinating, and when he approached her after a meeting to ask her to dinner to discuss an upcoming rally on campus, she was flattered.

He offered to pick her up at seven o'clock that Friday evening. Molly, ready early and unable to contain her excitement, decided to wait for him on the steps of her dorm. More than an hour passed and he never came. Feeling embarrassed and rejected, she went back upstairs.

The next day she was studying in the student union when he walked into the room. He immediately approached her and apologized.

"I needed to attend an emergency meeting," he said. "I didn't have the number for the phone in your dorm. There was no way to let you know." He invited her to drop her studying and come with him to the organization's office, to meet some of the people working on the new issue of the underground newspaper. Molly felt elated as they walked through a tranquil leafy neighborhood just off campus, happy that he was still interested, that the night before had been a misunderstanding.

They had just walked through the door of the newspaper's office— the ground-floor apartment of a two-story home—when she felt his hands on her, rough and violent, pushing her to the floor, pulling off her top. Molly was too shocked to respond at first, but she quickly felt herself fighting back, trying to push his hands away and pull her shirt back together. But he overpowered her, and before Molly knew it, in a fit of strength and force, he'd removed her clothes.

Lying on the floor at that moment, she knew she couldn't let it happen. She'd never been with a man before, had only kissed a boyfriend, and she was not going to allow him to assault her. She found a strength inside of herself, was able to gather every ounce of it, and pushed him off her. She crawled to the front door, but it wouldn't open. He had somehow locked it from the inside. She had no way out.

He dragged her into a bedroom in the back. It was only then that she had the wits to realize that this was not the organization's office. This was his house. In the bedroom, as he groped her and pinned her arms to the bed, she tried her best to steady her voice and reason with him.

"I don't want to do this," she said. "I'd like to just go."

"You can go," he said, with blatant cruelty in his voice. "After I have sex with you."

Molly was somehow able to break free. She ran into the bathroom and locked the door behind her, frantically checking to be sure he couldn't get in. In the mirror she saw that there were bruises on her skin and scratch marks on her arms and legs. Wrapping herself in a towel, she sat on the cold tiled floor. For the next few hours, she tried to comfort herself by silently reciting the nursery rhymes she remembered from her youth.

It was early the next morning when she heard him kick the bathroom door. "Get the hell out of my bathroom and out of my house."

Molly waited a few minutes before opening the door an inch and peering out. She saw him lying on his bed. Seizing the moment, she moved as quickly as she could to collect her tattered clothing. "You're lucky," he muttered. "I screwed some other girl the night before. I was tired last night. Otherwise you would have had no chance."

She walked back to her dorm in a daze, and when she entered her room—bewildered, bruised, and with her clothes torn—her roommate gasped. "We've all been so worried," she said, leading Molly to sit on her bed, where she covered her with a blanket before running from the room to summon the dorm mother.

"I was at this guy's house. He almost raped me," Molly managed. "I have to go to the police."

"Are you badly hurt?" the dorm mother asked her.

"I'm bruised and sore from fighting him off."

"Go take a shower."

"But I have to go to the police."

"You can't do that," the dorm mother said.

Molly looked at her in confusion. "Why not? I don't understand."

"You know how you feel right now? You'll feel much worse after going to the police."

"I don't understand," Molly repeated.

"You went to his house, right?"

"Yes, but I didn't—"

"They'll say you were looking for it. You have no defense."

Molly felt as if the room were spinning around her.

"I'm telling you, I don't want you to go to the police. I don't want you to have to go through that."

"But I should do something about it. I should try to stop him." Molly began to sob, finally allowing all the tears she'd been holding back. "What did I do wrong? I just went over to see about the newspaper. It was the middle of the afternoon—"

"Shhh," the dorm mother said. "Go shower. Get some rest. You'll feel much better."

The next morning Molly woke up feeling achy and alone. Someone had come to her with the name of a psychiatrist affiliated with the university's psychology department. She went to his office, still in a state of shock. Sitting across from him in a small, brightly lit room, she felt the devastation of what had happened to her sink in further as she repeated her story. "This person who I thought was doing good for society, who believed in peace and justice . . . I just can't make sense of it. He's talked so much about ending violence and the war." She began to cry again.

The doctor listened and when Molly was finished, he nodded his head. "I think I know why you're having such a hard time dealing with this."

"You do?"

"Well, you liked it, didn't you?"

Molly felt her stomach turn. "What?"

"You liked it. What he did to you. I think that's really why you're this upset."

"What are you talking about?" She stood up, fumbling for her purse. "How could you possibly imagine that I could have enjoyed that?"

Molly left the office feeling desperate for help. Unsure of where else to go, she found herself at the front door of the Lutheran church on campus, where she asked to speak to the pastor, a kind and ordinary man she had talked to once before. When she explained the situation, he clearly was at a loss for words, unable to offer her any guidance. "God will forgive you," he finally said.

"But I didn't do anything wrong," Molly stammered.

"Pray about it. You will find comfort in God."

Molly left, found a pay phone, and called her sister, Diane, now a student at Southern Illinois University. Diane's voice broke with concern when Molly, still in tears, told her what had happened.

"Molly, you need to talk to somebody who will understand. We'll find you the right person." Diane had a friend who had seen a counselor at the University of Illinois's student counseling center, and Diane called Molly later that afternoon with his phone number.

This man was the right person, or was at least the first one to try to assure Molly that what had happened was not her fault. "You absolutely should not feel any guilt about this," he said. Molly felt a wave of relief that someone, finally, understood what she had endured; that even though the physical assault was over, her suffering was only beginning. During her second meeting, he shared something that shocked her. "You're the fourth woman we know of that this guy has attacked. One girl who came to us says he tied her to the bed, raped her, and she was afraid she was pregnant. He left bite marks on her body."

"He's an animal," Molly choked. "What can be done to protect other girls?"

"Unfortunately, there's nothing we can do. His father is politically well connected. These events take place at his house. If people want to press charges, they don't have any proof. If I went to the police now on your behalf, they'd say he didn't rape you. They'd ask why you were at his house."

"I told you. I went under false pretenses."

"I know that. But can you prove it in court?"

Molly left his office feeling nothing but overwhelming shame. How had she gotten herself into this situation? How had she not protected herself better? She longed to speak to other women who had been through the same situation, but in 1967 there was nowhere to turn, no support groups for women in her situation, no female counselors she could find. Again and again, she returned to the advice the counselor had suggested: she needed to tell her parents.

Molly's hands were shaking a few days later as she stood at the pay phone dialing her parents' number. She hadn't wanted to do this. Her mother was not the type of woman who was comfortable speaking about sexuality. Molly had been too timid to even tell her mother when she got her first period, choosing instead to go to a friend's mother. The only sexual guidance Ann ever offered Molly was to remind her that kissing boys before marriage was dangerous. And after all, hadn't her parents tried so hard to protect her from bad things just like this? But Molly didn't know where else to turn. She'd become too distraught to study or attend classes, and she feared she was jeopardizing her education.

She didn't say much on the phone, other than that she wanted them to come for a visit. A few days later, Molly sat at a campus coffee shop across from her parents, the grief of her story heavy in their eyes.

"Where does this guy live?" Al said. "I'm going to beat him up."

"No, Dad, don't. He didn't end up raping me. I just wanted to tell you."

Ann was mostly silent during the conversation, but a few days later Molly received a letter from her mother. "Someone who has not suffered cannot live life in all its fullest, Molly," Ann wrote. "I would never want you to hide and be afraid and sit within your four walls. You go right on meeting life head on and do the best you can when you meet its vices and its virtues. . . . Somehow, as bad as I know this experience was for you, I feel that you will get so much from it. . . . I think you know such things existed, but until you are actually faced with all the complexities and the impacts of such an incident, you don't really know about it. Maybe now, because of this, you can save yourself or someone else from a much worse situation someday."

Molly found great comfort in her mother's letter, and she tucked it away in a safe place, thinking about it often. But after that day, she kept the experience to herself, and it would be many, many years before Molly would divulge her experience to another person outside of her family. She had been made to feel such shame about the assault, and she didn't know how to speak of it. She didn't want to rock the boat by going public about it, to bring further attention to what had happened, to be stigmatized from that point forward as either the girl who'd nearly been raped or the one who had caused all the trouble. She didn't know what else to do.

So she did the only thing she could do: she lived with the silence.

8

Démb ak Tey (Yesterday and Today)

By 1976, after living in Senegal for two years and having fully abandoned the idea that she was going to return to the United States anytime soon, Molly had come to an important realization: her true passion lay not in what she had come to Senegal to study—African literature written in French—but in the field of development and the study of national languages. "The African literature I was reading was frequently about people trapped between two cultures," she says. "But as I ventured out into Africa, to the markets of Dakar and the villages outside of the city, I realized that people were not torn at all. . . . They loved their culture and were confident in their way of life. They had a very clear idea of society based on family, friendship, warmth, and hospitality. They were proud to be African."

By this time, Molly had received her master's certificate from the University of Dakar. She went on to receive a master's degree from the University of Illinois at Urbana-Champaign, when her thesis on "The Role of National Languages in Development," which she wrote in Dakar, was accepted. In it, she argued for the use of national languages, particularly in education. Hoping for a way to apply her studies and insights, she showed up unannounced at the Peace Corps office in Dakar, where she asked to speak to Jack Schafer, the director at that time.

"I've come to pitch an idea," she said, taking a seat across from him. "I want to start a center for children not enrolled in school. A place where they can engage in cultural activities while learning to read and write in Wolof, through books written in their own language."

She'd had the idea a few months earlier, she explained. Since arriving in Dakar, she'd been volunteering at a city orphanage and had discovered a scarcity of books available to Senegalese children. Any children's books she could find in bookstores or libraries throughout the city were written in French, and their stories about Jacques's adventures on the Paris Metro or Marie's skiing trip to the snowy Alps were hardly geared to the children of Senegal. "How can children be expected to enjoy reading if nothing available for them to read is relevant to their lives?" she asked.

"I'm not sure," Jack Schafer replied, likely feeling confused.

"They can't," Molly continued. "And I think we can change that. We can produce the books ourselves at the center." She'd already worked it all out, beginning with having found the perfect location for the center—two rooms in the African Cultural Center, in a neighborhood called the Medina. Located near downtown Dakar, the Medina was established by the French authorities in 1914, after a severe outbreak of bubonic plague, as a so-called native quarter for the African population—a segregated area where Senegalese were forced to live separate from the areas inhabited by the colonizing Europeans. It had remained one of the most populated and poorest sections of Dakar ever since. Extended families were crammed into two-room apartments; children too poor to attend school roamed the narrow streets all day with little to do.

While this may have been the neighborhood that most visitors to Dakar would have preferred to avoid, it had always been one of Molly's favorites. She was drawn to the energy she felt, the vibrancy of life, in the neighborhood. She often visited a woman, the mother of twelve children and the grandmother of many more, who lived in the heart of the Medina. "Mama," as she was known throughout the community, always welcomed Molly with open arms, offering her a place around the bowl. As everyone knew, Mama was one of the best cooks around. Her small, simple, and comfortable house was always alive with dozens of children who, like the thousands of others living in such close quarters, had nowhere to go for play and learning activities. The time Molly spent there convinced her that the children of the Medina might really thrive at the center she had in mind, if given the chance.

"I've also been in touch with several different publishing houses based around the world," Molly went on to explain, "and have asked them to send children's books of African stories with beautiful drawings and simple text. I want to translate these into national languages and use them to encourage Senegalese writers and artists to create books that will interest Senegalese children."

"I'm not saying any of this is a bad idea, but maybe you don't understand how the Peace Corps works," Mr. Schafer said when she had finished.

"I know exactly how it works," Molly said. She knew it was a rigorous and competitive application process, requiring background checks, reference letters, and a health screening, after which selected volunteers were assigned to an existing position chosen by the Peace Corps. "But can't we make it work a little differently this time?"

"How so?"

"I want my job creating this children's center to be a Peace Corps position."

Perhaps it was her persistence or the strength of her idea, but the Peace Corps director said yes. Using a special exemption from normal procedures, Schafer created a three-year individual placement for Molly sponsored through Senegal's Ministry of Culture. The position came with a standard stipend of about $200 per month and a one-bedroom apartment in the center of the very busy and bustling Sandaga market, next to the *car rapide* terminal. Molly would go to sleep each night and awaken each morning to the sound of the conductors yelling out destinations throughout the city: "Grand Dakar! Grand Dakar! Yoff! Yoff! Yoff!"

Before opening the center and beginning her position with the Peace Corps, Molly returned to the United States to spend time with her parents. During this visit, her family received devastating news. Her father, Al, was diagnosed with colon cancer. Molly ended up remaining with her parents for five months, and she felt lucky to have this time with her father, despite how sick he'd become with the disease. After all these years, it seemed that he had changed.

"Molly, some of the people in this town are quite racist, and I don't like it," he said to her one day.

"But Daddy, you have had a racist attitude in the past. Have you forgotten how uncomfortable you were when my African-American friends came to the house when I was in high school?"

"Oh, that was a long time ago, Molly. People change. How could I not have changed being around you and your sister all these years? I've realized it's wrong, but that is how we were brought up then. By the way, I'm thinking about going into the Peace Corps now," he said with a smile. "Do you think they would take me with cancer?"

"They'd be lucky to get you," Molly replied. Al died one month later.

UPON RETURNING TO SENEGAL after Al's death, Molly opened the children's center, which she named Démb ak Tey (Yesterday and Today), and worked there for six years—the first three as a Peace Corps volunteer and the next three with funding she secured from the Chicago-based Spencer Foundation. The center became not only her livelihood but her life. As the only employee, Molly spent nearly every hour of her week at the center, a work ethic she would never abandon. Throughout these six years at the center, she adapted dozens of stories into Wolof, developing an impressive library of children's books written in national languages. Each day as many as sixty children, including of course

Mama's grandchildren, crowded into the center's two rooms to hear Molly read these stories aloud in her increasingly fluent Wolof.

The most popular book among the children of the center was one that Molly wrote herself, after a particularly painful experience at a party she'd attended in Dakar. Throughout her life, Molly had grown distinctly aware of the destructive effects of racism, at least as much as any white person growing up in America can be. While she'd always been in the majority, she was admittedly most drawn to people different from herself. She fondly remembered a time in junior high school when the students in her art class were assigned the task of choosing someone in the room to draw. An African-American student named Charles chose Molly, and when he showed her his final product, she saw that he'd drawn her as a black girl. Something about this really moved her and she asked Charles if she could keep the drawing. She brought it home to show her mother.

"Molly, this is a black girl," Ann said.

"It does look like that, doesn't it?" Molly said. "I really love it."

Ann probably didn't like it quite as much, and she liked it even less when Molly proudly announced to her parents during her sophomore year in college that she was in love. His name was Victor and he was a creative writer, who also happened to be African-American. Molly dated him for four years. She truly loved him, and when they walked down the street together and she noticed the glances and stares they received, she never thought it was because people felt uncomfortable by the sight of a biracial couple, but instead because she and Victor made such a handsome couple. Her mother struggled with the relationship, attempting at first to dissuade Molly from continuing it, informing her that couples who "share many things in common" have a better chance of staying together, that she'd get along better with someone with a similar background. Molly knew what Ann meant, but she chose not to address this. It didn't bother her that she and Victor were different; in fact, she preferred this.

"Why would I want to date someone who is the same as me?" she asked her mother every time the issue arose. "How utterly boring. Life is full of possibilities to learn new things, and being with someone different means I'll just learn so much more. It means I'll have the chance to see things differently, to take on a whole new perspective of what life might be."

Trying to be subtle, Ann eventually hinted to Molly that if she kept dating Victor, she and Al might stop paying for Molly's college tuition. Molly was furious and didn't have to give a second thought to her response. She applied for work at Marshall Field's and the Shoreline Hotel the next day and told Ann she would no longer be accepting another dime from her. The situation caused a serious rift in her relationship with her mother, but Ann did try her best. "Just a note to say that every day I am improving my attitude about your relationship with Victor," she later wrote to Molly in a letter. "Al has helped me so much to see that I have been keeping you tied to the umbilical cord. It *is* your life and I am constantly working toward the reality of you being an entity unto yourself."

Given this worldview, it was therefore never uncomfortable for Molly to be, as she often was since arriving in Senegal, the only white person in attendance at most functions. But at a birthday party for a Senegalese friend attended by some visiting African-Americans, Molly sensed an unfamiliar tension. Eventually, without any provocation, she was approached by one of the Americans and loudly asked to leave.

Confused, she asked this person to explain. "Why would I leave?"

"Isn't it obvious?"

"No, not to me. I was invited," Molly said.

"Well, you don't fit in," the woman said. "Hurry and eat, and then get your fat white ass out of here." Molly was mortified. She looked at the friend who had invited her, hoping he would intervene and defend her. When he remained silent, Molly discarded her plate of food, hot and untouched, and left the party.

She stayed at home and cried for three days. "I wasn't even so much crying for myself," she says. "It was just that for the first time I understood what discrimination feels like . . . what it does to people. It made me feel awful. Just because of the color of your skin you're told to leave by a person who's never seen you before, who knows nothing about you?" After allowing herself three days of brooding over what had happened, she sat down at the small table in her room and began to write a story.

In a village very far away lived a people with necks so long that everyone called them the Longnecks. They lived in peace in their small village until one day, to the great surprise of all the villagers, a little girl named Anniko arrived. She looked very strange to them. "What a short neck she has!" they whispered. They'd never seen anyone with a short neck and they didn't know what to make of her, but she seemed like a kind and sensitive girl, and they invited her to stay. Anniko accepted their invitation. She was a hard worker and a good dancer, and she made friends easily. But what the villagers liked most about Anniko was that every morning she walked through the village, awakening them with her singing. The Longnecks had never heard singing before, and everyone came to love the sound of her beautiful voice. Well, everyone except one man, who grew jealous of the way people loved Anniko.

"Why are you here?" the Mean Man asked her one day as she pounded the millet. "You have a short neck, and clearly you don't belong with us."

Anniko was devastated by his words and, without thinking, she ran far into the forest. By the time night fell, Anniko realized she was lost. The next morning, the people of the village started to worry when they didn't hear Anniko's beautiful morning song. When they learned that the Mean Man had insulted her, they confronted him. He was forced to admit what he had done and said that Anniko had fled to the forest. Not knowing what else to do, the Longnecks decided to try to lure her back home by attempting to sing as she had. At first, they were not very good at it, but they kept on trying and finally their voices rose from their long necks high above the trees and deep into the forest. Eventually, Anniko heard their singing, and she followed the sound of their voices until she found her way back home. "Anniko, the depth of your heart is more important than the length of your neck," the villagers exclaimed. "Don't ever leave us again!"

When Molly finished writing the story, she drew pictures to accompany it—elaborate, colorful images of Anniko and the land of the Longnecks. It took her a few weeks to finish the book, and afterward she sent it to the New African Editions publishing house, which chose to print and distribute twenty thousand copies in West Africa. When she finally read *Anniko!* out loud to the children at the Démb ak Tey Center, they sat quietly listening, inching closer to her with each page to better see the pictures. Molly knew how much they loved these experiences—hearing a book read aloud in their own language, filled with drawings of people who looked like them. When she finished reading, they remained quiet for a few seconds.

And then they asked her to read it again.

DESPITE HOW CROWDED THE center became, Molly never turned children away, and soon she expanded the center's offerings to include theater, puppetry, art classes, and drawing instruction. With the help of an artist named Malick Pouye and a theater student named Bolle Mbaye, who had both begun as volunteers at the center, she organized daily cultural and educational activities based on African oral traditions of songs, legends, theater, poetry, and proverbs. She and Bolle also started the first weekly Senegal radio program in national languages for children, broadcast for two hours each Saturday. Traveling to different villages

Molly *(right),* with her sister, Diane, and mother, Ann.

Molly in Senegal in 1976 with children from the Démb ak
Tey Center, where she used elements of traditional African
culture to teach out-of-school children in their native
Wolof language.

Molly with Bollé Mbaye and village chief Alaaji Mustaafa Njaay in 1984.

Molly, pregnant with Zoé, with women in Saam Njaay in 1985. This village is where Molly first developed the classes that would become the Tostan Community Empowerment Program.

Molly with Cheikh Anta Diop, her mentor and the man
who introduced her to the meaning of the word "tostan."

Molly's friend, Ousmane Sembène, in the study at his home
in Yoff in 1982. Like Cheikh Anta Diop, he was a leading
advocate for designating Wolof the official language of
Senegal and greatly influenced Molly's work.

Ourèye Sall, a former
traditional cutter who now
works with Tostan to promote
FGC abandonment in Senegal.

Maimouna Traore *(left)*, Ourèye Sall *(center)*, and Demba Diawara receiving an award from the president of Senegal for their work with Tostan in ending FGC.

The visit of the women from Malicounda Bambara to Keur Simbara in 1997, an event that encouraged Molly to continue Tostan's work on ending FGC.

Then President Bill Clinton
and First Lady Hillary Rodham
Clinton at a meeting in Dakar
with Molly and leaders of
the movement to end female
genital cutting in Senegal.

Poetry, dance, song,
and theater help Tostan
participants understand
and share new
information.

Demba Diawara, imam and village chief, is a major leader of the movement to abandon FGC in West Africa.

A public declaration where hundreds of villages announced the abandonment of FGC and child/forced marriage.

Participants at a declaration hold signs showing the villages they represent.

Women, men, girls, and boys participate in Tostan classes in rural villages in many African countries. Classes focus on many subjects including democracy, human rights, problem solving, health, literacy, and project management. Participants *(below)* learn how to read and write using SMS texting with cell phones.

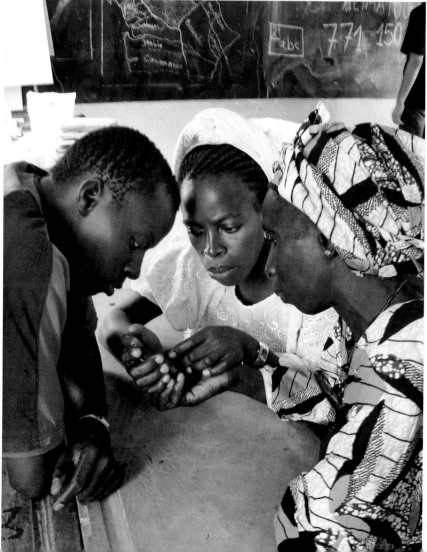

Molly and her daughter, Zoé, in 2004.

Molly visits the women of the Tostan class in Arabsiyo, Somaliland, in 2008. She congratulates Shamsi, one of the leaders of the movement to end FGC in Somaliland.

Participants during a Tostan session.

Kerthio Diawara during her visit to the United States
where she spoke at USAID about ending FGC in Senegal.

Tostan participant Marième Bamba studied six months at the Barefoot College in India and became a solar engineer, installing fifty solar units in her village, Soudiane.

Ninety-five percent of Tostan participants are Muslim. Traditional and religious leaders have been actively involved in creating Tostan sessions.

(Above, left to right) Ourèye Sall, Molly, and Demba Diawara at a publication declaration on the island of Niodior. Representatives from twenty-seven other island villages canoed to Niodior to participate in the April 2000 declaration to end FGC and child/forced marriage. *(Below)* Villagers at the declaration.

Women in Somaliland discuss the human right to vote and be elected. Four women from the class decided to run for elected office in 2008 with a platform based on human rights.

Dior, the coordinator of the Community Management Committee, explains monthly revenue and expenses to other members.

Tostan's philosophy comes from a core understanding that
African women love their daughters and want them to succeed.
That is why they practiced FGC and why they are now
abandoning it.

(Above and on the following page) Molly celebrates with the
women of Malicounda Bambara at festivities honoring the tenth
anniversary of their decision to abandon FGC in 1997.

in a Volkswagen bus she'd bought with funding support, she recorded the history and cultural traditions of the villagers. In the course of each broadcast, Molly inserted information on health and hygiene. The work allowed her to continue to get out of Dakar and into the villages, to better understand the problems people were facing in the communities and to experience the joys of rural life in Senegal. She truly loved spending time in the villages. Even though Dakar had its share of problems, the city at least offered access to health care and other social services; in the villages, there was almost nothing. Yet what Molly felt most was an incredible warmth and welcoming, a sense of exuberance and optimism.

In 1981, after six years at the center, the funding for activities ran out, and Molly started to question what might be next for her. The answer came to her on a day that had started simply enough, on her way to run errands in Dakar.

She met a woman she knew named Rama, who had recently given birth to twins. Rama was with her infant son, who looked dangerously ill. His eyes were hollow, his ribs protruded from his tiny frame, and his fontanel—the soft spot on his head—was depressed, as if the water had been sucked from his body.

"My son is very sick," Rama said, in great distress. "I'm on my way to see the *marabout*."

"Maybe you should also see a doctor," Molly suggested.

"No, I'm going to see the traditional healer because the baby has a sunken soft spot, and everyone tells me this is a sign that he's been possessed by evil spirits." Rama explained she was taking her baby to the best healer she knew, hours away by bus, who could help get rid of the spirits. Molly knew not to argue or judge, having come to understand just how deeply rooted the belief in the spirit world was in Senegal.

Upon her arrival in Senegal, she had immediately noticed many people wearing gris-gris, as they are called, small well-worn leather pouches usually tied around an upper arm or waist. Molly had been curious, and she'd asked a student what they were.

"The whole world is full of spirits, some good and some evil, bringing either great blessings or bad luck to people," he'd said. "Everyone here has a *marabout,* someone they consider to be a specialist in controlling these spirits. Often a *marabout* will write verses from the Koran, which people then sew inside the pouches for protection, to help ward off the evil spirits." He explained that other gris-gris are used for calling forth the good spirits to bring about healing or good luck.

Molly learned more about the spirit world during her work translating for Dr. Henri Collomb, a well-known French psychiatrist working in Fann University Hospital Center in Dakar. He'd become famous for being among the first in his field to take into account the cultural specificities of treating psychiatric patients in Africa. Like Cheikh Anta, he encouraged Molly to put herself in the minds of the people she encountered. "This is a different culture with a very different belief system and worldview than the one you're used to. When you see something in this culture that you don't understand, you must never judge by your own belief system, because it will only lead you to great frustration," he advised her. "Try to truly understand the people and the deeper reasons why they do what they do, and you will soon learn they feel they have no choice but to conform to certain practices and beliefs for fear of the punishments that could follow."

Molly kept this advice in mind, but a few days after meeting Rama, her concern for the little boy lingered and she decided to pay Rama a visit. When she arrived at her house, Rama was inconsolable.

"The *marabout* gave us blessings and a gris-gris," she said with great sadness. "But the baby died not long after we returned to Dakar."

Molly left Rama's house and went directly to speak to a Senegalese nurse she knew. She needed to understand what had happened to the baby. When she explained the symptoms, the woman shook her head in sadness.

"Molly, it's simple. The baby was dehydrated. He had diarrhea and desperately needed to be rehydrated." She explained that there was a simple, inexpensive remedy: a solution of water, salt, and sugar that can replace the lost fluids and rehydrate the body. "When the fontanel is sunken, the dehydration is severe," she said. "The baby should have been brought to the health post immediately. You should have insisted, Molly. You could have saved that baby's life."

Molly was distraught for days, unable to shake the idea that if she had only known that something as simple as identifying a sunken fontanel could have diagnosed the problem, for which there was an easy remedy, the boy would still be alive. She was devastated, acutely aware of her own failure to save the baby.

SOON AFTERWARD, MOLLY VISITED a small village an hour and a half from Dakar called Saam Njaay. None of the villagers spoke French, nor could they read or write in Wolof. Of the thirty-six villages in the surrounding rural community, there was only one public school, too far away for children to attend. The closest option for education was a Catholic school that was a one-hour walk away. But, Molly soon discovered, the residents of Saam Njaay were eager for education. She began to discuss with them an idea that intrigued her: creating an experimental program in their village, using African cultural activities to contribute to developmental education. Ready for another undertaking, she viewed this as an opportunity to combine the experiences of her eight years in Senegal and the materials she'd developed at the children's center into an educational program in national languages geared specifically to villagers, both children and adults. What she had in mind would be more than a literacy project; it would be an entirely different approach to development—a holistic program that encompassed not just reading and writing but discussions on problem solving, skills to build confidence, and an understanding of health and hygiene. She thought of a proverb she'd heard that referenced the *pagne*, the long, traditional skirt worn by Senegalese women: "No matter how beautiful one strip of cloth, it takes many strips to clothe a woman." Wasn't the same true when it came to the best way to approach development? Maybe if she could bring holistic, nonformal, basic education to the people of this village—people who'd never gone to school—offering it to them in their own language, she could prevent unnecessary deaths like that of Rama's son.

It was daunting to think of moving to this remote community and away from the relative comforts of Dakar, but she knew by now that life in the city was no longer best suited to her ambitions. "To go to villages and see people who have so little and yet never complain, who always seem to have the right attitude—I knew I had a lot to learn from them," she says.

So, she made a decision. She would move to the village for a short time and try to develop a program whose aim was teaching people based on their goals and desires, not what she may have thought best. And once they were given the knowledge, maybe they would, as Cheikh Anta had envisaged, spread it to others.

9

Njàng mu Xóot (Deep Learning)

M olly arrived in the village of Saam Njaay, population three hundred, in September 1982 at the age of thirty-two with a plan to stay for a few months. She would end up living there for three years, in a ten-by-ten-foot adobe hut with a thatched palm roof and a packed earth floor. During this time she would live without electricity, experience a severe drought, contract malaria, and discover during an eventual doctor's visit that her body carried so many parasites the list was six pages long. But she would also come to view her time spent living in this village as among the most important, interesting, and enlightening of her life.

The day Molly arrived in Saam Njaay was hot and clammy. She parked her Volkswagen bus in front of the small mosque in the center of the village and was delighted to find a crowd of people gathered in anticipation of her arrival. Dozens of children—boys in cutoff shorts and girls with tight braids—peeked shyly at her from behind their mothers' skirts. At first, the villagers seemed unsure of what to make of this Wolof-speaking American woman dressed in an African *boubou*, arriving with a small suitcase filled with educational materials, but they were gracious and welcoming.

A few young men carried her bags, as several girls escorted her to the hut the villagers had taken great care in preparing for her. It was furnished simply with a small cot and a wooden table, and woven straw mats covered the dirt floor. After she unpacked her bags, some women arrived with a bowl of food for her.

"We've made this especially for you," one of the women said, setting it on the table. "Enjoy."

"Thank you," Molly said. "I appreciate this, but I'd really like to come and eat with everyone."

The woman looked surprised. "But you're our honored guest. And we thought you might like to enjoy this here in your room."

"Not at all," Molly said. "I'd much prefer to join everyone else around the bowl. I'd much prefer to eat with you."

After dinner, Molly returned alone to her hut. As she lay in the stillness under a mosquito net, listening to the sounds of the village sinking into sleep, she felt as if she'd arrived in another world. It was the hottest time of year in Senegal, when the daytime temperature can reach 100 degrees Fahrenheit and the nights feel even hotter. The heat was intense in her room. She longed for fresh air but had been duly warned upon arrival to never leave open her door or small window, unless she wished to allow admittance to evil spirits known to enter homes at night.

Soon after falling asleep, Molly was awakened by a strange noise coming from the roof of her hut. In the darkness, she feared that it was one of the hyenas known to roam the area, or perhaps a human intruder.

"Hello! Hello!" she cried out in Wolof. "Who's out there?" When nobody answered, she yelled more loudly. "Help! Someone is breaking into my hut through the roof!"

Several young men, roused from sleep, rushed to help.

After a few minutes, Molly heard the sound of laughter. "Come on out and see the thief that was breaking into your hut, Sukkéyna," one of the boys said.

Molly cautiously crept outside to identify the culprit: a lone donkey feasting lazily on the leaves of the roof, paying no attention to the ruckus he had caused. For the next few weeks, Molly tried not to notice the giggles she inevitably heard from the young men as she passed them in the village.

The hut she'd been given was in the family compound of the village chief, a revered man named Alaaji Mustaafa Njaay, whose grandfather had founded the village around the year 1750. His title, Alaaji, was bestowed on people who had made the pilgrimage to Mecca, which he had accomplished as a young man, traveling across Africa by boat, plane, and on foot over the course of an entire year. He was now in his nineties and had become a wise and respected religious leader, attracting people from across Senegal who came to Saam Njaay to study the Koran with him or receive one of his blessings.

The village chief's compound included several individual huts inhabited by each of his four wives and their young children, surrounding a central courtyard where most of the daily activities took place under the shade of a large tree.

As Molly settled into life in the village, she and Alaaji Mustaafa Njaay passed many evenings together in the quiet on his verandah. Sitting in his hammock, adorned in an elegant prayer cap and always wearing a pair of glasses he had picked up at the used clothes market, he would speak to Molly about the workings of the village, the deeper origins of village traditions, and the important words that were key to understanding the hearts of the Senegalese. Offering her advice on how to be a strong and effective leader, he reminded Molly that she needed to let life be, to be open to its lessons, and to do the best she could in whatever it was she was setting out to do.

"A leader is like a Fulani cow herder," he said to her one evening, imparting a lesson she would never forget. "Sometimes he will lead the herd from the front. Sometimes he will remain in the middle and be part of the herd. And sometimes he will remain behind, allowing them to move forward on their own, following their lead. Like a skilled cow herder, a good leader always knows when to be where."

MOLLY BECAME A TRUE part of Njaay's family, referring to him as *baay* (father) and his children as her sisters and brothers. In the mornings, she would join them for a breakfast of millet couscous left over from the previous evening's dinner. In the hottest part of the afternoon, they would gather for tea in an ancient and intricate Arabic ceremony called *ataaye,* during which three small glasses of green gunpowder tea were prepared: the first strong and bitter, the second lighter, and the third very sweet.

"It's like friendship," Njaay would say, as Molly sipped her tea. "It just gets sweeter over time."

She especially loved the evenings. Because there was no electricity in Saam Njaay, the people of the village spent most nights gathered with their children on mats placed in a circle around a bonfire in the village square. Some would drum on upside-down bowls or buckets as people danced; some stood to tell jokes or share the traditional stories of the village. The women were masters of short Wolof poems called *taasu,* which they recited to rhythmic clapping and dancing. Before long, they began to create special *taasu* just for Molly.

"Sukkéyna Njaay, xobu lem la." (Sukkéyna Njaay is a leaf of honey.)

"Ku nu ko sexal." (When you taste it.)

"Doo yàbbi." (You won't spit it out.)

Repeated over and over, their clapping would lead to frenetic danc-ing, legs flailing, long skirts swirling about. Then people, lost in the excitement, would fall to the ground in laughter.

When it came to developing the educational program, the first thing Molly did was remember her ultimate goal: to find out what was im-portant to the people of the village before deciding what they needed. She knew the eventual success of any curriculum she created would depend largely on how she first engaged the residents, so for the first few months she devoted her time to getting to know the villagers and the way of life in Saam Njaay. With the help of Bolle Mbaye and Malick Pouye, her colleagues at the children's center in Dakar who had accompanied her to Saam Njaay, she recorded the history of the village, the local legends and proverbs, and the favorite activities and songs. She learned how the young girls made traditional Wolof dolls from tin cans and rags, and camels out of palm leaves; and joined the boys in fabricating wire cars and pony carts, which they would then wheel down the sandy paths.

She learned that the entire year's activities revolved around tending to the peanut, millet, and cassava fields. The planting of the seeds took place after the first rain in July. After the harvest in October and November, the crops were prepared and then brought to the market and sold sometime in December or January. Everything depended on the rain. Because the closest source of water was a well in a village one kilometer away, there was no way to irrigate the fields.

Molly was especially drawn to the experiences of the women. She had spent enough time in villages like Saam Njaay to know how hard women in rural Senegal worked, but to see it up close, to witness the extent of their work, amazed her still. She began to spend her days recording the activities of a woman named Kumba Sar, who was in her forties and the mother of three children, and of whom Molly had immediately grown fond.

Like the other women of the village, Kumba woke at five in the morning to walk thirty minutes or so to fetch water in the next village. She then prepared breakfast for her family, and after cleaning up the meal, she set out again, this time in search of firewood. Collecting enough to cook the day's meals meant Kumba had to walk several kilometers in the deep heat of the afternoon. She spent the next several hours on her remaining chores: preparing the evening meal for her family, sometimes having to feed up to twenty-five people, washing the dishes, and bathing and clothing the children.

Kumba had been doing this work, day after day, since she was a child. From as early as four years old girls were expected to fully assist their mothers and aunts with these tasks, and in addition to fetching water and firewood and helping with the cooking and cleaning, they were often responsible for tending to the younger children. Molly noticed that while the women worked, the men—if they weren't in the fields— often relaxed, and if boys were asked to help, they were given preferential treatment. The girls and women walked to the well, whereas the boys would load big tin barrels on the back of a cart and drive their carts to fill the barrels with water. At the end of the day, the best morsels of food were reserved for the elder males.

Molly understood that most Westerners who visited Senegal were often surprised, and sometimes outwardly critical, about the custom of polygamy, but Molly began to better understand how this system actually benefited women in villages like Saam Njaay. Another wife meant an extra set of hands to help with the chores. As she began to observe, the first wife would be in charge of the household for three days, including doing the cooking and cleaning. The second wife would then take over for the next three, lessening the other woman's workload at least for a few days.

Despite how hard the women worked, it was against their custom to speak aloud about the hardships they faced. Molly knew they had learned early in life to accept their work with no complaint, to see it as an honor. But it quickly became obvious to Molly how much energy women exerted trying to keep their families healthy, to simply survive. This was no easy task, as the village faced many hardships: the lack of water, the fact that during the dry season there was no work for the men of the village, and therefore no income. Nutritional conditions were extremely poor; many children were malnourished due to the lack of a balanced diet. The nearest health dispensary was twelve kilometers away, and the only way to get there was to walk or travel by horse and cart, which most families in Saam Njaay did not own.

Molly experienced these problems in ways she had never imagined. One day, after returning from a meeting outside the village, she spotted a woman named Anta Jiite sitting under a tree, her *boubou* wrapped around her knees, which she hugged tightly to her body. Anta was nearing the end of her pregnancy, and Molly had expected her to give birth any day. She went over to say hello and noticed that Anta looked sickly and pale.

"You look terrible!" Molly said. "Are you okay?"

The tears welled in Anta's eyes. "The baby died."

"What? What do you mean?"

"I can't explain. She came quickly, but she didn't survive. I don't know why. She died almost immediately."

Molly took Anta's hand. "When did this happen?"

"A few hours ago."

"Where is the baby?" she asked.

"My family took her. They've already buried her."

"Come on," Molly said. "I'm going to take you to the hospital."

"No, it's okay."

"What do you mean?" Molly asked.

"I don't want to bother you."

"We're going," Molly said, standing to help Anta from the ground. "We have to see that you're okay." On the twenty-minute drive to Thiès, Anta was silent. Molly knew that had she not insisted, Anta wouldn't have gone to the hospital; she wouldn't even have asked anyone to help her. She'd simply wake up day after day, knowing that her baby was buried in a field just beyond her house, knowing there was nothing she could have done about it.

It was simply part of being a woman.

10

Njàngale mi (Teaching)

Molly began to hold her classes about two months after she arrived in Saam Njaay. Because there was no room large enough to accommodate the class, the first lessons, which took place each evening, were taught in the courtyard of a family's compound. Everyone from the village was invited to attend, and on the first evening of class, nearly fifty people arrived at the scheduled time, dragging with them restless children and large woven mats on which to sit. A large majority of the villagers had expressed interest in learning to write, both to help them secure employment beyond their village and to send letters to family members who lived in other villages. Molly's first mission was to help her new students understand what reading is. With no books, magazines, newspapers, without even a sign hung anywhere in the village, many had never seen written text.

As far as she was concerned, the worst way to go about teaching people to read was the approach she'd observed in other literacy classes: assume the role of "teacher," stand before a class of people who had never even held a pencil, and ask them to memorize letters. She preferred to try another approach.

"What would you like to be able to read or write?" she asked the students on the first night of class.

Kumba spoke first. "I want to write a letter to my mother. She lives in a village ten kilometers away."

Molly asked Kumba what she'd like to say to her mother and then wrote it down.

She handed the paper to Kumba. "Now read this," she instructed.

Kumba was confused. "But I can't read."

"Yes, just tell me what you just said to me. It's all here."

"*That's* what reading is?" Kumba asked in amazement.

The students were enthralled. "I love proverbs," said a man named Cheikh. "I want to be able to write them down and share them."

"Okay," said Molly. "Let's do that."

She took a piece of paper and began to write. "If ten dig and ten fill in, there's lots of dust but no hole." She then asked Cheikh to read it back to her.

"I can read!" said Cheikh, as he looked at the paper in his hands.

To help the villagers become familiar with letters of the alphabet, Molly organized walks through the village, asking the students to identify familiar objects that resembled the letters she had shown them. The roofs of two huts became an *M,* the round mats the women wove were perfect *O's.* Then, sitting on mats on the ground of the courtyard, the students practiced writing the shapes they had observed—first a few letters, and then a word they particularly liked: rice, chicken, tree, *boubou,* necklace, braids, donkey. They then placed signs around the village identifying landmarks and objects: house of Mustaafa Njaay, baobab tree, chair, mat, fence. When they were fully accustomed to holding pencils and writing letters, Molly then asked them to learn the words other people in the class had chosen, until they'd built a village vocabulary.

After just five months, the students had made remarkable progress in reading and writing. Many knew enough to not only write the correspondence they'd hoped to send but some even started recording births and deaths in the village and rudimentary minutes from village meetings.

Molly was eager to include a discussion about health and hygiene in the evening sessions, knowing that the residents of Saam Njaay faced challenges far beyond their inability to read or write. She observed just how little the villagers understood about their bodies, their health, and the transmission of germs. Even though malaria was a significant problem, many thought it was transmitted through mangoes, an understandable assumption given that mosquitoes are most prevalent at the time of the rainy season when mangoes are ripe. They didn't understand the importance of vaccinations, or know that they could easily prevent many illnesses like diarrhea through hand washing and keeping the village clean.

She began to experiment with unusual and interesting ways of imparting the information on health. For example, she added a few drops of perfume to a small bowl of water and then passed the bowl around the class, asking each student to dip their hands into it. Although the students admitted they couldn't see anything, they knew there was something else in the bowl because they could smell it on their hands. This something is like germs, Molly explained—invisible, but rapidly and easily shared.

How did this student of French literature know how to so effectively teach literacy, to develop innovative and highly effective learning methods? Molly arrived in Senegal with some hands-on teaching experience, first as a substitute teacher after graduating college and then as a teaching assistant in graduate school, but she also has a passionate belief in the power of education and a true, innate gift for teaching, which runs in her blood. Her mother, Ann—herself a teacher for nearly twenty years—had always deeply believed in the power of education. Wanting only the best educational opportunities for her daughters, she encouraged both Diane and Molly to do well in school, perhaps because her own pursuit of education had been so difficult. After having to drop out of college during the Depression, she refused to give up on her dream of a college degree. In 1964, at the age of fifty-one, Ann enrolled in summer classes at the University of Illinois and eventually earned her bachelor's degree at age fifty-eight. "I gained a new respect for my mother when I saw her go, summer after summer, sitting among people in their twenties," Molly recalls. "She was so committed to achieving her dream of receiving a college diploma. It was truly amazing."

But for the most part, Molly taught herself to teach, fearless in her decision to try new, experimental techniques. When she started teaching in the early 1970s, working for a year as a substitute teacher, she was drawn to explore different pedagogical techniques than those that had defined much of her own education, such as rote memorization and the strict differentiation between student and teacher. She quickly came to prefer a more creative and holistic approach, which she later honed as a graduate student at the University of Illinois. Asked to teach an undergraduate course in French, she chose not to limit the lessons to grammar and vocabulary, as was expected. Instead, she transformed the class into one that explored French culture, taking her students to see French films, to study the works of French artists at the Art Institute of Chicago, to learn to cook French meals.

After arriving in Saam Njaay, she was given the book *Teacher*. Written by Sylvia Ashton-Warner in 1963, it confirmed Molly's idea about education. Working with Maori children, Ashton-Warner espoused what she called an organic approach to literacy, using not isolated syllables drilled over and over, but meaningful events in the context of children's lives. Ashton-Warner's approach was part of an emerging movement at the time, an approach to education meant to redefine the existing and dominant power relationships. Molly's reading of *Teacher* led her to value the approaches that would become the cornerstone of her teaching techniques in Saam Njaay: dialogue, role-playing, and student-focused learning.

"After reading that book, I thought, *I can do this,*" she remembers. "I didn't have to go back to the university and learn how to teach literacy. I just needed to find the best way to help people learn the things they wanted to learn."

Her approach to education would later be reinforced by her reading of the book *Women's Ways of Knowing,* in which the authors conducted a study of women's intellectual development and contrasted it to a famous study of Harvard men in the 1950s by a researcher named William Perry. The study found key differences in how women learned, especially in their need for what the researchers termed "connected knowing." The ideas in this book were especially relevant to the women in Saam Njaay. Their talents were innumerable. They could cook large, elaborate meals for more than thirty people twice a day. They could survive on little money and were able to use every resource at their disposal. Many could sew clothes, weave mats, or braid hair with great skill. And yet, Molly often heard the same sentiment: "There are people who are knowledgeable about things, and we women are not. We are ignorant and know nothing."

"This used to drive me nuts," she says. "I would say to them, 'Look at all you do. Look at how you braid hair. In my country, people would go to school to learn that skill. They'd charge a hundred dollars for one hairdo.' Or 'Look at how well you cook, and how you can live on almost nothing in the harshest conditions. People in the United States would be freaked out and unable to survive with the conditions you live with every day. You aren't ignorant. You just have bought into the idea that some people are learners and some are not.'"

Before long, she began to notice that when offered a more engaging, interactive, and relevant way of learning, the women of the village—the same women who once argued they could never become educated, could never be learners—quickly grasped the lessons they studied. She also noticed how excited they were to come to class and how eager they were to share their new knowledge with others.

Deborah Fredo, Molly's good friend and an educational activist, spent hours interviewing the women of Saam Njaay for her doctorate on non-formal education. "I look forward to attending class each day," a woman named Ndag Ndiaye told Deborah. "When I enter the room, I take off my *boubou* of discretion, feeling free for the first time to speak my mind and say what I think. Maybe one day, when I leave class, I won't have to put it back on again."

Molly especially cherished this type of growing confidence she observed among many of the women and, with that confidence, a new desire to change certain village conditions. Within six months, the Saam Njaay villagers successfully advocated to be included on a list of villages to receive safe drinking water. The men participated in digging the trenches to lay the pipes that would bring the water to a communal faucet in the village square. The day the water finally arrived was one of the happiest celebrations in the history of Saam Njaay. To mark the occasion, the women organized a baptism for the fountain. Everyone got dressed in their very best clothes. A large lunch of fish and rice was served, and people danced and ate until late into the night.

The water, it turned out, was just the beginning. Over the next few months, Molly's students built a classroom out of millet stalks and installed gas lamps so that classes could meet after sundown, when chores were finished and work in the fields was completed. They went on to organize the planting of a wood lot to provide wood for cooking, keeping them from having to walk several kilometers a day in search of wood for fuel. They built more than fifty clay-and-sand wood-burning stoves, which conserve heat and lessen the need for wood. In 1983, they established a health table, and then submitted, in Wolof, a project for a community health center, which was approved. One villager ran the center, keeping daily records of every patient who arrived from the twenty-seven surrounding villages, meticulously recording the twenty-five cents paid by each patient for receiving basic treatments for malaria, conjunctivitis, wounds, diarrhea, or *fatiguement* (general fatigue).

But Molly's work in the village was not without its mistakes. After learning that the villagers had long craved a garden to improve nutrition, help sustain them between weekly trips to the market in Thiès, and earn them income from the sale of the vegetables, Molly worked with them to write a project to fund a well and purchase start-up equipment, seeds, and fertilizer. Despite her best intentions to leave all decisions to the villagers, Molly and Bolle announced that the garden would be cared for communally. After all, they thought, this is Africa; shouldn't things be done collectively here? When everything was finally completed—the well dug, the land plowed, and the seeds planted— forty people showed up to begin watering and caring for the plants. The next day, thirty came. Within a week, only ten people were coming, until eventually only Molly and Bolle were working in the garden. Molly called a meeting, feeling more than a little perturbed. "What is wrong? Why have you stopped working on your garden?"

The villagers were silent, until a man named Magueye Ndiaye spoke. "Well, it's *your* garden."

"What do you mean?" Molly asked.

"The way the garden is organized is not the way we do things here," Magueye responded.

"How do you do things?"

"Well, we would have assigned rows in the garden for each participating family who would plant the seeds and continue to look after the plants."

"I don't understand," Molly said, feeling surprised and a little embarrassed. "Why didn't you tell me this earlier?"

"Because you never asked," he said.

Molly was speechless.

"And you were so excited, and none of us wanted to discourage you," he added.

After the meeting, Molly went to the village chief. "Did you know that I was making this mistake?" she asked him.

"Of course I knew it," he replied.

"Why did you allow me to do that? Why didn't you tell me what I was doing wrong and direct me?"

"A good leader must make her mistakes," Alaaji said. "If I had told you, you wouldn't have fully understood the lesson. You needed to find your way to this answer on your own."

The garden was quickly reorganized. Each family was given a small plot of the garden and agreed to contribute a thousand francs (two dollars) for fertilizer and general maintenance. To this day, thirty years later, the garden of Saam Njaay still thrives.

A YEAR AFTER SHE arrived in Saam Njaay, Molly received a two-year grant from USAID to continue and expand her educational work in the village. The grant included an annual salary for Molly of about $30,000. She was thirty-three years old, and it was the most money she'd ever earned. But receiving so much payment for her work made her highly uncomfortable, especially when those around her had so little, and she often gave her money away to those who needed it more. (Like her work ethic, this too became a behavior Molly would never shed. After she turned sixty, her board of directors insisted she finally establish a retirement fund.) She was, however, careful to set aside a certain amount each month to send home to her mother, who promptly deposited it in a savings account in Molly's name. While Molly didn't see the need for a savings account, she hoped this gesture might diminish Ann's relentless pestering about her future security. Molly knew that in the largely white, conservative Arizona town where Ann now lived, Ann struggled to explain to people what her youngest daughter did for a living and why she insisted on remaining in Africa for so little money when she could just come back to the United States, get a good job, buy a house and a car, and secure health insurance for herself. Molly knew that Ann would never understand this, but what she was doing—living in a small African village, developing an education program—did not feel like a choice. It was just what she *did,* what she had always been meant to do. "I knew that I could never do any other type of work," Molly says, "and I also knew that my mother loved me. But it was conditional love, tied to this idea of who she wanted me to be. For so long all I wanted was her approval, the one thing I couldn't get."

But having her mother's approval had begun to matter less. Molly had come to realize that trying to make Ann understand her choices was a little like trying to water the desert with a garden hose. And anyway, the people of Saam Njaay certainly understood. They knew this woman was special. As Molly's friend Carrie Dailey recalls, "Every time I visited Molly in her village, I developed an even greater respect for her. I'd lived in Senegal for more than thirty years and had adapted well, but never like Molly did. She lived like the people of the village. She ate what they ate. She showered outside, behind a makeshift screen made of cornstalks. But the most amazing thing to watch was how she interacted with the women and children. She was not even aware of the difficulties there. All she saw were the people, whom she truly loved."

The villagers felt the same way. Molly was one of them. She took part in every birth, wedding, and funeral. When the evenings turned cooler, women and children would come to Molly's hut and coax her outside, where they would show her new dance moves, which she'd later showcase at the nightly village gatherings. They loaned her a horse, on which she'd travel bareback down the long, dusty paths, visiting the farmers in the fields, investigating what was happening in nearby villages. As Alaaji Mustaafa Njaay told her often, she was the salt in their rice. Without her work in the village, life would be flat and tasteless. To them, she was a woman who had everything.

Well, everything except the one thing a true Senegalese woman needed: a husband.

11

Jabar ak Ndey (Wife and Mother)

Molly met Walter Williams the following year, in August 1984. Born and raised in Mississippi, he'd recently taken a job with an American-based NGO that had a project in a village very close to Saam Njaay. A former Peace Corps volunteer himself, he'd arrived in Senegal after years spent working in some of the most difficult communities in the Democratic Republic of the Congo, then called Zaire.

Molly was amazed to discover that an American was working nearby and that he also happened to be recently divorced, three years older than she, and very good looking. She was thirty-four at the time. Although she'd dated during the ten years she'd been living in Africa—a few Senegalese she'd gotten to know through work or friends, an American working in Kenya whom she'd met on a plane—she had partly given up on the idea that she would marry. It was unlikely she could ever adeptly fill the role of a Senegalese wife and all that was expected of a woman in that position—cooking, making the arrangements for every religious and other holiday, and holding an entire extended family together. The last thing she thought might happen after moving to a remote village miles away from any modern amenities in western Senegal was that she'd meet a handsome, alluring, and very eligible American bachelor.

Molly and Walter fell in love quickly. She was taken by his charm, intelligence, and sincere dedication to his work. Most mornings he would be out of his hut by four o'clock, walking from village to village to rouse people, to get them working on whatever project was on the agenda. He visited Molly most evenings, and they'd sit in her hut or in front of a bonfire and talk about their lives. After high school, Walter had been drafted to fight in Vietnam. Not unlike her father and his experience fighting in World War II, Walter was reluctant to talk about the realities of his time in Vietnam, but he could never fully mask the pain of it.

A few months after they met, Walter showed Molly the amulet he'd been given by a *marabout*. "I asked him for something to shield us from anything bad happening," Walter said, "so that we'll always be together."

They married in March, seven months after meeting, in a simple civil ceremony in Dakar. Molly wore a long white *boubou,* and Carrie Dailey was her witness. When Molly called Ann a few weeks earlier to tell her the news that she was getting married, Ann was surprised but supportive. Like Victor, Walter was also African-American, but by this time Ann had grown more comfortable with Molly's choices, recognizing that she could not keep Molly from doing what she wanted. A few weeks after the wedding, Molly and Walter settled into a new home in Dakar: an airy three-bedroom apartment in a comfortable neighborhood called Fenêtre Mermoz. It was a very happy time. The couple would both continue their work and return often to their respective villages, but Molly was happy to return to life in Dakar. She especially loved being married, feeling a thrill each time she returned home to find Walter's African caftans hanging in their large closet beside her collection of *boubous.* Their new apartment was more spacious than anywhere Molly had lived in Africa; she'd grown so accustomed to living in the simplest quarters, she didn't know what to do with it all. But it wasn't long before they filled the space with the one thing that Molly had, throughout her life, wanted perhaps more than anything else: a daughter, Anna Zoé Williams.

IN 1987, WHEN ANNA ZOÉ—or Zoé as everyone came to call her—turned two years old, Molly took a part-time consultancy position with USAID to evaluate a literacy program being implemented in 242 centers throughout Senegal. What she learned surprised and disheartened her. Sitting in dozens of classes, she discovered that few villagers remained enrolled for long, and the ones who continued to attend were frequently bored, finding it hard to keep their eyes open during the long lectures. If the students spoke during class, it was only to recite letters and syllables at the request of the teachers. Although the teachers had been told to be "participatory" in their classrooms, they hadn't received training on how to do this. They drew, therefore, from the only model of teaching and learning they knew: an authoritarian one.

As Molly had learned from her teaching experience in the village, isolated word fragments, without context or meaning, would fall from students' memories like coins from a pocket. The teachers were frustrated, the students felt lost, and Molly began to understand just why the national literacy rates were so abysmal.

Her observations reinforced her growing belief that literacy teachers needed a different kind of training and that literacy programs needed to be more holistic: educational, fun, engaging, and most of all, emerging from people's experiences in their daily lives.

At about this time, Molly was asked by another NGO, through funding from USAID, to help develop a literacy program in the Kaolack region. A three-hour drive from Dakar, Kaolack is known as the peanut basin of the country. The communities here were similar to those in which Molly had been working, but they felt hotter, dustier, and even poorer and more desolate. She went to work immediately, eager to draw from her past experiences to create a new educational model. She took the materials, especially the learning games, posters, and stories she had developed in collaboration with the villagers in Saam Njaay, and began to organize them. She found that they could be broken into modules, such as problem solving, hygiene, and health. She integrated literacy and numeracy into the modules and started the program with important questions: What do we want for our community? Why come to class? Why learn to read and do math? In creative bursts, she wrote what would be the first modules of her new approach to literacy.

By the following year, the program Molly was implementing in Kaolack began to bear fruit. Engaged students were flocking to class, hungry for more. Responding to their enthusiasm, she created more activities—games, drawings, plays, poems, and stories. But then she received devastating news: there was no money to fund the second year of the program. Her work could not continue. "I was horribly frustrated and depressed," she says. "I knew I had created something that people wanted and that worked. When the program collapsed, it felt like some-one had stolen something I held very precious."

Adding to this blow, Molly and Walter were starting to have problems in their marriage. Walter had been assigned to work in Guinea-Bissau, a fifteen-hour drive from Dakar. While Molly longed to be closer to her husband, she did not want to leave Senegal, or the chance to somehow keep the Kaolack program alive, in order to join him. She was dealing with being a new mother, sensing a physical and increasingly emotional distance with her husband, and also feeling that she had failed. To this day she remembers it as "one of the darkest times of my life."

A CHANCE ENCOUNTER IN 1998 with the new UNICEF country representative in Dakar, Denis Caillaux, helped to turn that around. Upon their meeting, Denis explained to Molly that he was interested not only in development to improve the lives of the millions of children in Africa but also in "preparation" for village development, a concept Molly found intriguing. When Molly told him of her work, and her discouragement at being cut off midstream from her successful program in Kaolack, he invited her to meet him at his Dakar office.

"I'm interested in what we have to do prior to bringing in projects to villages . . . laying the foundation, if you like," Denis told Molly, within the first few minutes of their meeting, "because I have seen so many projects start up and then fail."

"Yes!" Molly responded, knowing she had found a kindred spirit. "People first need basic education in their own language, drawing from their own cultural experiences. Only then can they effectively manage projects. This is especially true for the women I have been interacting with in the villages."

"I'd like to see your ideas for education in action," he said.

Molly took him to Saam Njaay to speak to the villagers about all they had learned and to see the health center and millet machine they had successfully managed on their own. It didn't take long after this visit for him to approve the proposal Molly submitted to UNICEF to continue her work. With the support of Ndioro Ndiaye, the minister for social development, they decided to pilot Molly's education program in villages close to Thiès, where Molly and Zoé had recently moved into a four-bedroom house and where Walter had joined them. After much discussion about their future, Walter had resigned his post in Guinea-Bissau and returned to Senegal to create his own NGO, called Culture for African Development, through which Molly would receive the UNICEF funding for her project. The idea was that Walter and Molly would work together. She would continue to focus on the work she loved: developing dynamic, interactive materials for use in the village classroom and training teachers on how to use cultural traditions to create a truly participatory and engaging class environment. Walter would direct the organization, manage staff, take care of general administration, and be responsible for implementing the community projects: digging wells, starting gardens, doing reforestation and animal fattening.

Molly hoped that Walter's return to Senegal and the joint collaboration would help strengthen their marriage, but working together proved to be an even greater challenge. While Molly had received funding for her educational program, Walter had difficulty finding support for the high-cost capital projects he wanted to implement, causing him great frustration. Over the next year Molly and he grew further apart, and in August 1990, Walter decided to move back to Dakar. Molly soon found out that he was living with another woman. They divorced a few months later, five years after they'd married.

12

Lu Guddi gi Yàgg-Yàgg
(However Long the Night)

In early 1992 Molly received a call from a son of Alaaji Mustaafa Njaay. "Sukkéyna, our father has grown very ill," he said. "He is requesting to see you. Can you come to Saam Njaay?"

Molly drove immediately from her home in Thiès to the village, which she still visited on a regular basis. Along the way, she felt a cold panic rising inside of her at the thought of losing Alaaji Mustaafa Njaay. It had been more than fifteen years since her father, Al, died, and six years earlier, Cheikh Anta Diop had died unexpectedly from a heart attack at the age of 62. Despite the fact that Alaaji Mustaafa Njaay was 104 years old, Molly didn't feel prepared to lose him too. She had come to love him as a father and she looked to him for support and guidance, which she needed now more than ever. Two years earlier, after her marriage had dissolved and, along with it, her desire to continue working for Walter's organization, Molly had decided to establish her own organization. The decision had not been an easy one. In spite of the success Molly had enjoyed to this point—running the Démb ak Tey children's center for six years, building a highly successful educational program at the village level, working to develop literacy projects—she questioned her ability to run an NGO and was consumed with self-doubt that she could pull it off.

A lot of her doubt stemmed from the confusing and often contradictory messages she had learned growing up in Danville, Illinois, in the 1960s. While Molly's mother, Ann, certainly believed in education and economic independence for women and was one of the few mothers Molly knew who worked after she and Diane started going to school, she'd also instilled in her girls her own ideas of the limited capabilities of women. "My mom lived with very specific social norms around gender," Molly's sister, Diane, recalls. "She wanted us to be good at school and economically independent, but she'd been shaped by the idea that girls have very clear limits. Women weren't expected to be good in science or math, for instance. We could only hope to go so far." Many of Molly's female classmates at Danville High School (where the girls' basketball team was relegated to playing half-court games) had the same idea. They seemed to believe that a girl's best opportunity for happiness was to grow up and marry well. Even by the time Molly entered college, women were encouraged to pursue typically female jobs—as a secretary, social worker, or nurse—and with her interest in foreign languages and cultures, Molly had always believed her ultimate career choice was to become a translator. "Wouldn't it be fun to be the wife of somebody doing something important and exciting, and with whom you could travel?" a friend once asked her. Molly didn't think anything of this at the time and never would have dreamed of asking, "Well, why wouldn't *we* be the ones with the important and exciting jobs?"

Which is why, in 1990, when she was confronted with the idea of starting her own organization, she was terrified. Despite her accomplishments, despite her incontrovertible intelligence and fierce sense of independence, she still hadn't resolved these inner contradictions, and she deeply doubted her ability to lead an organization. As far as she understood it, her natural talents lay in her ability to bring innovative ways of learning to people who had never been to school, through creating materials and activities based on dance, theater, song, and storytelling. Those things she hadn't had to learn. They were second nature to her. But the idea of managing and hiring staff, writing budgets, running an office . . . not only were these tasks that didn't interest her, they were also skills she felt she didn't have and didn't want to spend time developing. She'd always considered herself to be the visionary, with decisions around day-to-day management best left to others. And she certainly didn't have any role models to look to for guidance, women who successfully sat at the helm of their own organizations.

"Coming from a childhood where the women's role was to support men, I didn't even think it was possible for a woman to become a director of an NGO. But I had no other choice," she says.

The UNICEF Senegal funding she'd been receiving was critical to her work, but according to UNICEF protocol, she needed to be part of an official organization in order for the funding to continue. Left with no other choice, she gathered every ounce of her courage and, in December 1990, returned to the United States to begin the process of incorporating her new organization, which she named Tostan to honor the memory of Cheikh Anta Diop. She would receive the documentation making Tostan an official NGO two months later, on February 7, 1991, the fifth anniversary of Cheikh Anta's death. Over the next few months, she hired more than twenty staff members, every one of them an African. In fact, Molly would remain the only American on the Tostan staff for the next fifteen years.

By the time she received the call that Alaaji Njaay was ill, Tostan had been in operation for nearly one year. It had been a hectic and, at times, anxious period for Molly. The Tostan offices were located in three crowded rooms in the front part of the house where she and Zoé lived with their pet monkey, Zita, a dog named Dalva, a rabbit, and a swan they called Charlie, who spent most of his time in a small pond Molly had dug in the front yard. Every day, as Zoé (five at this time and fluent in English, French, and Wolof) gathered with her friends in the small yard, the house was abuzz with activity—dozens of people coming in and out for meetings, volunteers searching for a space to work, and others from the neighborhood who stopped by just in time for the communal lunch of fish and rice that Tostan provided each afternoon at one, served Senegalese style from a shared bowl on the floor. At the center of everything was Molly, forty-one years old, a single mom, the head of an NGO, and trying to manage it all on her own.

The program was doing well—Tostan classes were in place in forty-four villages—but Molly's confidence was wavering. She struggled as a manager, often allowing her emotions to get the best of her and viewing her staff more as friends than employees. As her sister, Diane, remembers, "Molly has always been open and trusting of others—a characteristic, perhaps, of having been raised in a Midwest town at a time when there was little crime and she was free to play and wander throughout our neighborhood without many restrictions. She'd never given up her trusting nature, even in the face of interactions where her best interests were not in the mix."

In his position with UNICEF Dakar, Samir Sobhy got to know Molly well. "She is a fantastic thinker," he says. "She's a true visionary with an incredible imagination and heart. But she's also extremely emotional, which never helped her as a manager. She'd cry if she had to fire someone, and at times her emotions caused her to be a terrible judge of character."

Molly is quick to admit her failings as a manager in these early days. "I felt as if I had just been thrown into things, and I never really owned the fact that I was the director," she says. "If there was a mistake to be made, I can assure you that I likely made it."

ALAAJI MUSTAAFA NJAAY WAS lying on a mattress in his hut when she arrived. One of his sons, Magueye, was sitting beside him.

"I'll give you some time alone with him," he said to Molly. As Magueye left, Molly sat down on the bed beside Alaaji. She took his gnarled hand, so thin that she could feel his bones. A light breeze drifted through the open window of his cluttered room, delivering the scents of smoky firewood and smoldering incense, which had been set on the verandah outside.

"I'm glad you came to see me," Alaaji said in a voice just above a whisper. "I needed to speak with you."

"What is it, *baay*?"

"I'm preparing to leave soon. I am not long for this life."

"Don't say that," Molly said, feeling her throat tighten with his words.

"We all have our time, and mine is coming soon. But I want you to know, even after I am gone, I will be with you." He paused, sinking farther into the thin, foam mattress, taking in a long, difficult breath. "You are trying to accomplish great things, but nothing is going to come easy for you. You will have problems along the way, many problems in life. You will need to experience these problems in order to get to a better place, the place you are meant to be."

Molly gently fanned the air around his face with the soft end of her scarf.

"I have blessed you many, many times, and in the end, you will find your way," he said. "Your work will be like electricity: it has a beginning, but no end. Continue to listen and learn from the people, and you will move forward together." He closed his eyes and his breathing deepened. Molly gently placed his hand on the mattress, thinking he had fallen asleep, but after a few moments, he spoke again.

"Sukkéyna Njaay, things will become even more difficult for you. But always remember my words and never lose hope." She leaned closer to hear him better. "Lu guddi gi yàgg yàgg, jent bi dina fenk," he said. "However long the night, the sun will rise."

13

Sañ-Sañi Doom Aadama
(Human Rights)

Tostan continued to grow. By 1994, what had begun three years earlier in forty-four communities was now in place in more than three hundred and fifty villages, reaching fifteen thousand participants in five national languages. At the center of Tostan's approach was the Community Empowerment Program (CEP)—a three-year curriculum with classes meeting three times a week. Initially the CEP covered six learning modules: problem-solving skills, health and hygiene, preventing child mortality caused by diarrhea or lack of vaccination, financial management of village projects, leadership and group dynamics, and, finally, conducting feasibility studies for proposed income-generating projects. Literacy and numeracy sessions were integrated into each module so that by the time the program was complete, participants had acquired basic reading and math skills to support the projects that arose from class discussions and decisions.

From the beginning, Tostan's philosophy was in stark contrast to the authoritarian pedagogy prevalent in traditional school systems in

Senegal. Teachers in Tostan were called "facilitators" and students "participants." Almost always of the same ethnic group as the participants, facilitators—all of whom were required to have at least four years of primary school or be literate in national languages—were trained to unlearn the typical idea of teacher as "master" and student as passive recipient. Young men and women flocked to apply for the positions, and once hired, they lived in the villages in which they taught, used the language of the villagers, and earned the same salary as other literacy teachers in the country, approximately fifty dollars a month. All villages participating in the CEP agreed to provide housing for the facilitator and a place for the classes to meet. They also agreed to establish a Community Management Committee, comprised of seventeen members—at least half of them women—who would coordinate activities with the class and manage any development projects started by participants.

According to several external evaluations, the Tostan classes were successful in teaching villagers to read and write and to implement and manage their own projects. The rate of vaccination increased, and participants were found to have a better understanding of the causes, consequences, and preventative measures of the most common childhood illnesses. Participants were also able to apply problem-solving methods to resolve real issues affecting their villages and initiate changes in the dynamics of their communities. Many participants reported an increased sense of self-confidence, greater participation in community activities, and a greater ability to assume responsibility. In 1993, just two years after Tostan classes were established, UNESCO selected the organization as "one of the most innovative nonformal education programs in the world."

Due to the early success of the program, Molly was eager to further expand Tostan's offerings, and in 1994 she received funding through the American Jewish World Service (AJWS), a New York–based social justice organization, to develop a new module on early childhood development. This seventh module would be implemented in villages that had already completed the eighteen-month CEP, offering information specifically designed to help women understand how to improve the health and development of their children.

Before writing the module, Molly and five Senegalese staff members—all women—embarked on an intensive period of participatory research, interviewing thousands of women throughout rural Senegal in five national languages. Their aim was to gain an understanding of the types of information women wanted to know about the health and well-being of their children, which would form the cornerstone of the new module. But what Molly came to discover through this research was something she hadn't expected. While women were interested in learning more about the health of their children, they felt they first required knowledge about something else: their *own* health.

Perhaps it was because many of the women being interviewed had completed the Tostan program and had, through that experience, grown more accustomed to speaking their minds and sharing their honest opinions, but Molly and the other researchers were stunned, and often moved to tears, by the stories women shared about their health problems—problems, Molly knew, they had likely never publicly discussed before.

"They talked about how much violence they endured, often as part of their daily existence," Molly explains. "And not just physical violence at the hands of their husbands—which was certainly a common complaint—but violence that came in many other forms: Being ignored by their husbands. Not being given enough money to buy food for their children. The long and strenuous work days, and the toll they felt this took on their health."

They also shared how little they understood about the workings of their bodies, especially when it came to reproductive health. They didn't know about family planning or menstruation—when it started and why or when it stopped. In one local language, the word for menopause is translated as "getting down from the bed" and, as women had come to understand, to stop menstruating often marked the time in a woman's life when her husband stopped having sex with her and took a younger wife. The women had never been taught about healthy sexuality, didn't understand anatomy, and had never seen pictures of sexual organs. Many admitted they wanted to be able to better educate their daughters about these issues, but how could they when they didn't understand their own bodies, when they knew so little themselves?

Without this knowledge, they faced problems when accessing health care, and it was the stories around these experiences that upset Molly the most. Women shyly confessed that when they went to the health center—often having to walk an entire day to get there, sometimes even being transported on the back of a bicycle or, if they were very ill, carried there on a stretcher—they were often treated very poorly.

One young woman named Soxna from a village in northern Senegal explained that soon after her husband returned after a two-month visit to Dakar, she began to experience "itching and pain down below." When she finally decided to be examined at the health center, the doctor looked at her disapprovingly and questioned if she had been unfaithful to her husband. "I will never go to a health center again," Soxna said. "It is too humiliating."

Issues around childbirth were particularly jarring. Women were culturally forbidden from crying out or complaining during childbirth and would often be hit by a midwife for doing so. Molly thought back to her own labor with Zoé—several painful hours without any pain medication—and was so shocked to hear this that she arranged to have a researcher spend time observing births at a public hospital. When the researcher reported back to Molly, she was very upset. She'd witnessed women being hit or ridiculed while in the midst of labor and had seen one particularly difficult birth, after which the doctor had to stitch the woman where she had torn. When he instructed the new mother to move down and she didn't hear him, he jerked on the thread, causing the woman to cry out in pain. *"Move down!"* he yelled. The Tostan researcher returned to the hospital to further interview the midwives and doctors and was told that this behavior was justified and was even in a woman's best interest. Were she anything but stoic during birth, a woman would lose the respect of her community.

Like Soxna, many women admitted that they had stopped seeking health care, believing it was simply better to try to manage their pain or illness—or that of their children—on their own or solely through the prayers or medicinal herbs of a traditional healer, rather than suffer the humiliation and shame to which they had been subjected. This reality was certainly reflected in some pretty stark statistics. In 1990, 750 out of every 100,000 women died in childbirth; and 139 out of every 1,000 children in Senegal died before the age of five, 70 before their first birthday.

After a full year of conducting these interviews, Molly became obsessed with trying to fully understand what was at the heart of what she was learning. While she'd once believed the main problem with health care in the villages was what she had witnessed during her previous work and her time living in Saam Njaay—mainly, how difficult it was to access and the costs associated with it—she was beginning to understand that the issue was far more complex.

"Women were so accustomed to being mistreated and so often the victims of discrimination that they didn't believe they were worthy of any other type of treatment," she says. "What they needed was not just closer hospitals or better trained medical workers, but a way of envisioning an alternative existence in which they understood their right to be treated with dignity. Only if they believed they were entitled to better treatment could they demand it and bring an end to these harmful customs."

She knew, also, that these behaviors and beliefs were so deeply entrenched in the culture that Tostan facilitators could not simply appear in a village and instruct women to demand better. She needed to find a strategy that would take into account the basis of the behavior, the social norms that perpetuated it—something that could do no less than shift a woman's thinking, to help her begin to understand that all people, women included, had the legal and God-given right to dignity.

ON DECEMBER 10, 1948, former First Lady Eleanor Roosevelt stood before the United Nations General Assembly in her role as chairman of the Human Rights Commission, created two years earlier after the unspeakable atrocities committed during World War II. Unlike the other members of the commission, Eleanor Roosevelt was considered neither a scholar nor an expert on international law, but with her deep commitment to human dignity for all people, a belief that every individual should be allowed the opportunity to flourish, and a distinctive intelligence and sense of compassion, she was chosen by the other delegates to serve as the chairman of the commission. For the next two years, she would expend an extraordinary amount of energy working toward the adoption of a Universal Declaration of Human Rights, writing parts of the text herself, envisioning a document whose enduring principles would be perpetually recognized by all nations. "We stand today at the threshold of a great event both in the life of the United Nations and in the life of mankind," Mrs. Roosevelt stated in front of the General Assembly, as she submitted the final declaration for official review. "This declaration may well become the international Magna Carta for all men everywhere. We hope its proclamation by the General Assembly will be an event comparable to the [French Declaration of the Rights of Man and of the Citizen] in 1789 and the adoption of the Bill of Rights by the people of the United States." The declaration, which was adopted by the UN that day—an event Mrs. Roosevelt would later describe as one of the most important accomplishments of her life—stipulated that all people were legally entitled to full equality before the law and mandated that everyone, regardless of sex, had the right to property, that couples had the right to marry, and that people had the right to thought, conscience, and religion.

This declaration set in motion a decades-long discussion about human rights, and nearly twenty years later, the UN General Assembly continued what Eleanor Roosevelt had started with the adoption of two legal covenants: the International Covenant on Civil and Political Rights and the International Covenant on Economic, Social, and Cultural Rights. Both reinforced the universal declaration, a moral declaration committing its parties to work toward the granting of labor rights, the right to an adequate standard of living, and freedom from forced marriage, as well as people's right to life, freedom of religion, speech, assembly, and the right to a fair trial.

While these documents were an important and groundbreaking step in addressing the issue of human rights for all individuals, a growing awareness began to take shape in the 1960s about the many ways in which women in particular were subject to discrimination. As the feminist movement began to crystallize, women activists from all corners of the world called for a global commitment to specifically address the protection and promotion of the rights of women. The UN responded, taking steps to outline women's rights more specifically, culminating in a decision in 1974 to prepare a single, comprehensive, and internationally binding instrument to eliminate discrimination against women. Five years later, the Convention on the Elimination of All Forms of Discrimination Against Women was adopted. The CEDAW, as the convention became known, went into effect on September 2, 1981, faster than any previous human rights convention. It focused on three key areas: civil rights and the legal status of women, including a woman's right to vote, hold public office, and be free of discrimination in education and employment; reproductive rights, including the right to reproductive choice and family planning; and cultural factors influencing gender relations. This last point required ratifying nations to address the social and cultural patterns that perpetuated gender discrimination, affirming that men and women have equal responsibility with regards to their family life, education, and employment.

As the most comprehensive and detailed international agreement to seek the advancement of women, the CEDAW was celebrated among women's rights activists around the world and would go on to become one of the most highly ratified international human rights conventions in history, having the support of 186 nations (the United States not among them).

When Molly first came upon this information, she was surprised to learn that Senegal had ratified the CEDAW in 1980 and put it into effect in 1985. By accepting the declaration, the Senegalese government agreed to incorporate the principle of equality of men and women and to ensure the elimination of all acts of discrimination against women.

Eight years later, in 1993, the Declaration on the Elimination of Violence Against Women was adopted by the United Nations. This document proclaimed that all women should be free from all forms of violence: physical, sexual, and psychological, including family violence, marital rape, and dowry-related violence.

"This is it," Molly thought, as she read through these documents. "This is what I've been looking for." Here it was in black and white—a way to help women understand that despite certain customs and accepted norms, they at least had the legal right to demand protections against abuse and discrimination.

Of course the big question was how to use these instruments. She looked everywhere to try to find examples of other organizations in Africa using human rights in village education programs. As far as she could determine, they had never been applied on a practical level or implemented as a means of changing social norms and expected behaviors.

The question remained: Could she somehow find a way to apply these seemingly abstract principles at the level of an African village, where women clearly remained subject to the type of discriminatory and abusive practices these documents specifically protected against?

MOLLY WOULD SOON GET the chance to attempt to answer this question. At about this time, a Tostan staff member named Lala gave birth to her fourth child. Each of her pregnancies and deliveries had been difficult, and her doctor had warned her that if she carried any more children, she could face dire health consequences. On her doctor's advice, Lala had agreed to have her tubes tied after the birth, but when she woke up from her cesarean section, she learned the procedure hadn't been done.

"Why not?" Lala asked the doctor, exhausted and incredulous.

"I went to get your husband's permission," the doctor explained, "but he refused to grant it. He believes it is a wife's duty to have children."

Startled and angered by the doctor's decision, Molly began to investigate its legal basis. Working with a local human rights lawyer, Sidiki Kaba, who later became president of the International Federation for Human Rights, she sought to understand if the CEDAW might be applied in this case, to help the doctor understand how his decision had violated Lala's rights. A few days later, with copies of the CEDAW in hand, Molly and several female researchers nervously walked to the hospital to meet with its director.

"Did you know there is a legal human rights instrument that has been ratified by the government of Senegal which allows for women to decide on health issues related to their own bodies?" Molly asked from across his desk, piled high with papers. "And did you know that a doctor in your hospital denied this right to a female patient, and her life is now at stake because her husband did not agree to a procedure she needed?"

"It's true," the director admitted. "We have always required a husband's permission for such procedures. It's also true we've never had anyone question this practice before."

Molly's three colleagues leaned forward as she prepared to deliver the lengthy and emotional defense of Lala she had prepared.

But it wasn't necessary. Peering over his glasses, the director held up his hand to silence Molly. "I recognize that you're right. I promise we will listen to the woman and decide in favor of her health in the future."

"I couldn't believe it," Molly says. "I couldn't have imagined that sort of response. To be honest, I was expecting we'd be run out of the hospital. But this is when I knew. We may have found a very powerful tool for improving women's health."

14

Ngir Sunuy Doom yu Jigéen
(For Our Daughters)

In 1995, after the participatory research was complete and Molly was in the midst of writing the new module on women's health, she was approached by three Tostan staff members who had been part of the research team. They wanted to talk to her about an idea they'd been debating: including a discussion about the tradition of female genital cutting in the new health module.

Molly was taken aback. "Of course I knew by this time just how sensitive and secretive this topic was," Molly says. "My first response to the idea was 'Are you crazy? No way.'" Since first learning about the custom of cutting girls' genitals to prepare them for marriage, she had gone on to have a greater understanding not just of the tradition but also of the complicated politics that surrounded any efforts to stem the practice, especially if those efforts were attempted by a Western organization. Some Africans condemned the mere idea that Westerners should become involved in what they saw as a very African problem. Knowing

that Tostan's success rested entirely on local trust and a deep overall respect for traditional culture, Molly was extremely hesitant.

She'd already run into enough trouble, given the fact that she was the
director of an American organization based in Senegal. As Samir Sobhy,
the UNICEF representative in Senegal at the time, recalls, "Molly had
made some enemies simply because she is not African. Members of
other NGOs were envious of her success and the support she got from
our UNICEF office and the fact that a foreigner was getting funding
they believed should have been going to local NGOs."

But the three Tostan women, all of whom themselves had been
cut, were adamant. During their research, they'd been approached
several times, often in quiet corners after the large group discussions
had ended, by women ready to share their misgivings about the tradition. While these women believed it to be required under Koranic law
and were reluctant to say too much about it, they were curious, they
admitted, if some of the problems girls faced were perhaps due to the
procedure and not solely to evil spirits. They talked about seeing their
daughters hemorrhage afterward, how some young girls had even died.
They had themselves experienced their own difficulties during sexual
relations with their husbands and certainly during childbirth. They
wanted to understand more.

"I just don't think this is an issue that Tostan should take on," Molly
responded. "People will not be comfortable with the idea of an American working on this."

But the Tostan women wouldn't let the topic die. "Tostan is hundreds of Africans, Molly. This is not about you, the only American in
the organization," one said weeks into their debate. "We are African
women who need to discuss this issue. We have suffered and some of
our daughters have died. The question of FGC is a human rights issue,
and we believe it's time to discuss this openly. You have a choice. Will
you support us on this?"

IT WAS AN EXPERIENCE with Zoé that helped Molly make up her mind. By this time, Molly's daughter had grown into a beautiful, vibrant nine-year-old. But life was not always easy for Zoé, growing up in Thiès, the biracial daughter of two Americans. "At this time of my life," Zoé, now twenty-seven years old, recalls, "it was impossible to pinpoint my own identity. I wasn't completely black or completely white and was much lighter skinned than all of my friends. I was officially American, but I grew up in rural Senegal and considered myself Senegalese. I could speak fluent English, French, and Wolof by the time I was five but have a hard time saying what my first language is. When asked to describe myself, or say where I'm from, I know that I'm not just one word. I'm a whole paragraph. I'm proud of this now, but as a child it wasn't easy. Like all young girls, I just wanted to fit in."

It was this desire to fit in that prompted nine-year-old Zoé to approach Molly with a very serious concern one day, after spending an afternoon with a few Senegalese girlfriends. One had reported that her cousin was preparing to be cut. When Zoé asked her to explain, her friend said the tradition was an important part of Senegalese culture that a girl had to experience before she could be considered ready for marriage. Girls who were not cut would have a hard time finding a husband.

"I don't understand why you haven't done this for me," Zoé said to Molly, on the brink of tears. "Why would you keep me from this? Do you think I'm not brave enough to endure it?"

Molly was stunned.

"Zoé, sit down," she said. "Do you know what cutting involves? Do you know what they do to you during this procedure? Sit down so that I can explain everything to you."

Greatly alarmed, Molly rushed to her room to get the pictures she'd collected of the different types of FGC to show Zoé and explain exactly what happens, as well as the consequences that follow for the rest of a girl's life. Molly could hardly get the words out fast enough.

Zoé's eyes widened as she poured over the drawings and listened to her mother. Imagining the pain of having the most sensitive organ of her body amputated, her hesitation grew. Molly explained what she had learned from women who had seen their daughters hemorrhage or who had to treat painful cysts resulting from botched operations.

"I didn't know this, Mom," Zoé said in a hushed voice. "I just didn't know."

"It blew me away," Molly now recalls. Here her own daughter, an American, was feeling the pressure of the tradition. "It was a very decisive moment in my own understanding of the power of FGC, and I knew what I now had to do."

Over the next several months, Molly threw herself into her work, searching for how best to bring information on women's health—including a discussion of human rights and FGC—to village women. When she felt she'd finally gotten it right, she went back to the director of AJWS and explained that thousands of women interviewed had asked to do a module on their own health before discussing that of their children.

"We agree you should always listen to the people whom you are serving, so go ahead and do this module first," the director responded.

The new module on women's health, including a discussion of human rights—Module 7—was piloted with several thousand women in twenty villages, in four regions of Senegal. The reactions to the sessions were almost immediate. Just a few weeks after it had been completed in the villages, Molly began to receive feedback that made her head spin. "I was so surprised," she recalls. "I heard that the women from one village formed a delegation to confront a man known to beat his wife, explaining that this was a violation of her human rights and they would no longer accept it. I learned of the women's excitement, because for the very first time they understood the phases of pregnancy and could now plan for the day they'd give birth." She received poems

from women in response to the module. "Before, we felt unsure and op-
pressed, we walked with our heads lowered! But now our heads are held
high," wrote the women in one village, in a poem they entitled "Human
Rights."

Women from the village of Ngaparou wrote another poem entitled
"Who Is Module 7?" reading, in part:

Ah! Module 7!
You came to Ngaparou and chased away illness from our families.
Come, Module 7!
Help our Senegalese women know their rights,
especially their right to health.
Help them to learn about their bodies.
You, women of Ngaparou,
share your knowledge with your daughters,
especially at puberty.
Speak to them about menstruation, about sexuality.
Don't be ashamed any longer!
Women of Senegal, answer Module 7's call.

"The women's stories were keeping me awake at night trying to understand what was happening," Molly says.

But nothing could have prepared her for the call about to come a few
weeks later, in late June 1997.

"I DON'T UNDERSTAND WHAT you mean," Molly said into the phone
to Malick Gueye, a Tostan coordinator from the region of Thiès.

He said it again: the women of the Tostan class in a village called Malicounda Bambara had, after completing Module 7, convinced the people
of their village to end the practice of female genital cutting. It had been a
long process, he explained, involving many months of intense discussion
and debate.

"The facilitator in the village, Ndey, had me interview many people yesterday because I couldn't believe it myself. The women have clearly made up their minds, and no girls were cut this year." Malick paused. "Molly, I never thought anything like this could happen. But this is real. This is really happening."

15

Yeewu-Yeete (Showing the Way)

News of the Malicounda Bambara decision traveled fast, capturing the attention of villagers throughout Senegal. "It was such an anxious and uneasy time," Molly remembers. "We all knew things could go either way—the decision would either be understood as an act of bravery, or the women would be ridiculed and ostracized. All we could do was wait and see, and pray for the best."

At first, the coverage appeared positive, portraying the Tostan participants of Malicounda Bambara as intelligent women who had made a thoughtful decision based on their new knowledge of human rights, the negative health consequences of FGC, and a desire to end a practice they had finally come to question.

But as Molly had feared, it wasn't long before another story began to emerge.

As reported in some newspapers, many villagers were shocked and felt angry and betrayed by the women's pronouncement. Accused of being under the spell of Western influence or of having been paid to stop the tradition by an American, they were labeled "revolutionaries" and accused of turning their backs on tradition. An article in *Le Soleil*, a Senegalese daily newspaper, was accompanied by a cartoon of women burning down the "circumcision hut" and a young girl behind them saying *anitche* (thank you) in Bambara.

With every disparaging article, the men of Malicounda Bambara grew increasingly incensed and Kerthio Diawara, Maimouna, and the other women of the Tostan class increasingly discouraged. As one of Kerthio's male relatives said angrily to her, "When we agreed to your decision we never dreamed you would be putting your intimate parts out in the village square. These are private matters that should not be discussed publicly. If you had just made the decision and quietly carried on we would have no problems. But you are discussing secret things related to our culture that make us look bad."

A few weeks after the announcement, Molly returned to Malicounda Bambara to check how the women were faring. The exuberance of their previous discussions was gone. "They are calling us revolutionaries and traitors to our culture, but we are not these things," said Maimouna. "We are making peaceful change in an effort to promote women's health. We are not attacking our traditions. We are trying to change a practice that has dangerous health consequences for our daughters."

Over time, Molly couldn't help but question the choice of going public with the decision, knowing that it might only get worse. "You can't control what journalists write or put on television, and things may become even more distorted," she said to the women one afternoon. "But it's not too late. If you want to stop discussing this with the media, we can do that. We can stop bringing people here to speak with you so that others will no longer write about Malicounda Bambara."

The women debated the best way forward, and as they did, Kerthio sat quietly in her chair, one hand fanning the flies from her face, the other resting on her stomach. Inside her, she'd recently discovered, another baby grew, her fifth. While she'd been happy with the news, she couldn't help but feel the familiar pangs of sadness and worry that accompanied the discovery of another pregnancy, bringing memories of the day a decade earlier when she'd lost her daughter, Mariama. She caressed her swollen stomach as she listened to Molly and the women of her village debating the possibility of no longer speaking to the press about their decision.

But she knew. Because of what she and the other women were doing, because of the information they'd been given and the courage they'd found, this child inside her, if she was a girl, would never be cut. She would never have to experience the pain and suffering, or the risk, of a custom that no longer made sense. That was enough to convince her that no matter what, no matter the hardships that might await them for what they were doing, no matter how many times they might be met by anger or disappointment, no matter the names they were called, for the health of this baby inside her, and for all the daughters of Senegal, she was never looking back.

She spoke to the group. "We will not stop speaking of this to others. Before something is beautiful, it might have to be difficult. We made this decision and believe in what we did. We must therefore have the courage to explain to other women why we ended the tradition here. We cannot forget our sisters and our daughters. Change like this takes time, and we must persist."

THE WOMEN WERE TRUE to their word. A few weeks later, they received news that the women in the nearby village of Keur Simbara, where many of their relatives lived, were preparing to cut their girls. Despite the tension they continued to experience in their village, the women of Malicounda Bambara remained committed to spreading the knowledge they'd received. After all, theirs was a village of just three thousand residents, and while their efforts would spare their daughters pain and suffering, thousands of other girls in the region would still be cut.

Kerthio called Molly at the Tostan office in Thiès. "We've decided we'd like to visit our relatives in Keur Simbara to share our knowledge with them and speak about our decision. Can you help us get to the village?"

Molly agreed to rent a bus for the occasion, and a few days later the women prepared for the two-hour journey from Malicounda Bambara to Keur Simbara. Despite everyone's excitement and nerves that day, there was something else on their minds: the weather. It typically begins to rain in mid-July in Senegal; here it was August, and it had barely rained at all. Once on board the bus, the women kept glancing at the sky, hoping to spot rain clouds. Molly found herself doing the same. Having lived through a drought during her years in Saam Njaay, she fully understood the suffering, hunger, and poverty that accompany a lack of rain.

As the bus drew closer to Keur Simbara, the women put aside their worries about the weather, and stirring with excitement, they strained to hear the sound of drumming and music that always welcomes guests—especially visiting relatives—to any village. But when the bus finally slowed to a stop in the village square, the women were surprised to find there wasn't any drumming or music. While a few people were there to greet them, they climbed off the bus to complete silence.

Kerthio took her mother's hand. "Has something happened? Is there a funeral today we weren't told of?" she asked.

Maimouna shook her head in confusion and looked at Molly for a possible explanation, but she was as bewildered as the rest of the group. She had, of course, called ahead to give notice that the women were coming to discuss their recent decision. "I distinctly remember the sinking feeling I had at that point," Molly says. "I'd expected a celebration and much joy from people, happy to see their relatives, who'd made considerable effort to get to Keur Simbara. That was the moment I began to grow very unsure about what we were doing."

More people eventually began to arrive in the courtyard, and chairs were brought and placed in a large circle under the great neem tree in the center of the village. The village chief greeted the women, and after everyone had solemnly taken their seats, Maimouna explained that the women had prepared a theater about their recent decision to end the tradition in their village. There was silence as the women stood to take their places, and throughout their performance, there was very little reaction from the audience.

Afterward, Maimouna stood to speak. "We know you may be upset that we made this decision, and we want you to know why we made it. We're here to talk to you, our relatives, so you can understand what we've learned through our Tostan classes and why we've chosen to do this. We are part of the same ethnic group, the same family. And we want you to join us."

Molly, seated in a chair in the circle, noticed a few women from Keur Simbara exchanging annoyed glances, others wrestling with the desire to take leave of the conversation, and she felt the uneasiness rising inside her. The heat was stifling in the courtyard. Beyond the large circle, children looked on with curiosity. Demba Diawara, one of the most respected men in Keur Simbara, stood to speak.

A slight man with deep-set eyes and a graying goatee, Demba was born—at least according to the identification card he keeps in a small leather billfold—in 1937, which made him, on that day, sixty years old. Demba's family had been among the first to settle the village of Keur Simbara in the late 1800s, when his mother's father first came to Senegal from Mali in search of richer soil for his peanut crops.

"Thank you very much for coming all the way here," Demba began. "We appreciate the effort you've made. As you know, the tradition of which you speak comes from a very long time ago, from our mothers and their mothers. As a way of recognizing our ancestors, and showing them the respect they deserve, we hold this tradition in very high esteem. We are a very small village, a small community, but we are also part of a large community beyond this village. You have made a decision to do things your way, but that is not how we operate here." He paused to clear his throat. "You have all come here and you have told us why you have stopped. But you made your decision without consulting with others. You have not included your family members in the dialogue. I know you now want us to join you, but we will not."

Molly looked around the circle at the crestfallen expressions on the faces of many women from Malicounda Bambara, and though she was loath to admit this to herself, the nagging doubt she'd been feeling over the last few weeks finally took hold of her. She leaned closer to Bilal, the head of training at Tostan, who had come to witness the meeting. "Come with me," she said with some urgency. They stepped away from the circle. "Maybe we shouldn't be doing this," she whispered.

"What do you mean?" he asked.

"I don't know. I'm no longer sure. Maybe this is too sensitive an issue for us to address. Maybe we made a mistake in getting involved in all of this."

"Why are you saying this now?" he asked.

"This is much deeper than I may have realized. People are not welcoming their own relatives. The tension here is so thick, and the women are being ridiculed in their own village. I'm beginning to wonder if we know enough about what we're doing, if Tostan has a right to be doing this."

Bilal pointed toward the seated crowd of people. "They are the ones doing it, Molly."

"I know, but Tostan is an American NGO, and I've seen too many instances of outside groups trying to impose their own ideas on villages like this. I've been so committed to not making that mistake. Maybe we should not be dealing with these cultural issues, which run so deep. Maybe it's too much."

"We'll talk more about this later," Bilal said.

They walked back to the circle, and just as they did, Molly felt it: the first drop of rain. People jumped from their chairs as the leaves above them shivered softly with raindrops.

"Rain. At last! Rain!" people shouted, catching the drops on their uplifted cheeks and down the backs of their *boubous*.

Kerthio, who had noticed the look of concern on Molly's face, rushed to her side. "This is a sign," she said. "I know this is difficult, but the rain is telling us something. This is what we have been waiting for. We are doing the right thing."

"Let's move inside," Demba suggested, as above the wispy gray clouds thickened with moisture. Everyone grabbed a chair and moved into a small circular hut nearby. One by one, people placed their chairs around the room, and because there was not enough space for one large circle, the chairs took the shape of a spiral. Molly was among the last to enter, and she placed her chair in the middle of the circle. Just as she did, she had the strangest feeling of déjà vu, as if she had been here before, in this exact place.

And then she remembered. This was her dream.

She'd had it more than twenty years earlier, in the weeks just before she was scheduled to first come to Senegal for the six-month student-exchange program. The trip had been proving to be highly disorganized. Molly had come to regret her decision and was about to give up her efforts to make it happen. But then she'd had the dream. In it, she was in the middle of a circle of Africans, in the belly of a pregnant woman, and she felt safer than ever before, filled with a feeling of tremendous well-being and peace. She woke the next morning awash in the vividness of the dream, feeling a lingering sense of joy, and she decided that despite the challenges she might face, she was going to Africa.

Now, two decades later, standing in the middle of a hut in Keur Simbara, she looked around the room and suddenly felt flush with the emotions of the dream, as if she were being cradled in a spiral of harmony and comfort. Despite the number of years she'd lived in Senegal, she hadn't quite absorbed the people's deep belief in spirits and signs. But maybe this *was* a sign: the dream and the rain, which had become a downpour.

Maimouna spoke to the room. "Take your time and reflect upon this as we did. At any rate, we share the same traditions as you, and we have made up our minds and are convinced of what we are doing."

Molly went over to where Bilal sat. "I take back everything I just said," she whispered.

"What do you mean?"

"We have to support these women no matter what. No more hesitation. No more vacillating. No more turning back. In fact, we're going to see where we might take this. And we're going to do it together."

"Are you sure?"

Molly looked around the room, at the spiral and her empty chair in its center, knowing that she had arrived in this place, in this moment, for a reason. "Completely."

BOOK TWO

Where, after all, do universal human rights begin? In small places, close to home—so close and so small that they cannot be seen on any maps of the world. . . . Such as the places where every man, woman, and child seeks equal justice, equal opportunity, equal dignity without discrimination. Unless these rights have meaning there, they have little meaning anywhere. Without concerted citizen action to uphold them close to home, we shall look in vain for progress in the larger world.

—ELEANOR ROOSEVELT,
WRITING ON THE TENTH ANNIVERSARY OF THE ADOPTION OF
THE UNIVERSAL DECLARATION OF HUMAN RIGHTS

16

Yewwiku (Deliverance)

Not long after the meeting in Keur Simbara, in a nearby village called Nguerigne Bambara, a woman named Ourèye Sall finished rinsing a dinner platter before placing it on the mat beside the washing tub and calling to her six children.

"Finish your chores," she said to them. "And remember you're to obey your aunts this week. I'm not sure how long I'll be gone." She wrapped her *pagne* tightly around her waist and slipped her feet into a pair of plastic sandals that sat by the door of her hut. After grabbing the small bag she'd packed, she began the walk to meet the bus that would take her on the long journey to her home village of Sinthiou Bamambe, many hours away in an area traditionally called the Fouta, located along the Senegal River.

Once on board, Ourèye rested her head against a diesel-stained window and spent the daylong trip watching the small villages of Senegal pass by, thinking about the first time she'd made this trip many years ago. She was fourteen then, on her way to be married to a man she'd never met, from a village she'd never heard of, called Nguerigne Bambara.

"It's a long trip from here," her mother had said, with very little ceremony as they readied the millet couscous for that evening's dinner. "Prepare to leave early tomorrow morning." Ourèye was speechless. She hadn't any idea her mother had found her a husband or that a week earlier he'd sent a representative to Sinthiou Bamambe to ask for her hand in marriage. She didn't know her mother had been working for months to arrange this marriage, that she had fed this man her best rice dish and told him only about Ourèye's best qualities: her peaceful and friendly nature and her ability to cook and clean house.

Apparently, Kadidiatou had sold the man on Ourèye's value as a bride, and Ourèye accepted the news that day, smiling at her mother and nodding. But as she quietly stirred the leaf sauce over the couscous, her head became crowded with questions: Who was this man? What was he like? She knew it was best to keep these questions to herself. Marriage was not between two people; it was a joining of families, and she was now expected to be obedient and trusting.

Her sisters and brothers were called. They collected on the mat around the bowl and dug into their dinner, but Ourèye had trouble eating. Trying to contain her mounting nervousness, she focused on the fact that this was very good news. After all, no girl wanted to grow old without a husband.

As soon as the meal was finished and she had helped her mother and sisters with their chores, Ourèye hurried to find Gedda. Gedda was not only Ourèye's closest friend—closer even than any of her five sisters— she was also her *sehil am wonki ngooti*. The term means "friends of the same heart" in Ourèye's language, and that was exactly how Gedda and Ourèye felt about each other—as if since the day of their births they had shared the same heart, beating deep in each of their chests in one perfect, unbroken rhythm. Ourèye spent most nights sleeping in Gedda's room, their bodies sprawled next to each other on a thin mat, their arms touching. Long into the night—especially nights far too hot and sticky to find sleep—they discussed the events of the day and wondered aloud about their futures: their anticipation of marriage and children, their hope that they wouldn't be worked too hard by their mothers, or later by their husbands. Gedda had cried with surprise that evening when Ourèye told her the news that she was going to be a bride. In Gedda's room, under the bright blue glow of the moon, they mulled over their questions. Ourèye had been able to discreetly wrestle a few key details from her mother: her husband's name was Modou, and he was a peanut and millet farmer. But what was he *like*? Would she know how to please him and thus bring honor to her family? Would he be kind? Gedda encouraged Ourèye to remain confident. Of course her mother had chosen a generous and peaceful man, she reassured her, one whose family would welcome her as one of their own. What they did not venture to discuss at all was the one detail that might break their shared heart: Nguerigne Bambara was many hours away from where Ourèye and Gedda lived. This was likely the last night the two would get to spend together for a very, very long time.

The next morning, before the sun rose, Ourèye's aunts Binta and Myriam, the eldest sisters of each of her parents, arrived to accompany her to Nguerigne Bambara. Ourèye did her best to appear strong and stoic, and although she knew it was impossible, she wished that Kadidiatou could come with her. Ourèye was a woman now, and it was time for her to set off on her own. Before leaving to catch the bus to Nguerigne Bambara, Ourèye and her mother stood outside the dusty courtyard in front of their family's compound, trying not to show their grief in parting. Ourèye was unsure of how to say good-bye to her mother. She didn't dare tell Kadidiatou of the fear she felt—so uncertain of what the future held, unable to imagine days without her mother there to orient her to life as she always had, like the most brilliant among the stars in the northern Senegalese sky. Ourèye's father joined them, and he held out his hands to offer a blessing for Ourèye.

"Don't be afraid, my daughter," he said when he had finished. "God is great and all will be fine." Ourèye accepted her father's blessing in her cupped, outstretched hands and slowly pulled them to touch her fore-head, so that his words were sure to cloak her entire being.

It took many hours to reach Nguerigne Bambara, and along the way, outside the window of the crowded bus, the world opened up before Ourèye. The sky was endless and deep blue, like the feathers of the blue-necked birds she and Gedda had once chased through the nearby fields before stopping to peer at the boys sitting under a tree studying their books at Koranic school. The bus passed forests of baobab trees as villages came and went, most just like the one she had come from and the one that would become her home. It was nearly midnight of the following day when the bus finally turned down a dirt path and she ar-rived, exhausted and sticky, the taste of diesel and dust on her lips, in Nguerigne Bambara.

Hundreds of people stood in the courtyard, the women dressed in their most vibrantly colored *boubous*. Men drummed and women banged on the dried, round calabash gourds resting at their feet, and the warm welcome helped to calm Ourèye's fear. A few young men were called to help unload her belongings: one small trunk crammed with a few articles of clothing and the bowls and pots she had brought as gifts for her mother- and sisters-in-law. Ourèye was led to the small, simple hut where she would live with her husband, at least until she became a mother, when Modou would get his own room and Ourèye would share her bed with her children. Inside, several women and girls, many of them her new in-laws, waited to greet her. They welcomed Ourèye with gifts of their own: intricate fabrics and several large cooking pots. The women remained with her until the sun rose, all of them dancing to the sound of the drumming.

It was early the next morning when Ourèye heard a man's voice outside the hut. She felt her heart race as she caught her first glimpse of the man she guessed to be Modou. From behind her veil, which she had worn through the night, she couldn't discern his features; all she could tell was that he was tall and many years older than she, perhaps the age of her grandfather. The women in the room laughed and cheered, knowing it was time for Modou to welcome Ourèye to his village. But first, according to their family tradition, Modou was required to give Ourèye's friends a gift for the honor of unveiling her, and the crowd applauded and sang as he made his way around the room doling out coins. He then returned to where Ourèye stood, and without hurry, he raised the cotton veil, revealing first her neck and then her chin.

The darkness lifted, and in the soft light of early morning, the man—her husband—was smiling down at her. She was relieved to find kindness in his eyes. Years later she would find him charming and gentle, but on this day, she was a child still—just fourteen years old—and all she could do was shyly avert her gaze.

THE FOLLOWING YEAR, SHE had a son. He had shiny skin and eyes the shape of almonds, and she named him Ousmane. The next year, Ourèye's second child arrived, and more children kept coming. By the time Ourèye was twenty-one years old, she was the mother of six. As much as she valued her role as a wife and mother, she knew before long that the time had come for her to set out to work, as she always knew she would: assuming the role of the traditional cutter. Like the women's tradition itself, the job was bequeathed from a mother to her daughters, and for generations the women of Ourèye's family had held this important and revered position. Knowing the job would someday be theirs, Ourèye and her sisters had begun at a very young age to accompany Kadidiatou on her visits to the surrounding villages—to observe her work and learn, just as generations of women had before them, the precautions to be taken, the prayers to be recited, and the care needed immediately following the procedure.

Ourèye was paid well for her work. Some days she might cut as many as ten girls and could earn more than forty dollars as well as bars of soap, fabric, and extra razor blades. She was proud of the money she could contribute to the household, and she savored the responsibility she held, the vital role she played in one of the most important moments of a girl's life.

But through it all she felt an uneasiness about her work. She never admitted this aloud to anyone, but at times, while throwing scoops of feed to the chickens or on long, dusty walks back from the well, Ourèye couldn't help but think of what had happened to her own daughter many years earlier, on the day that she was cut. Ourèye had done everything a mother was meant to do. She'd arranged for her own mother to come and do the cutting. Throughout the procedure, she'd recited all the appropriate prayers. But despite this, things did not go as planned. Her daughter bled too much, and they had trouble rousing her. For hours afterward Ourèye and her mother treated the wound, pressing it with leaves Ourèye had collected from the neem trees, known for their medicinal properties. This usually brought some relief, but her daughter's screams only intensified, as did the amount of blood that flowed from her body, staining the straw mat and the hardened ground underneath.

As the hours passed and her daughter suffered, Ourèye considered taking her to the closest health center in the city of Mbour. But the only way there was on the back of a *charette* (horse-drawn cart), and her daughter was in no condition to endure that sort of travel. Instead, she kept the girl cradled in her arms, trying to soothe her with the words of a traditional lullaby:

Live little baby, so you can grow and help your family. Long life my little baby. God will make you strong so that you will help your family and your people. Live little baby.

By morning, Ourèye had been able to stop the bleeding, but her daughter remained on the mat, sick and weakened, for several days.

When she was finally well enough to travel, Ourèye took her to see the local *marabout*. He prayed over her daughter, and when he was done, he confirmed Ourèye's worst fears. The child had been touched by evil spirits, and it was these spirits that had caused her to fall ill.

The memory of that day never left Ourèye, and it was made worse by the fact that her daughter never seemed to fully recover. As she got older, she was often in poor health and seemed weaker and frailer than other girls her age. After she married in her teens, she had excessive hemorrhaging during childbirth. Ourèye knew these same ailments were sometimes suffered by other girls she cut. A girl might bleed too much or contract a serious infection in the months following her procedure. This happened despite the fact that Ourèye always did her best to be careful, performing the operation with reverence, and always to a mother's liking. She did it just as Kadidiatou had taught her, one girl after another, often using the same razor blade on different girls. She had nothing with which to disinfect the blade and no medicine to help ease the pain. Instead, she relied on the girl's aunt or grandmother— very rarely her mother, as it was often too difficult for a mother to witness her daughter's pain—to bring neem leaves, which they would pound into a paste and apply to the wound. Afterward, Ourèye would leave the girl to the care of the elder women and move on to the next village, where more girls waited for her.

These problems troubled Ourèye, but she knew they were beyond her control: the work of evil spirits. She would never speak of the problems aloud, of course, for fear of angering these spirits. What was the point of speaking about the tradition anyway? Even if Ourèye had been able to express her misgivings, there was nothing she could do. The tradition had been an important part of being a woman for centuries and would continue to be that way forever.

At least this is what Ourèye had always understood, until a few months earlier when education had arrived in her village, through a program called Tostan. Because of this education, women were some-how finding the courage to speak about the tradition for the first time. And as she had recently come to understand, one group of women from the nearby village of Malicounda Bambara had not only begun to speak about it.

They had decided to abandon it.

17

Yoonu Diisoo (Choosing Dialogue)

Hours later, still lost in these memories, Ourèye awoke with a start to find that the bus had arrived at her childhood home. Her mother, Kadidiatou, was waiting to greet her. Exhausted and hungry, Ourèye dropped off her bag at home and went in search of Gedda. While she wanted to remain awake all night talking, Ourèye bid her friend good night early and returned to her family's hut to sleep. After all, this trip was different, and she needed her rest.

Ourèye woke very early the next morning feeling tired and anxious. She knew it was best to hurry and do what she had come to do, lest she lose her courage. As soon as she and her sisters had finished fetching the water from the well and preparing the millet for the day, she asked her mother and her four sisters who had remained in the village—and all of whom, like her, had become cutters—to join her in a circle under the tree.

"I have to tell you something," Ourèye said after they were all seated. She had rehearsed what she wanted to say many times, and yet she struggled to find the best way to begin. But then her words tumbled forward before she could stop them.

"I've begun to participate in an education program in Nguerigne Bambara called Tostan, and I've learned some things I didn't know before," she began. She went on to explain how much she'd been awakened through her education and how much the program had helped the women of her village. Not only were they learning to read and write, but they also now understood so many things—the importance of vaccinations, how germs are transmitted, financial management, and, most important, the existence of human rights. Ourèye spoke of the protections granted to women under the law and about every woman's right to health and freedom from all forms of violence.

"As part of this discussion, we've been having a long and honest dialogue about the women's tradition," she said, registering the flash of surprise on her mother's face. "The women in a village not far from mine have gone through the same program and have made a brave and exciting decision as a community. They are going to stop cutting their girls. They are going to abandon the tradition."

"Ourèye," one of her sisters said, "be careful what you're saying."

"The information I've received has really changed my mind about things," Ourèye continued, "and that is why I've come. I have made a decision, but I needed to come and talk to you about it first, before I share it with anyone else."

She told them about the afternoon when Fatimata, the Tostan facilitator, first spoke of the tradition. Ourèye had sat as still as stone, feeling the blood drain from her face, as Fatimata told the class about the decision the women of Malicounda Bambara had made and then spoke about the potential problems associated with the tradition. When Fatimata finished her presentation, Ourèye took in a long, slow drink of dusty air, trying to recover her breath.

The other women in the class were quiet at first, stewing in their dismay and disbelief. Some eventually spoke up, voicing their anger and confusion, but Ourèye remained silent. She understood.

What Fatimata spoke about was exactly what had happened to her daughter so many years ago. She had hemorrhaged, and her wound had become infected. That was why she had suffered; why, throughout her life, she'd always had problems.

It was me, Ourèye thought. *It was because of what I did.*

As soon as the class was finished, Ourèye hurried from the hut to find Marièma Ndiaye, her closest friend in Nguerigne Bambara, feeling heavy under the weight of her shame. She explained to Marièma what Fatimata had said, and as she did, everything seemed to come into perfect focus. Her daughter's problems, Kadidiatou's inability to stop the bleeding. What had happened that day wasn't because of evil spirits. "Marièma," she found the courage to say to her friend one day. "I've witnessed the same thing happen to other girls I've cut myself."

Marièma could say nothing to calm or comfort Ourèye. That night, and for the next several nights, while cooking dinner for Modou and her children, while taking advantage of the mild afternoon air after her work was complete, Ourèye was withdrawn and quiet. The money she earned cutting the girls of her region was a great help to all the members of her family, allowing her to buy shoes and clothes for the children, and her work brought her much respect from the women in her village and the surrounding communities. But if what she did possibly led to health problems, if what she did brought suffering—not peace—to people, how could she continue?

Ourèye's mother and sisters remained quiet as Ourèye explained how afraid she'd felt since first hearing Fatimata speak of the tradition in class, afraid that she and the other women of her family had brought pain to others; and how, despite many years of believing otherwise, she'd become truly convinced that the information she'd learned was true. Since hearing about the events in Malicounda Bambara, she had spent many hours speaking to the well-respected imam in Nguerigne Bambara. He had assured her that what Fatimata had told the Tostan class was true: the Koran did not require women to practice the tradition.

As her mother and sisters kept their gazes fixed on the horizon, Ourèye explained her belief that the problems with the tradition extended far beyond the potential health consequences. "Look at how it's led us to discriminate against others," she said. "We would never allow our sons to marry an uncut woman, even if that was their desire. We exclude and ridicule the women from ethnic groups that do not practice the tradition. We refuse to eat their food. We call them insulting names."

Ourèye was guilty of this herself. For so long she had believed that not being cut made a woman impure and unclean, and she had herself discriminated against women who had not had the operation. For the last few weeks she'd been especially saddened by thoughts of one woman in particular to whom she had been unkind. Her name was Atti, and she was from an ethnic group that didn't practice the tradition, but she had married a man in Ourèye's village. None of the other women would consent to being her friend, and Atti, in her loneliness, was very unhappy. Every time she washed any dishes or clothes, the other women would rewash them. When she walked into a circle of women, they would get up and leave. Eventually Atti decided she was miserable enough to take drastic measures. That year, when the cutter came to perform FGC on the girls of the community, she asked to be cut. She was in her thirties at the time, and while it was highly unusual to perform the operation on a woman of that age, the cutter had agreed. Atti's procedure was very painful, and it took her weeks to recover. But afterward, she got what she had wanted: acceptance from the other women. She was asked to join in their activities and cooking, to share in the meals for the first time.

"Imagine the pain that sort of discrimination causes women," Ourèye said, "on top of the pain of the operation itself."

"Enough," her mother said. "I don't want to talk about this anymore."

"I know, Mother," Ourèye said. "I didn't either. But none of us sitting here right now can say we haven't witnessed suffering. Any cutter who tells you this is trying to hide something."

"Those problems are not caused by our actions," her mother said. "They are the work of the bad spirits."

"They are the result of infection," Ourèye said. "I learned in Tostan that there are scientific reasons for the problems that occur. I wouldn't be saying this to you if I didn't truly believe it myself. I know now in my heart the tradition does not reflect the values of our culture. It comes down to this: if we are truly about well-being and peace, this is not the right path."

Kadidiatou gave her a stern look. "You have lost your mind," she said. And with that, she got up from the circle and walked away.

Ourèye remained with her family in the Fouta for a few days, trying her best to ignore the icy way her mother and sisters spoke to her. When she returned home to Nguerigne Bambara the following week, she felt discouraged but undeterred. Meanwhile, the discussion in her Tostan class about the tradition, and the decision made by the women of Mali-counda Bambara, grew increasingly intense. Ourèye knew that many of her classmates were looking to her for direction on the subject. Not only was she the coordinator of their Community Management Committee, but she was also the cutter. If she wasn't going to support it any longer, how could they?

She knew what she had to do. Despite her family's refusal to support her, there was no going back. After all, she'd always considered herself a woman of peace. In fact, her desire for peace was the organizing principle of her life. Life in villages like hers was not easy. The lack of drinking water, the fear of drought and disease, and the scarcity of firewood often made the mere act of survival very difficult, and Ourèye's main priority was to help, in every way she could, to bring happiness and peace to her community. For without peace, what was life but struggle and existence? And now, if she truly was committed to the values she'd always held so dear, if she really was a woman of peace, what other choice did she have?

Carefully, and with all the respect and sensitivity she could gather, she began to approach the women of her husband's family, and then her neighbors; she was determined to speak to every woman in the village, especially those not enrolled in the Tostan classes. Marièma often accompanied her on these long walks to communities surrounding Nguerigne Bambara, and before long, others from the Tostan class also joined her. The women she spoke to were surprised. Here was the cutter herself coming to tell them of the dangers of the tradition, to educate them about what had happened in Malicounda Bambara, and to ask them to consider giving up the tradition.

Ourèye spent nearly every free moment during the course of the next month doing this work. While it was tiring and trying, she was proud of these efforts. She wished she had been able to convince her family— her mother especially—to support her decision, but perhaps that might happen in time.

Several weeks later, in November 1997, she was walking down the path in her village, lost in these thoughts, when she heard Marièma calling to her from ahead, motioning her to hurry. "Come on!" Marièma said. "She's arrived."

Just then, Ourèye heard the sound of Molly's car approaching. She quickened her step to join the twenty or so other women in welcoming her.

MOLLY, DRESSED IN A beautiful light-green *boubou,* stepped out of the car into the sticky November heat and stopped to greet each of the women. Ourèye could sense the shared excitement among the Tostan students as the group made its way to the small, dark room used as a classroom. Everyone took a seat in a circle, the stale air inside buzzing with flies. Molly had come with a journalist from the French magazine *Point de Vue* who was reporting on the Malicounda Bambara declaration, which had taken place four months earlier, and who wished to talk to women in a village where the tradition was still practiced.

Molly began the meeting by asking the women to speak about their experience with Tostan. A few took turns explaining all they had learned in school, how important it was for them to finally have the chance to be educated, how they wished Tostan classes could exist in every village in Senegal. When the women had finished, Molly looked at Ourèye. "I'm especially happy you're here today," Molly said. "As the cutter, you can offer a unique perspective on the tradition you practice here."

"Yes," Ourèye said, as the journalist jotted down notes. "For generations the women of my family have held the position of cutter. I inherited it from my mother, who inherited it from her own. For years I have been traveling to the villages of our region performing the operation, and I have cut thousands of girls. All of my life I have believed in this tradition. Like everyone here, I was taught it was necessary and sacred. But then I came to these classes and I learned differently."

Molly smiled at Ourèye, unsure of where this was heading.

"Molly, I'm proud to tell you today that our community has made an important decision. We have been inspired by the courage of the women of Malicounda Bambara. They are our sisters, and they have shown us what is possible. To support them, and for the health of our daughters and granddaughters, the village of Nguerigne Bambara has decided to follow suit. A few days ago, the village chief and imam called a meeting of the entire village after the afternoon prayers, and we've discussed this as a community. We, too, have decided. We will no longer practice the tradition in our village."

18

Tànki Jàmm (Feet of Peace)

For weeks after the meeting in Nguerigne Bambara, Molly reveled in the excitement of what was happening. "All the doubts I'd been feeling had disappeared," she recalls. "Instead of thinking about what might go wrong or the problems that might arise, I became obsessed with dreaming of the possibilities."

Ourèye's pronouncement about the decision in her village had been followed by something equally significant. A few weeks later, on November 22, 1997, the president of Senegal, Abdou Diouf, gave tremendous support to Tostan's efforts and the women of Malicounda Bambara in his speech to the Thirty-Third Congress of the International Federation for Human Rights in Dakar. "We must vigorously fight against female genital mutilation," he announced during the congress's opening ceremony, in front of nearly five hundred people, including Molly. "Today, this traditional practice can no longer be justified. In relation to this issue, the example of Malicounda Bambara deserves to be cited. In this Senegalese village, the women became aware of the dangers of this practice and engaged in dialogue with their husbands, the imam, and the village chief. Through a collective decision, the community decided

to never again practice FGM. I today make a solemn appeal for the Malicounda experience to be followed and to spread throughout Senegal."

Molly left the ceremony feeling jubilant. She hadn't known he was
planning on mentioning this, as FGC had been a subject long avoided
by Senegalese politicians out of fear of losing the support of their con-
stituents. After all the anguish the women of Malicounda Bambara had
suffered, she knew this was just what they needed to raise their spirits.

Following the meeting in Keur Simbara in August, things had continued to go badly. In October, less than three months after Malicounda
Bambara's declaration, a newspaper in France published an article about
their pledge in which the journalist erroneously reported that all villagers performed infibulation on their girls, meaning they were sewn shut
after their procedure. The men of Malicounda Bambara had been sent
the article by relatives in France. Incensed by the description in the article, they immediately called a meeting of the entire village.

In the oppressive heat of mid-October, they pulled chairs into a large
circle in the village square while the women nervously instructed the
children to find something to do with themselves. One by one, the men
expressed their indignation over the article, reiterating their frustration
that while they had agreed to support the women's decision, they did
not expect them to be so public about it, inviting strangers to come and
misrepresent the tradition. They'd had enough, and they were now demanding that the women stop their work. Tene Cissoko, Kerthio's best
friend, answered courageously. "We have learned our human rights," she
said. "Not only do we have the right to make important decisions like
the one we made, but we also have the right to voice our opinions. We
respect you and are willing to listen to your opinion. But we also know
that it is our right to disagree."

Kerthio, Maimouna, and the other women met to discuss the meeting, and while they too were unhappy with the language of the article,
their dedication to bringing about change remained. Molly knew that
the fact that the women were willing to defy their husbands' wishes was
a testament to just how far-reaching the transformation in Malicounda

Bambara had been. But she also knew that something needed to be done to bring the men into the process, to include them in these efforts.

During such moments, Molly often thought back to her experiences with the social movements of the late 1960s, while she was a student at the University of Illinois. "I watched the events unfolding around me with interest and observed the different strategies being used to try to bring about social justice and change," she says. "I could certainly understand the anger and revolt that I witnessed on campus, but I wondered if this would ultimately lead to the deeper social changes we were seeking." Reading about Mahatma Gandhi and Martin Luther King Jr., she had been drawn to their peaceful, inclusive methods, which appealed to the deeper values of humanism. "They held firm to their beliefs without blaming, shaming, accusing, or creating an enemy to fight," she says. "Rather, they were promoting a positive vision for society to which everyone could aspire."

She thought back to one particularly memorable experience during her days in France as a college student, when she had attended a political meeting organized by students struggling to change the system. People from the workers' movement had come in hopes of coordinating activities with student groups. One worker started his speech by attesting to his belief in Jesus Christ, a statement that brought jeers and ridicule from the students. The workers walked out in anger.

Molly left that meeting sharing their frustration. Placing blame, insulting people's personal beliefs, or trying to force one's values on others was not the way to go about solving problems and creating peace and justice. As far as she saw it at the time, if people were out to end the oppression they felt, anger did not seem the best way to go. All anger accomplished was to stop the dialogue, at the moment when dialogue was needed most.

AROUND THIS TIME, MOLLY relocated the Tostan office from her house to a small, five-room building in the Dixième, a leafy neighborhood in Thiès, on a quiet street lined with large cailcedrat trees and colonial-style buildings, their red-tiled roofs reminiscent of when the city was French-controlled. Inside, the simple offices were sparsely furnished with teak furniture crafted by local artisans, the walls hung with batiks Molly had collected during her travels to other African nations. Not long after the move, Demba Diawara, from the village of Keur Simbara, paid Molly a visit. She'd first met him eight years earlier, while developing a literacy project in his village, and she'd since come to deeply respect him. He was a wise and patient man who spoke beautiful Wolof, rich with proverbs. Originally from Mali, a large nation to the east of Senegal, the Diawaras had once served as Malian kings, ruling over sixty-eight villages. By the late 1800s the land in Mali had become depleted from overfarming, so Demba's grandfather came to Senegal seeking fertile fields for his peanut crops. He found the earth in Senegal to be rich and generous, and he decided to remain. He built a home among the fields and named the area after his eldest brother, Simbara, who remained in Mali. He married and had many children in Keur Simbara, and was later blessed with too many grandchildren to count, who now populated several villages around Thiès.

For a man of Demba's age, the skin on his face was smooth and bright, and his small frame was whittled with muscle, a lingering effect of when, in his much younger days, he was considered one of the best wrestlers in the area. As an adult, he'd made it his mission to represent his family in a way that would make his grandfather and mother, a strong and respected woman, proud. Without any formal education, other than Koranic school as a very young boy, he was known by all to be an extremely intelligent, fair, and generous man.

Through the years, Molly had come to depend on Demba as a trusted adviser, and he always seemed to know when she needed guidance. By the look on his face that afternoon, Molly could tell this was likely one of those moments. He accepted the glass of water she offered and took a seat across from her.

"I've been thinking a lot about the meeting in my village with the women of Malicounda Bambara a few weeks ago, and Molly, I need to be honest with you," he began. "I trust you very much. You are part of our community, you have learned our language, and you have always shown us great respect. But this time, my friend, you have gone too far. You are involving yourself with our oldest tradition, and I have come to tell you I think you should stop what you are doing."

"Oh, Demba, I'm sorry you're upset," Molly said. "I had misgivings about it myself in the beginning. But just as the women have learned so much, so have I. You need to understand. After what the women of Malicounda Bambara and Nguerigne Bambara have done, after what I've learned, I can't just stop. We need to keep talking about this tradition."

Demba's gaze was severe. "But Molly, you are concerning yourself with something you don't know enough about. If this had happened just ten years ago—if you had come to a village like ours and talked about the tradition so publicly—I'm not sure you would have made it out of the village unharmed. That is how deep our sentiment is around this tradition."

Molly hesitated. "Demba, I have to ask you something. Have you ever talked to the women in your village about their experience with the tradition?"

"Of course not."

"Why? Why haven't you asked them about it?"

"You know men never discuss these things. It is taboo to talk about this."

"But do you realize what the health consequences are?"

Demba was silent.

"Demba, the information we're giving to the women, it is all based on facts. For as long as I've known you, you have been keen to learn new things. I'm not trying to get you to stop anything. I just want you to be informed. And I want you to do three things for me before you ask me again to stop what I'm doing."

"Three things?"

"Yes. I want you to go talk to a doctor about the tradition, and I want you to speak to imams. Have a discussion with both. Ask them their opinions. When you are done, speak to the women in your community. They respect you, and I think they will tell you the problems they have experienced. Do that, and when you are finished, please come back to see me."

ON A STEAMY MORNING a few months later, Demba left Keur Simbara at seven in the morning and began the ninety-minute walk to the Tostan offices in Thiès, where he quietly took a seat in the front lobby and waited in silence until Molly opened her door. He followed her into her office, removed his dusty prayer cap, and took a seat across from her.

"In life, you're bound to make mistakes and bring bad things to others," he said. "That I can accept. What I do not accept is someone who is not big enough to say, 'I made a mistake and I'm sorry.' Well, Molly, I'm sorry. After our last conversation, I was ready to shake what you'd said from my ears. But now I know. If I had understood what I do now, I never would have sat in silence. I would have stood up a long time ago."

He'd gone first to other religious leaders. "If any of them had confirmed what I've always believed—that the tradition was a religious obligation under Islam—I would have stopped right there," Demba told her. But in every meeting, he was told the same thing: nowhere did the Koran encourage or require women to perform the tradition, and no truly learned Muslim could claim it was a religious obligation. Demba left each meeting feeling bewildered that for so long, for so many generations, his people had held such a deep misunderstanding of what their religion required on this matter.

He then went to a doctor, who explained exactly what was done to a woman's body during the procedure, how painful it could be, as well as the potential health consequences. Slowly, and with some trepidation, he then began to engage in conversations with the women in his family. "I had no idea, no idea!" he said, shaking his head. "I have heard unbelievable stories—of girls suffering, and women's pain and difficulty during sexual relations and childbirth, especially if they were sealed. The women never talked about this, never showed pain, never told us about the problems before. Like me, most didn't realize this pain is linked to the tradition." They had, of course, all assigned it to another cause: evil spirits or the will of God. Although Demba had once shared their belief that sickness is often due to the mysterious, invisible forces that exist everywhere, both he and the women were now beginning to understand through the Tostan health module that this was likely not the case. "They were surprised by what they learned in Tostan. They thought all women had the same pain, that it is natural to suffer in this way."

"Demba, are you saying your village is going to stop practicing the tradition?" Molly asked when he'd finished speaking.

"Molly, we can't. I need to explain to you what you did wrong, my friend. This tradition is a very old custom that no one in our community has ever questioned. To decide to stop it—that is not a decision an individual can make alone. It is not a decision that one village can make alone. Our daughters intermarry in ten other villages. If we stop today, tomorrow our daughters will not have husbands, and no mother would do that to her daughter. That would cause insurmountable problems in a girl's life. This is why there have been so many problems in Malicounda Bambara. The way the decision was made there is not how decisions are made in this culture. The worst thing you can do in Africa is to pull yourself out of your group, to make an individual decision. That is what the women did, without consulting the larger community."

"I don't understand," Molly said. "They decided as a village to stop."

"Yes, but a person's family is not their village. The family includes one's entire social network: their relatives in many surrounding villages, in all of the places they marry, even in far-off countries like France and the United States. If you want this work to continue, if you truly want to bring about widespread change, you must understand something. When it comes to important decisions, they must *all* be involved."

Molly knew immediately that Demba was right. It wasn't that the decision of the women in Malicounda Bambara was wrong; it was that they had employed the wrong strategy. "I should have known," Molly said. "What do we do?"

"I'm going to help you, and if I can, I will work to get more villages—many more villages—to follow the lead of the women of Malicounda Bambara and Nguerigne Bambara. I will go to the ten villages where my closest family members live, and I will speak to them myself. I don't know how they will respond, but I know we must include all of them and share the knowledge we have learned."

"I want to help," Molly said.

"Well," he replied, "I do not want to offer any false promises that I will have any effect. And I do not want people to think I am earning money from anybody. My feet are feet of peace, and they alone will carry me far."

THE NEXT WEEK, DEMBA began to walk. From village to village, with nothing but the clothes he wore and his prayer cap, he walked. Some days he walked five miles, other days as far as fifteen, returning home only a few nights at a time over the next month. Arriving in each village with an aching back and skin slick with sweat, he was greeted warmly by his relatives and offered food and a place to sleep. These initial encounters were always cheerful and warm until, after a meal had been shared, Demba called the people of the village together to explain why he had come. Many looked at him with disbelief, others with anger, that he—an elderly man, no less—had the audacity to speak aloud about something so intimate and private.

In the first village he visited—a small, remote community of about eight hundred residents called Diabougou—a few women rose from their chairs and left the circle as he spoke. As a respected elder, Demba was not accustomed to this treatment. "Come back. Sit down," he said calmly to the women, concealing any signs of his quickly beating heart.

"I'm not saying you have to change your behavior. I'm simply asking you to listen." But the women kept going. In another village, he was seriously challenged by one of his nieces. "Just try to tell me to stop," she said when he'd finished speaking. "Not only do I refuse to ever give up this tradition, if I hear of a girl who hasn't been cut, I will take her and cut her myself."

"I understand you're upset," Demba said to his niece. "But I also understand there are three parts to life: yesterday, today, and tomorrow. Most of us live wholly in the first two parts, and we have trouble envisioning tomorrow. To do that requires a lot of introspection and thought. You are angry now, I understand. I was too when this issue was first brought to me. But we must not react. Rather, we must pause and think. We must envision tomorrow."

Again and again—in Samba Dia, Sorabougou, Soudiane—his message was met with anger, but he remained patient when he spoke, pausing to touch a knee when he wanted someone to pay closer attention, to deepen their understanding of what he was saying. At the end of each evening, when the discussion had waned and the people of the village were ready to retire, Demba thanked them for their time, inviting them to meet again the next day. In a few instances he was politely asked to leave, but his resolve remained. He quietly explained he had come in peace, and while he respected their request, he preferred to stay another night so that in the morning they might continue the dialogue.

He was soon accompanied on these journeys by his nephew, Cheikh, and before long, his niece, Duusu. In her thirties, Duusu had never been able to have children, and only after going through the Tostan class in her village did she link this with her own operation. She'd also seen many young girls suffer after their procedure, and one young girl from her village had died afterward. She went to speak to Demba one morning, to offer her assistance. "What you're doing is so important, because when you are confronted with problems like I have seen, and you can't do anything about it, it's very frustrating," she said to her uncle. "Maybe women have wanted to stop this for a long time and didn't know what the solution was or how to do it. When your girls are suffering, there is no peace. I want to help you. I believe we have a way to end this practice, and we must speak up. I must also now raise my voice."

As the weeks passed and he, Cheikh, and Duusu visited more villages, Demba came to realize that visiting each community just once would not be enough; people needed time, as he had, to absorb the information he was bringing, to discuss the issue among themselves. The weeks stretched by, and on his second and often third visits to each village he was pleased to discover that people had softened to his message and were more open to discussing the information he had come to share. In the village of Faajal, a young man spoke honestly to Demba and Cheikh. "We men would like to see the end of the tradition, because to tell you the truth, we're tired," he said. "We want our wives to have sexual pleasure, but it takes so much effort that we sometimes just give up. Men in our ethnic group often marry a second wife from an ethnic group which does not practice the tradition just for this reason."

Despite the progress they were making, Cheikh often felt frustrated by people's stubbornness on the matter, but Demba advised him to remain patient, to allow the conversation to occur as it was meant to. "Even if you know what the answer is, and you know what is right, you must let people discover it themselves," Demba told his nephew. "You know human nature, and you know if you tell people to stop, they won't."

And Demba knew he would not abandon this mission. The more that women slowly began to open up to him about what they had endured, about the suffering of their daughters, the more he was convinced of the significance of his work. He had also begun to hear stories about the hardships that came with other aspects of their culture, particularly the custom among some ethnic groups of marrying their daughters as young as eight years old. Custom required a husband to wait until the girl was older before the marriage could be consummated, but as Demba understood, you don't put gas and fire together and expect them to stay apart.

One evening, after Demba had been on the road for more than two months, he, Duusu, and Cheikh sat in front of a fire in the small village of Kobongoy. They were hours away from their own village, and it had been weeks since they'd been home with their spouses and children. Cheikh turned to Demba, a troubled expression on his face. "Uncle, what is your greatest goal?" he asked. "What is it we are ultimately after?"

Demba sat in thought for many minutes before answering. "I know what we are doing is oftentimes frustrating and that our legs are very, very tired. But I know that I can't sit at my home drinking tea and yell out to others to do something. If I want to bring about change, I have to get up and move. Even if I'm tired, I have to get up and move. And what you'll find is that when you do, God will bring you the strength. I know we are working not just to bring knowledge to our family, but to also bring hope."

The fire reflected in Demba's eyes as he watched the fading embers. "What is my greatest hope? My greatest hope is that after I'm gone, the children sitting out here among us will one day say, 'We once practiced this harmful tradition because we simply didn't know any better. Can you believe we did that, and for thousands of years? But we don't anymore.' And that will be because of people like you and me." Demba reached to rest a wrinkled hand on Cheikh's knee. "Life has legs and continuously walks. We must walk with it or we will be left behind. Remain with me. Let's keep walking."

19

Biral gi (The Public Declaration)

Four months after Demba first set out on his journey, he walked back to Thiès, arriving at the Tostan offices before noon. When Molly met him at the door, he looked weary and drained. His caftan was dusty and shredded at the hem along his ankles, revealing cracked, dirt-rimmed toes peeking out from his tattered plastic sandals.

"I'm here to invite you to accompany me to a few villages that I've visited, to meet my family," he said to Molly. "We talk about you a lot. People are aware that you are concerned about this issue, and it's important you meet them. Also, I want you to see for yourself what has happened."

A few days later, Molly and Demba visited four of the villages where Demba had been working, and in each, they were graciously welcomed by a large gathering of people playing music and dancing. Again and again the villagers discussed their experiences over the last few months: how they had resisted Demba's message when he first arrived to speak to them, how they had spent days sitting together in a circle, discussing the issue from every angle. And most important, how they had all decided after much debate and dialogue that they were no longer going to cut their girls.

"It's true," Demba said to Molly. "And the same is true in every one of the ten villages I have visited. We are going to make this decision, and we are going to make it as one."

Molly spent the day in a state of disbelief. If this was true, if the people of these ten villages were serious about what they were saying, this would mean that a significant number of Senegalese—at least eight thousand people—would be abandoning the practice, that the decision would affect many thousands of girls.

They remained in the last village until after dinner. As night fell, Molly steered her Land Cruiser along the darkened, unmarked roads back toward Keur Simbara. Demba was silent on the ride back, speaking only to direct Molly on which road to take. Molly enjoyed the silence. She'd come to love the way the Senegalese were able to be with one another without having to fill the space with mindless chatter and unnecessary observations. It had taken her a while, but she'd eventually grown comfortable with the quiet between two people. Even so, as she neared Keur Simbara, her curiosity overwhelmed the tender silence.

"Do you believe it will really happen?" she asked into the darkness. "Will they all keep their word?"

Demba turned to look at her and paused to reflect. "I know the people of these ten villages are very serious about what they're saying, and I trust they will remain true to their decision to stop the practice. But we need to all come together as one family, one community, and voice our decision aloud."

"What do you mean?"

"We need to make our decision public. Doing so will give everyone the assurance that the tradition will not be abandoned only by certain people, only in isolated instances. They need to know that every village present will keep their oath. Otherwise, those who do not cut their daughters will always fear they may be the only ones doing so and may be limiting their daughters' opportunities for marriage."

WHEN MOLLY WAS LITTLE, her mother, Ann, would sometimes read her and her sister, Diane, stories about Albert Schweitzer, a German physician who had founded a hospital in West Africa and went on to win the 1952 Nobel Peace Prize. Driving into the village of Diabougou on February 14, 1998, Molly was reminded of these stories, of their descriptions of African villages that seemed to Molly—a girl of eight—to be too remote and magical to actually exist. But now here it was—Diabougou.

The village had been chosen, at Demba's suggestion, as the location for the meeting of the ten villages he had visited. In its center stood one of the thickest, most verdant neem trees Molly had ever seen. It was surrounded by paths, like the spokes of a wheel, spreading in every direction to huts made of palm leaves. The Bambaras of Diabougou were known for their dancing, and when Molly stepped from her car into the cool morning air, she was greeted by the sound of drumming and scores of women dressed in colorful *boubous* and head scarves. The sounds and the sight took her breath away.

Hundreds of people were present, joined by villagers from Keur Simbara, Malicounda Bambara, and Nguerigne Bambara. Dozens of girls danced among the group, each dressed in her finest clothes and with her hair plaited in intricate patterns. The women tended to the guests, some ensuring they had seats while others carried a large tub of drinking water to a cool spot in the shade. The participants of the Tostan classes in Malicounda Bambara and Nguerigne Bambara had been invited as special guests, and Molly took a seat in one of the chairs under the tree to wait for Maimouna, Kerthio, Ourèye, and the others to arrive. In minutes she was pulled from her chair and into the circle of dancers. She loved dancing among the African women, loved the way Africans seemed to dance not just with their bodies, but with their souls. She moved fluidly and effortlessly beside them, her *boubou* catching the wind. Eventually, the village chief raised his hand to ask for silence. The music stopped, and all eyes followed him to where the women of the Malicounda Bambara Tostan class, joined by Ourèye, proudly strode into the square. The village chief walked to greet them.

"You are pioneers who have lit the way for us," he said. "You are the ones responsible for all of us being here today. We stand to honor you." And with that, the hundreds of people gathered in the cool February morning stood and applauded.

THE DAY WAS LONG. One by one, people spoke about their experiences with the tradition, some bravely sharing the problems they'd witnessed because of it. Several hours into the meeting, Molly decided to leave Diabougou to allow the villagers some time to talk among themselves.

Later that night, under the gauzy veil of a mosquito net in a hotel room forty minutes away, Molly was unable to sleep. She lay on the thin bed, the sound of drumming echoing in her thoughts. She didn't know what, exactly, would come of the discussion happening in Diabougou, but regardless of the outcome, the magnitude of what was happening began to sink in.

If these ten villages did decide to collectively and publicly abandon this tradition, if this was the way to end the practice of female genital cutting and spare thousands of girls years of needless pain and a lifetime of potential problems, then what would now be required of her? She felt unprepared for what might lie ahead, for the responsibility that Tostan might have in all of this. Taking the movement any further would mean reaching out to hundreds, if not thousands, of social networks across Senegal and maybe even into other countries where FGC was practiced. She didn't know how she would do that—after all, Tostan was a small organization, with a small staff and a budget of just $300,000—but if the men and women at Diabougou declared an end to the practice, she knew she had to find a way.

She gave up on the idea that she would get any sleep and dressed quickly, before driving back to the village and making her way among the unlit streets, back to Demba and Ourèye, to find out what the representatives of the thirteen villages had decided. It was nearly four in the morning when she arrived, yet a large crowd of people was still gathered under the neem tree. She went to the schoolroom being used to host the guests who had come from other villages and found mattresses strewn across the floor. Demba and Ourèye greeted her, the smell of the fire lingering on their skin.

"I couldn't wait any longer," Molly admitted. "How is the discussion going?"

"We've made a decision," Demba said, handing her the text someone had written in Wolof. "This will explain it all."

Molly took the paper and sat down, straining to read by the dim light of the gas lamp on the table. She read it several times before beginning the work of translating it into French. It took her two hours to finish, checking with several people to make sure she was getting each word correct. She and the others were exhausted when, later in the morning, journalists, UNICEF staff, and local and national government representatives began to arrive in Diabougou to hear the news of what had happened that weekend in the village. Demba's niece was chosen to read the statement. She stood proudly before the crowd, her amplified voice echoing throughout the village.

"We, the fifty representatives of more than eight thousand people residing in thirteen villages declare our firm commitment to end the practice we call 'the tradition' in our community," she began, "and our firm commitment to spread our knowledge and the spirit of our decision to our respective villages and to other communities still practicing. We would like to take this opportunity to express our deep appreciation and gratitude to the women of Malicounda Bambara, Nguerigne Bambara, and Keur Simbara who, under difficult circumstances, led the way and indicated the path to follow for the government and other communities who are committed to assuring that girl children and women will no longer be subjected to the dangers of cutting. Our meeting here in Diabougou today is the result of the determination of these courageous women."

THE NEWS OF THE Diabougou declaration spread quickly across Senegal through media coverage and word of mouth. Four months later, on June 2, 1998, eighteen villages that had also been through the Tostan program came together to hold their own public declaration in the village of Medina Cherif, in the region of Kolda.

These declarations captured the attention of First Lady Hillary Rodham Clinton. A year earlier, in 1997, Ms. Clinton had paid a state visit to Senegal. At the request of the U.S. ambassador, Molly had accompanied Ms. Clinton on a visit to Saam Njaay. Though twelve years had passed since Molly had lived in the village, it had continued to thrive, and since that visit Molly had written to Ms. Clinton of the extraordinary events surrounding the declarations in Senegal. The First Lady wrote back encouraging letters of support. Molly soon received the news that Ms. Clinton, who was scheduled to return to Senegal with President Bill Clinton, wanted to take time to meet with and personally congratulate the people behind these courageous decisions.

The meeting took place at Dakar's Le Meridien Président Hotel, where the Clintons were staying. "It was not easy for women and men to come together to stand against and speak out against a key ancient custom," Ms. Clinton said to Maimouna, Kerthio, Ourèye, Demba, and the others who had come to meet with her, some traveling hours by bus from their villages. Afterward, she invited them to a roundtable discussion of human rights presided over by President Clinton, who asked the villagers to stand and be recognized as leading activists for human rights at the grassroots level, an example for all. Not long after, at a 1999 National Democratic Institute dinner in Washington, DC, President Clinton spoke of this meeting. "We walked in that room in Senegal, and all those women came up with their men supporters," he said. "I'm telling you, it made chills run up and down my spine. And I wish that every American could have seen it."

The news of these pronouncements, as well as the Clintons' visit, received full-page coverage in several daily newspapers. Unlike in the aftermath of the public declaration in Malicounda Bambara, Molly spent her days fielding phone calls from people around the country congratulating Tostan on its efforts and expressing their astonishment at the number of villagers coming forward to share these brave decisions with the world.

This increased recognition of Tostan's efforts further consumed Molly, who became obsessively focused on her work and even more aware of the extent of the problem. The World Health Organization had recently announced a startling finding. While they'd previously reported that two million African girls were being cut each year, new research showed that this number was a gross underestimation; they now believed that number to be as high as three million.

"The work engulfed me," Molly recalls. "We had so much to do still but were always in a state of crisis because we had very little money. I was scrounging for funding. I was traveling a lot. Tostan took up so much of my time, at the expense of all other aspects of my life. For one thing, I could have been a better mother. Things were not always easy for Zoé."

By this time, Zoé was thirteen and living in Dakar, where she attended a bilingual school, while Molly stayed in Thiès. Living with a family friend of Molly's, Zoé had—perhaps by necessity rather than choice—grown into an independent and adaptable girl. The following year she chose to leave Dakar to spend her sophomore year in the United States, enrolling in a school near Boston and living with another friend of the family.

Zoé enjoyed her time in America but struggled to feel as if she totally belonged. Some aspects of American culture confused her—the focus on physical appearance, the way so many women felt pressure to be thin, some even making themselves sick to achieve this. "I was going through a lot in high school," Zoé says now. "And while I always knew that my mom loved and supported me, I also knew that everything in her life revolved around her work. I understand and appreciate it now, but it wasn't always easy. She was away a lot, and when she was here, she was at work. In the evenings or on the weekends all of our conversations were about Tostan. All of her friends are associated with Tostan. All of our visitors—and we always have visitors—are here because of Tostan. For my entire life, there's never been a separation between my mom's personal life and her work. I don't know how she does it. It's emotionally draining sometimes. She breathes her work. She lives it. She *is* it."

The struggle to balance her roles as a mother and as the head of Tostan is one Molly would never completely resolve; despite the conflict she felt, it was a sacrifice she needed to make at the time. As Molly saw it, her organization may have uncovered a means to facilitate the widespread abandonment of FGC, and she was determined to bring the Tostan program to as many Senegalese villages as possible. While she'd hoped others working on the issue would share her enthusiasm for what was happening, she was surprised to find this was rarely the case. She was frustrated to learn of conferences on FGC to which Tostan had not been invited or meetings among grassroots organizations that didn't even mention the public declarations or Tostan's work.

Whenever Molly was given the opportunity to present the Tostan approach, people often responded with skepticism, believing the public declarations that had taken place to be isolated one-day events, the result of Tostan staff visiting a village and telling them to end the practice, which seemed too easy. They didn't grasp that the decisions came at the end of a three-year education program, followed by months of outreach to interconnected villages. At these conferences, Molly listened to anti-FGC presenters describing their own approaches to end the practice. One emphasized the importance of passing and enforcing laws against FGC, encouraging people to call the police to report any incidents of the practice. Another approach targeted the traditional cutters, who would be brought together for a three-day seminar, during which they would be offered an alternative source of income to cutting. At the end of the three days, the cutters would ceremonially bury their knives, declare an end to their practice, and be given a diploma and the funds to pursue another project. Another approach was to host meetings in communities, during which known anti-FGC activists used large plastic models of women's sexual organs to explain FGC and its consequences, urging people to stop the practice.

Molly disagreed with the narrowness of these approaches. Encouraging neighbors to report one another would divide communities, and paying cutters to stop did nothing to address the demand for the practice. Even if some did pledge to stop, others could be found or people could cross borders to have the procedure done elsewhere. But the approaches that most bothered the villagers—and, by extension, Molly—were those that tried to bring about change by shocking or shaming. It was obvious to Molly that the techniques of publicly condemning the tradition and the women who practiced it, through bloody posters or radio and television messaging ("Stop now!"), only made women feel defensive, and any strategy that didn't take into account the existing social dynamics that made it almost impossible for individual families to stop the practice on their own was doomed to fail.

She also knew that it wasn't just the strategy that mattered. It was also the language. The terminology used to describe this practice had, over the years, undergone a number of important evolutions. When it first caught the attention of the public beyond the practicing communities, it was most commonly referred to as "female circumcision." This term, however, was quickly considered flawed, as it drew an inaccurate parallel with male circumcision, which unlike female genital cutting sometimes carries a medical benefit: namely, helping to prevent the transmission of HIV/AIDS. In its place, many activists and NGOs began to use the term "female genital mutilation," or FGM. Thought to better reflect the practice's deeply rooted gender inequalities and profound physical and social consequences, it first became popular in the late 1970s. In 1990, the term was adopted at the third conference of the Inter-African Committee on Traditional Practices Affecting the Health of Women and Children in Addis Ababa. The next year, the World Health Organization—in the hope that the term would create a clear linguistic distinction from male circumcision, and to emphasize the gravity and harm of the act—recommended the United Nations adopt the term FGM, which they largely did when referencing the practice.

But this term and much of the accompanying language—calling the practice "barbaric" and "primitive" and referring to it as torture—was highly problematic at the village level. It deeply offended villagers who certainly did not believe they were "mutilating" or intentionally harming their daughters. While Molly had, in the beginning, used the term "female genital mutilation" herself, she decided to abandon it in favor of the less judgmental term "female genital cutting," largely at the request of Demba, Ourèye, and Maimouna. In the months since the Diabougou declaration, Demba had continued his social mobilization efforts, traveling to hundreds more villages to educate his relatives about the movement under way and to encourage them to organize a public declaration of their own. He'd begun to notice, he told Molly, that any language that implied judgment, such as the words "mutilation" or "barbaric," only served to shut down dialogue.

This issue was a thorny one that continued to plague Molly for years, as some representatives of organizations often voiced frustration at the use of the term FGC, arguing that any attempt to water down the language just hurt the cause by failing to emphasize the gravity of the situation. Molly didn't agree. "Judging or shocking people rarely proves effective in getting them to see another side," she argues, "or to change their views on any topic." In this case, her instincts told her to follow the lead of the villagers.

Whenever she was confronted by this, Molly thought back to a children's story she loved, about a competition between the sun and the wind that transpired after both spotted a man walking alone down a road.

"I bet I can make that man take off his coat sooner than you," the wind said to the sun.

"Go ahead and try," the sun replied. "We'll see who wins."

The wind huffed and puffed with all his might, hoping to blow the man's jacket right off him, but this just made the man pull his coat more tightly around his body.

"Let me try now," said the smiling sun, after several minutes of watching the wind nearly exhaust itself. With much gentleness, the sun beamed warm rays of sunlight down on the man. The man loosened his grip, and soon, basking in the warm sunlight, he happily removed his coat.

20

Jëf, Gëstu
(From Practice to Theory)

Four months after the Diabougou declaration, in June 1998, a junior research fellow named Gerry Mackie sat in a quiet classroom at Oxford University in England proctoring an exam. It was a boring assignment, and Gerry passed the time flipping through a copy of the *International Herald Tribune* he'd hidden on his lap under the desk. On one of the last pages, he came across an article about the practice of female genital cutting in Senegal that made him catch his breath. "Despite outraged arguments . . . that cutting off genitals violates girls' rights, Western exhortations have had little effect in Africa. In fact, they have often been met with defensive hostility by Africans. . . . But now, in this small West African country [of Senegal], with barely eight million people, one education program is having dramatic success." The journalist, Vivian Walt, went on to detail Tostan's work, the pioneering efforts of the women of Malicounda Bambara, and the public declaration held in Diabougou. After re-reading the article a second and third time, Gerry spent the remaining hours of the exam feeling at first dumbfounded and then exuberant. As soon as the exam was over, Gerry Mackie, the forty-eight-year-old Oxford academic, ran out to St. Giles Street and, under the canopy of plane trees, literally jumped up and down.

That night he wrote Molly a letter, explaining that two years earlier he'd published an article in an academic journal called the *American Sociological Review* in which he posited a theory about how female genital cutting might end in one generation. And what Tostan was doing sounded just like an application of that theory.

In his paper Gerry compared the practice of FGC to foot-binding, a common practice in China that is thought to have been in place for a thousand years, starting sometime around the tenth century. Like FGC, foot-binding was considered necessary for proper marriage and family honor. The practice typically took place when a girl was between six and eight years old and involved bending and breaking her toes as they were pressed toward the sole of her foot. Her feet would then remain wrapped in this position until each had reset into the ideal shape: a four-inch-long appendage. The process was extremely painful and, afterward, girls could rarely walk without support, thus keeping them largely housebound. The practice often led to infection, ulceration, gangrene, paralysis, and even death. Like FGC, foot-binding was considered a tradition of the women, who were primarily the ones who defended and perpetuated it.

Despite the efforts of many well-meaning organizations endeavoring to bring an end to the dangerous tradition, the practice was so deeply entrenched and considered absolutely vital to a young girl's future, it was commonly believed that it would take many generations to end it.

Until a woman named Mrs. Archibald Little got involved.

Born Alicia Bewicke in 1845 in England, she settled in China in 1887 after marrying Archibald Little, a successful entrepreneur who lived in Chongqing, in south-central China. Unlike many wives of expatriates, Alicia Little studied Chinese, taught English, and traveled extensively throughout the interior of China to rural villages typically not on the route of foreign women. She had always been sensitive to the practice of foot-binding, and despite the stories she heard of the pain it caused girls and the problems they suffered afterward, she didn't morally condemn it, as many Europeans did. Rather, she set out to understand it. She spoke to people who practiced it and learned that a mother's decision to bind her daughter's feet was considered an act of love, one that would ensure a proper marriage, protect the virtue of the girl, and bring respect to her family. Mrs. Little also paid close attention to the efforts that had been tried—and had failed—to convince women to reform.

One day, during her travels, she made a surprising discovery. As she entered one town, many of the women ran to greet her. She had never seen women in China do this before, as most had been hobbled by their bound feet. After asking the parents why they had chosen not to have their daughters' feet bound, Mrs. Little learned that the women had decided as an entire community to abandon the practice so no one girl would suffer the consequences on her own. The experience was a turning point for Mrs. Little, helping her understand the need for *collective* abandonment, rather than a decision by one individual. As she saw it, this was perhaps a strategy that could be replicated, helping bring about change on a wider scale.

She became involved in a reform movement seeking to accomplish three things: through a modern education campaign, to explain to Chinese women that the rest of the world did not bind their girls' feet; to explore the advantages of natural feet and the disadvantages of bound feet in Chinese cultural terms; and finally, to form natural-foot societies whose members publicly pledged not to bind their daughters' feet nor allow their sons to marry women with bound feet. The pledge associations were critical.

At the core of this, Mackie pointed out, was an important idea from game theory known as the Schelling convention. Applied to foot-binding, the essential insight is the interdependence of families' decisions: what one family chooses depends on what other families choose.

In other words, a family in an intra-marrying group that practices a custom related to marriageability cannot give up that custom unless enough other families in their group coordinate to do the same. As Demba Diawara seemed to know instinctively, even if every family in a community believed the custom to be wrong or undesirable, without a collective public pledge, this would not be enough to bring about its end: any family abandoning the custom on its own would ruin the future of its daughters.

In 1895, Mrs. Little helped create the Natural Foot Society of China, and she served as its first president. At the same time, a number of native Chinese-run societies had begun to spring up, demanding reform. They used the discovery Mrs. Little had found of pledge societies and catalyzed the movement, helping it spread like a grass fire. By 1907, Chinese public opinion had turned decisively against foot-binding, and—extraordinarily—the practice was considered to be largely abandoned among eastern coastal populations by 1911, just sixteen years after the founding of the Natural Foot Society.

Gerry Mackie concluded his paper with a prediction: the formation of a similar kind of pledge association in interconnected communities that practiced female genital cutting—one that included a critical mass of individuals who publicly declare a communal decision—could help bring about a swift end to the practice of FGC.

Gerry's letter to Molly arrived at the Tostan office in Thiès five days later. As soon as Molly read it, as well as the copy of his article that he'd sent, she (as she would later put it) "went nuts." She wrote back to him immediately.

Gerry was equally thrilled to get her response. "Since publication in 1996, I sent out my article at least two dozen times to anyone who had policy or journalistic interest," he says. "I never once heard back." Over the next several weeks, Molly and Gerry corresponded often, through letters, faxes, and phone calls. They finally decided to meet in Paris to discuss Tostan's experiences in Senegal and his theory. While in France,

Molly came to the realization that what Gerry was explaining to her, and the theory he posed, was going to be key to her work.

"What happened in China was astoundingly similar to what was happening in villages across Senegal," Molly says. "In Gerry's theory, I found a way to understand and explain the movement occurring." He especially helped her grasp the critical importance of public declarations, which marked a shift in expectations of all those who mattered in the group.

Best of all, Gerry's work, as well as his enthusiasm for what was taking place, lent scientific credibility (and from an Oxford academic, no less) that she hoped might help donors, other NGOs, the Western media, and the remaining skeptics understand that the three public declarations that had taken place—and the many others she sensed were imminent, from reports in the field—were not just a fluke, that maybe they really had discovered the mechanism for bringing about lasting change.

But before she could convince others that this might be the case, she knew she had to address one nagging question of her own.

ALTHOUGH SENEGAL IS NOT a particularly large nation, its fourteen regions, further divided into thirty-two departments, vary vastly. The first public declarations had happened in Bambara communities in or near the region of Thiès. Here, the Bambaras are an ethnic minority surrounded by communities of Wolof, the nation's majority ethnic group. The Wolof do not practice FGC, and yet they are considered prestigious people and good Muslims. Molly had begun to question if the declarations occurred, in part, due to the Bambara's proximity to a nonpracticing population, or the fact that they were a minority group practicing a tradition not embraced by the majority. Perhaps this had helped them more easily imagine an alternative.

The same dynamic was not true everywhere in Senegal, and certainly not in one area in particular: the Fouta, in northern Senegal. Extending about two hundred and fifty miles along the Senegal River and the border of southern Mauritania, it is inhabited mostly by members of the Toucouleur ethnic group, who speak the language of Pulaar. The Fouta—where the tall shepherds with their heads wrapped in indigo turbans so only their eyes show, stand out against a horizon hazed by the dust of the nearby Sahara—had always fascinated Molly. As a teacher in the village of Ndioum once explained to her, there were spirits everywhere in the Fouta: the *jom mayo,* who live along the depths of the Senegal River, the *jom ledde,* masters of the trees that inhabit the forest, and the *waande,* who find a home on the large, rock-like pillars of sand that dot the landscape.

The Fouta is also a land of traditions and fierce adherence to custom. Considered Senegal's cradle of Islam, it is where the religion first found its way into the nation, and a very strict interpretation of Islam rules here, creating a highly conservative and hierarchical society in which an ancient caste system is still observed. Nobles—members of the highest caste—have a very important role in society, holding sway over the lower castes.

Tostan first began operating in seventy villages in two departments in the Fouta in 1992, and Molly had always taken extra care to be sensitive to the cultural dynamics in play. She knew the women here had very few rights and were expected to conform scrupulously to tradition and religious obligation, to be shy and reserved. She'd observed this herself while visiting the classes when they first began, noticing how the women responded to questions with their heads slightly turned to the side and spoke very softly with their head scarves pulled over their faces to cover their timidity. Compared to the region of Thiès, where 7 percent of the population adhered to the custom of female genital cutting, here it was practiced by 94 percent of women, and sometimes even the most severe type, after which girls were sealed shut. The procedure meant they later had to be cut open on their wedding day.

Ourèye Sall was born and raised in the Fouta, and since the declaration in Nguerigne Bambara, Molly and she had grown very close. "Girls in our villages are cut soon after birth," Ourèye explained to Molly one afternoon over tea in her hut. "And the way we do it leads to far more serious health risks than in communities like Malicounda Bambara or Keur Simbara. Because they are cut so young, many girls spend their entire lives thinking the problems they suffer are normal and expected, part of what it means to have a female body. I know. I lived this myself."

Ourèye shared with Molly a story neither of them would ever forget. A pregnant woman who had been sealed and was still scarred had gone into early labor, and because the woman's vulva now blocked the baby's head, the baby burst out, ripping apart her scarred labia, which the doctor could not sew back together. The story had deeply troubled Molly, but she also understood that broaching the subject of female genital cutting and its health consequences in a place like the Fouta carried great risks. Tostan could not simply introduce the modules on human rights and women's health in the region without the potential for serious opposition from many different factions, especially the religious community. After the president of Senegal had voiced his support for the efforts of the women of Malicounda Bambara, one religious leader from the Fouta had sent a letter to deputies in the national assembly voicing his opposition to any efforts to end the tradition. He claimed that FGC was a religious obligation and that any woman who was not cut could not control herself around a man because the clitoris makes a woman sexually uninhibited.

At about this time Molly was offered a job opportunity to start a basic, countrywide education program elsewhere in Africa. It would have been good money and a great opportunity, but with barely a thought, she turned it down. Because now that she understood the theory behind what was happening in villages across Senegal, now that all her years of hard work may have truly unlocked a way of bringing about widespread, lasting change that could improve the lives of women and give them a sense of power, she had one pressing thought she couldn't escape. They had proved that the Tostan approach could bring about changes in Thiès, but could it happen elsewhere, especially somewhere as conservative as the Fouta?

21

Alhamdulilaa (Thanks Be to God)

In July 1998, a few weeks after receiving Gerry Mackie's letter, Molly sat on a mat around a communal bowl of fish and rice at the Tostan office in the town of Bokidjawe, in the department of Podor in the Fouta. As she ate her lunch, she did her best to ignore the concerned looks on the faces of the eight staff members seated around her.

"You can't even think about bringing up that subject here, Molly," Abou Diack, a Tostan supervisor, warned her. The uneasiness was evident in his voice. "It's not like the Thiès region. The tradition is far too sensitive an issue here, and we will all have tremendous problems if you even mention it in the communities."

"He's right," said Gellel Djigo, another supervisor. "Now is just not the time. Perhaps we might add the topic to our classes here in a few years, but for now, we're begging you, please don't bring it up." He relayed the story of how another Senegalese development organization recently had planned to host an event in a nearby village to raise awareness about the harmful effects of FGC. When their staff arrived, they were met by an angry crowd, likely organized by local religious leaders determined to prevent the event from taking place. They threw rocks at the speakers, and when the situation threatened to become more violent, the staff fled the village, abandoning their efforts.

"Don't worry," Molly told them. "I understand." She simply wanted to spend the week visiting some of the villages where the Tostan program was in place, she explained, which was at least partly true. While she had no intention of doing anything rash, including speaking carelessly about the tradition in any of the villages she'd planned to visit, she did hope to get a sense of the atmosphere there. If Molly felt that even speaking about the subject would cause trouble, she would of course reconsider her goal of finding a way to introduce the modules in villages throughout the region.

The next morning Molly woke early in her hotel and pulled on her finest *boubou,* which she'd had specially starched for the occasion. The staff had asked her to spend her first day visiting the village of Keddele, where a Tostan class had been established one year earlier. The village was extremely remote, accessible only by traveling several miles to a village called Ranwa, on the banks of the Senegal River. They would cross the river in a canoe and then flag down a bush taxi—a pickup truck fitted with benches in the back—to take them an hour or so across the parched, unmarked land to the village. But after Molly and the Tostan staff accompanying her had crossed the river, they discovered that no bush taxis were operating that day. Their only available choice was to hop aboard one of the waiting horse-drawn carts.

"You think this can carry all five of us?" Molly asked.

"It'll have to," Gellel said. "You know the people in Keddele are excited about this visit. They will be quite disappointed if you don't come."

Molly and the others climbed aboard the cart, the planks of gray, weathered wood creaking under their weight.

"How far is the ride, exactly?" Molly asked as the horse slowly pulled the cart over the terrain with the temperature nearing 110 degrees Fahrenheit.

"Oh, not far at all," Gellel replied with a smile.

She settled into the ride, pulling her wide scarf over her head to ward off the brutal rays and heat of the midday sun. Once they lost sight of the river, there was not a tree or bush to interrupt their view. The only thing that lay ahead was a seemingly endless expanse of flat, baked land where no sign of human activity was evident. The earth cracked under the weight of the cart, and looking around her, Molly felt as if she were slowly traveling back in time. An hour later, a desert village appeared on the horizon. Molly paused to take it all in: narrow, winding, sandy streets with low thick-walled houses that seemed to grow out of the ground, built of mud bricks made from the sand on which they rested.

It seemed as if every one of the eight hundred residents had gathered to greet them when they arrived in Keddele, so touched and apprecia-tive of the effort Molly and the Tostan staff had made to travel to their village. One of the older women took Molly's hand and led her from the cart to a shaded porch, where she offered Molly a glass of milk, which Molly gladly accepted. Afterward, lunch was served and mats were laid out on the large adobe verandah. The villagers called for everyone to gather for a discussion. Feeling a soft and welcome breeze, Molly looked up and saw the clouds begin to thicken. The young women took seats on Molly's left, the men and boys on Molly's right, and the older women sat on blankets spread under a nearby tree. Molly was given a position of honor, on a fine woven blanket spread atop a mattress, in the shadiest spot on the verandah.

With Gellel translating for Molly from Pulaar to Wolof, the women of the village spoke of many things, especially the hardships that ac-company life in a village like Keddele. "You can see how isolated we are here, miles from any type of health care," a woman named Dieynaba said. "It takes hours to travel to the nearest health post, and in the rainy season we are literally trapped. The land often floods, and our carts can't get by. Those are the hardest times for us."

Molly knew that primary school enrollment in the Fouta was lower than in the rest of Senegal, and so most had never attended formal school. The women thus spoke enthusiastically about the Tostan education classes and the changes that had taken place in their village. They now knew what to do when their children became ill with diarrhea, and they had built latrines to help stop the spread of germs. They held regular cleanup activities in which everyone in the village—even the men—participated. They were particularly proud to announce that they had started a community solidarity fund, through which they pooled their money to make sure all the children of the village could follow the necessary vaccination calendar. An hour into the discussion a young woman seemed eager to say something, rising to her feet in the midst of the group of women. She spoke softly for a while in Pulaar, and when she stopped, Molly waited for Gellel to translate.

"She said the women of this village have received news through family members of the declarations that have taken place," Gellel said with obvious surprise. "They want to know how many villages have decided to abandon the women's tradition."

"Since the first in Malicounda Bambara, forty-three others have declared," Molly said. "And many other declarations are being planned."

The woman smiled and continued. As she spoke, Gellel whispered to Molly. "I can't believe she's saying this."

"What? What is it?"

"They, too, have begun to speak about the possible dangers linked to the practice of female genital cutting. They say they realize these are the same health problems many girls and women here suffer. They would like to learn more about the health risks," Gellel said, "but they fear the reaction from their husbands and religious leaders on this matter."

The woman continued to speak. "Childbirth here is hard enough," she said. "So many women suffer greatly in the process, and because we are so isolated and far away, there are no professionals to offer help." She paused. "If there's anything you can do to help bring the information we need, to help us possibly do as other villages have . . . to bring about an end to this practice, I know I speak on behalf of all the women here to say that we would be very grateful."

One of the men spoke up. "You've never asked us about this before, so how do you know what we think? We need information also."

Molly chose her words carefully. "Well, the way it happened in Malicounda Bambara, and every village since, is that the women discussed the problems they had experienced with the men. Afterward, they decided together to abandon the tradition, with the men supporting the women. Tostan has never tried to tell people to stop the tradition. But perhaps I can find some way to bring the module on human rights and health to this region."

Molly felt a gentle nudge on her back. She guessed it was one of the facilitators, warning her not to say any more, not to take this too far. Another woman, an older one, spoke up then. "We all have to remember, what can be ended in other villages in a few months might take generations to end here. We're very isolated. Women don't have a voice here. We would need some extra help just to begin."

The sky suddenly grew darker, and everyone looked up.

"The rain is coming," Gellel said. "This isn't good. I hate to say this, but we really need to go now. Once it starts, we won't be able to get back to the river."

"Now?" Molly said. "I hate to leave this conversation." She noticed many of the women glancing nervously toward the sky.

"I know, but we must," Gellel responded. "It won't be safe to stay. If it rains, the parched earth will quickly turn to mud and the cart will sink. We could get trapped in the middle of nowhere. It's best if we hurry." Within minutes, as the rain clouds continued to gather, everyone at the meeting seemed to share Gellel's sense of urgency. They crowded around Molly and the Tostan staff members, placing their belongings atop the waiting cart. As soon as they had climbed on, the driver was yelling at the horse to move, frantically whipping the ground next to its hooves.

"This is not good," Gellel said. "We shouldn't have waited so long."

"But what they were saying was so important," Molly said. The horse took up speed as the wind rose around them. "What are we going to do?"

"The only thing we can do. Pray."

Molly felt the tension in the staff members around her, but she had a hard time sharing their concern. She knew she'd just experienced a very critical moment in the village of Keddele and what was, perhaps, a turning point in the movement that had begun in Malicounda Bambara. For these women to speak of the tradition as they had, to ask for her help . . . it was so unexpected.

More than an hour later, just as the river came into view, the rain began to fall. Molly spotted a few men sitting near the river's banks, crouched under a tree for cover, their canoes tethered to large rocks along the bank. Gellel jumped from the back of the cart and ran to the men. Molly watched as they shook their heads no.

"They're not going to let us cross," Abou said. "The wind is too strong."

But Gellel was relentless and was able to finally convince one of the men to ferry them across the river. "Okay, Molly," Gellel yelled into the wind once they were inside the canoe. "When we get to the other side, you're going to have to run."

"Run?" Molly yelled back. "Why?"

"Because we need to get to the paved road before this gets any worse. The rain will be torrential when it reaches full force, and it can flood these fields at any point. If we're not on the main road, we'll find ourselves floating in the middle of a lake or worse."

"Hurry! Run! Run!" the driver of the waiting Land Cruiser yelled when the canoe reached the far bank. Molly ran as fast as she could, sprinting up the riverbank, her *boubou* covered in mud and sand. They were barely inside the vehicle when the driver sped them away, the car roughly bumping through the field as the rain came down harder. Just as they reached the paved road, the skies opened wide. The wall of rain that poured down around them was so thick, it was impossible to see out the window. The car stopped and all were silent.

"Alhamdulilaa. Thanks be to God!" Abou said. "We were saved from the flood, and this must be a sign from God that we are doing the right thing. Maybe it is time to bring a discussion of the tradition to the Fouta." He looked at Molly. "God is great."

Molly smiled at him, shaking the rain from her hair. Knowing they had made it safely, knowing that the women of that village were ready for change, she had to agree.

THROUGHOUT THE WEEK, IN visits to several other villages in the Fouta, Molly continued to encounter women eager to speak about the tradition. They were curious about the declarations that had taken place and keen to understand how exactly they had come about. In a village called Gollere the women told Molly of their efforts to begin a discussion about the harmful impact of the tradition. "We would like to help change attitudes here on this subject," a woman named Bani Bousso said. "A lot of women who have dared to speak of it are worried now, as they have been shunned and ridiculed by the men in our community. But we have no intention of stopping."

Concerned, Molly asked if this was too much for the small group of women to take on.

"Molly, where there are two determined women, it is already enough; where there are twenty determined women, there is great hope."

Often when Molly was taken aside by women, she was told a similar message: the women wished to better understand the harmful consequences of the tradition, but they were afraid the men of their village would never allow it. They were even afraid to speak of it to them. Molly was not surprised to hear this. In a society where women were dependent on men for their very survival, it was unimaginable to question one's husband. But she had also come to understand that because men never discussed the subject—not with each other, not with their religious leaders, not with their wives or mothers—they typically did not have an informed opinion on the matter, and they certainly didn't understand what exactly the tradition entailed. The only understanding they had of it was an erroneous one, that the tradition was a religious obligation and thus impossible to question. Once they understood otherwise, many had been open to, and even very supportive of, a move to end the practice.

The religious leaders were a different story. Because of a fatwa (a scholarly opinion on a matter of Islamic law) issued by a religious leader in the Fouta against ending FGC, others believed the topic should not be brought up for discussion—in public or privately. Therefore, any steps to include information about human rights and female genital cutting in the Tostan curriculum in the Fouta would need the explicit support of the local religious leaders, which was perhaps impossible to get. After realizing how much the women wanted to receive the module on their own health, Molly knew it was time to take a bold step to make this happen and decided to arrange a meeting with one of the most respected and revered religious leaders in all of the Fouta, Thierno Amadou Bah, who had long been supportive of Tostan's work.

When Molly informed the staff that she would be paying a visit to Thierno Bah the following day, Abou needed to be convinced this was a good idea. "If you're thinking of bringing up the tradition with him, I'd strongly advise against it," Abou said. "To even mention the subject to the *marabout* would be to risk the entire Tostan program in the Fouta. Should Thierno Bah feel insulted or become angry, participants might decide they are too scared or intimidated to continue their work with Tostan. Classes could fold, villages could shun the organization."

"Well, let's go see," Molly said. "I promise to be careful."

The night before the meeting with Thierno Bah, Molly had trouble sleeping. In the quiet of her hotel room, she tossed and turned, wondering if she was doing the right thing. If she upset the *marabout,* all the efforts she and Tostan had made in the Fouta over the last six years could be in jeopardy, and it might be decades, if not longer, before they could hope to reinstate the organization in the region. But she couldn't help but wonder what might happen if, after asking for his support, he offered it. The idea seemed like a long shot, but it wasn't impossible. After what she had witnessed in Malicounda Bambara and Diabougou, after receiving the support of imams in the other forty-four villages that had decided to end the practice, she was beginning to believe that the impossible was, perhaps, possible.

She was still awake when the cock crowed outside her window, accompanying the first hints of morning light. As Molly rose sleepily from her bed to prepare for the day ahead, she thought about Kerthio, Maimouna, and Ourèye, about all the risks they had taken on behalf of themselves, their families, and the daughters of their region. Maybe it was time for Molly to take a risk of her own.

THEY ARRIVED AT THIERNO BAH'S house at ten in the morning and were led through a labyrinth of dark, cool hallways. Outside the closed door of his room, people gathered on mats on the floor, waiting to speak with him, to receive a blessing or guidance on a problem or help for an illness. Molly and the eight Tostan staff members who had accompanied her took seats beside the others to wait their turn.

At one point Gellel leaned toward Molly. "Remember, don't mention anything about the tradition," he reminded her. "We need to be very careful today."

Molly smiled at Gellel but remained quiet.

They were eventually summoned inside the darkened room. There was just one small window slightly open in the corner providing a shaft of dusty light. Thierno Bah sat on a woven mat on the floor. He was an old man, yet he sat up straight with his legs crossed before him, a red turban wrapped around his head, and soft white robes draped across his shoulders. His vision had grown poor, and he wore thick glasses. His son, Cherif Bah, sat beside him, and scattered on the floor around them were small pots of ink, pens, and sheets of paper with writings from the Koran. Molly took a seat on the mat facing him and, after extending her greetings, she asked about the health of Thierno Bah's wife, whom she'd met once before and liked immensely.

"Tell me how Tostan is doing here in the Fouta," Thierno Bah said. Molly updated him, telling of the progress that had been made in the villages—the cleanup projects and the increased rate of vaccinations and use of oral rehydration therapy. She then took a breath and steadied her voice. "As you know, I've greatly appreciated your support."

Thierno Bah smiled at her.

"And I want you to know that there is a very important purpose to my visit." As she spoke, she sensed the budding tension in the room and the surprised, cautionary posture of the Tostan staff members. "I would like to know if I can ask you something," she said.

"Yes, of course."

"As you may know, in other parts of Senegal, the women and men have started to learn about problems related to health because of the women's tradition. So far, forty-four villages have decided together, with the support of their religious leaders, to abandon the practice. I've spent some time this week speaking to women here in the Fouta. They are telling me that they, too, have experienced terrible problems related to this. They are afraid to talk about it with others, but the health consequences can be dire. I thought it was serious enough to bring this matter to you." She paused again and waited to allow Gellel to translate. "The women have complained of many things. Severe pain at the time of the cutting. Hemorrhaging. Problems during childbirth. A health agent in one village near here showed me official records indicating three young girls died this year following the procedure. I know that Islam seeks the health and well-being of everyone, and Tostan would like to implement a module on women's health, which would include information on the tradition. We have been doing this in other parts of Senegal, providing information about the health consequences, all of which are based in science. But before we do anything here in the Fouta, I came here to speak to you. If you tell me that no, this is not the thing to do right now, because I trust you . . . I will follow what you say."

Some of the Tostan staff members audibly gasped as Molly's words were translated. For several minutes, as Molly grew more nervous and uncomfortable, the *marabout* sat very still and said nothing. Finally Cherif, the son of Thierno Bah, broke the tense silence.

"My father cannot answer this now," he said, the aggravation evident in his voice. "No one has ever asked him this question before. This is a very complicated issue. He will need time to think about it."

Thierno Bah lifted his hand, silencing his son. "No. Stop, son. I will answer." He looked at Molly. "I know you, and I have known and observed Tostan since 1992. You have always held respect for our culture and our religion, in this and nearby communities. You tell me that the women have told you that there are health problems, and if you tell me this, I believe you. And if this is true, if there are indeed health problems, this needs to be addressed. Do you want my decision?"

"Yes, I do," Molly said.

"Here it is. Go forward with what you need to do. Work on this. If it is for the health of women, Islam is behind you and I will support you. It will not be easy for you, but if anyone asks you why you're doing this in the Fouta, if anyone challenges you, you must tell them to come and see me."

The words were such a surprise, so unexpected. Molly stared in disbelief, and then, unable to hold back her tears, she began to cry. They were tears of relief that he had not been furious with her as everyone had predicted. Tears of sadness for all that the women who had confided in her had to endure under such harsh conditions. Tears of joy in realizing that the support from this religious leader would make all the difference. Tears of hope for the future and what this might mean for thousands of women across the Fouta.

"Molly, don't cry," Gellel said, touching her shoulder.

"No, tell Molly it is all right to cry," the *marabout* said. "But it is not necessary. She will be happy. This is a noble thing she is doing." Molly lifted her head to look at him. "God is on your side, and you will be victorious."

22

Njàmbaar (Courage)

Six months later, on January 13, 1999, the Senegalese government enacted a law making the practice of female genital cutting illegal. The law set a prison sentence of six months to five years for anyone who practices FGC and life imprisonment with forced labor in cases where a girl died. The day before the vote, a delegation of villagers, including Demba Diawara and Ourèye Sall, accompanied Molly to the parliament to try to convince legislators to reconsider the bill. While everyone should stop practicing FGC, they argued, passing a law at this time was not the means to end the practice. Rather, they believed they had found the way: human-rights-based education, outreach, and open dialogue about the potential health consequences, plus a collective decision by interconnected communities to end the practice.

"I can assure you that if I hadn't gone through the Tostan program and you passed a law telling me to stop the practice or face imprisonment, I would have chosen jail," Ourèye stated before the deputies. "Please understand. Your efforts could actually hurt the movement under way. Give us time to do the educational work that needs to be done. Trust that we have found the right path."

Despite these efforts, the law passed. The next day, in the region of Kédougou, one hundred girls were cut in protest.

A few days later, Ourèye called Molly at the Tostan offices. She knew that after Molly's meeting with Thierno Bah, Tostan had begun to implement the health and human rights modules in more than sixty villages across the Fouta. "If you are going to take the risk of speaking publicly about the tradition in the Fouta—in a place where, growing up, I wouldn't have dreamed a woman could feel empowered enough to even mention it aloud—I'm going to be a part of it," she declared. "It is not enough that the tradition has ended here in my village and others. We need to end this tradition for good, in Senegal and beyond."

Knowing how deeply entrenched the practice was in the region, Ourèye expected the women of these villages would face deep resistance, as she did with her own mother and sisters, and she now wanted to embark on an effort to help raise awareness among her vast network of relatives in the Fouta about the health risks of the tradition and show them that an alternative was possible.

"We've all learned from Demba what is possible with effort," she told Molly. "I am a traditional cutter. People will listen to me because I am the one who has seen the consequences of this practice. I will go for as long as it takes."

Molly was overjoyed to hear of Ourèye's interest. While she remained hopeful about the possibility of change in the Fouta, she also knew that it would likely not happen as readily as it had in the villages around Thiès. Patience and a longer process would be required, made possible, Molly hoped, by the momentum of change occurring in other regions of Senegal. With help from Tostan, to pay her transportation and food costs, Ourèye set out a few weeks later with a team of other concerned village participants from the Fouta. They traveled mostly by bush taxi, but frequently the villages they visited were so remote they could only be accessed by a horse-drawn cart. For weeks at a time,

Ourèye endured several hours a day on the back of a cart, making its way slowly through the flat, treeless landscape.

She went first to the villages where Tostan classes were operating. Like Demba, Ourèye faced trouble and resistance. In one village, a woman spit on her. "We will stop this tradition over my dead body!" she yelled. "I will curse you." But Ourèye remained steadfast. Her Tostan education had trained her how to approach people—always in a peaceful, nonaggressive way, determined to find solutions rather than focus on the problems. And her message was always the same: "I am the one who defended this tradition the most," she said repeatedly. "I was even paid for it and have given up my only source of income. I am now here to speak to you not because I have chosen to turn my back on my traditions, but because I seek peace, well-being, and health for our granddaughters."

At the end of her travels, she would return home for a short time to check on her family before setting out again. Her days were long and difficult, filled with fatigue, heat, hunger, and a deep loneliness she felt at missing her children, the youngest of whom was just seven. But Ourèye knew in her heart that change and peace were coming, and she chose to focus on this rather than on the hardships of the travel, knowing that time and patience were critical here in the Fouta.

Every time she left a village, she promised to return again to continue the discussion. "All of us, every woman of Senegal, should come together united to promote peace and health for our children," she would say. "If we do this together, if we all come together to celebrate our best values, if we do this in the spirit of peace and health, all will be right."

GIVEN THE DIFFICULTIES OF working in a region as conservative as the Fouta, many NGOs had long refused to invest their efforts there. But since 1998 Tostan had been receiving funding for its work in the Fouta from the German National Committee for UNICEF, one of the few funding organizations willing to take the risk of investing in the area. Christian Schneider, the director of the German National Committee, explains: "We were immediately impressed with Tostan because it never pointed a moralistic finger at anyone. With Molly, you have someone who really wants to change things but is always very respectful."

In April 2002, Molly decided to invite two representatives of the German National Committee—Claudia Berger, the communications director at UNICEF, and Katja Riemann, a well-known German actress who served as the UNICEF ambassador for Tostan—to accompany her to the Fouta to witness for themselves the tremendous progress being made.

It took ten hours to travel the rough potholed road from the Tostan office in Thiès to the town of Ourossogui, and Ourèye was waiting for them when they arrived. Molly had organized a meeting with Tostan participants, spearheaded by Mère Habi, an energetic, dynamic woman who led the Community Management Committee in the Matam region.

The next morning, after an early breakfast of bean paste and omelet sandwiches at their hotel, Molly, Ourèye, Claudia, and Katja prepared to leave the hotel to meet Mère Habi and the other women of the Tostan class. Before they left, Molly noticed from her hotel window that a large crowd of two hundred or so men had gathered on the street below, chanting something she couldn't decipher. Behind them was a mountain of fiery tires, sending black plumes and the rancid smell of burning rubber into the hazy morning air.

"Oh no," Molly said. "There seems to be some trouble outside. I'll go check and see what it is." When she got to the hotel lobby, a few of the Tostan coordinators were there. They stopped her from going outside.

"Don't go out there, Molly," one said, gently taking her arm.

"Why not? There's something happening outside. I want to see what's going on."

"They're here because of you and your delegation."

"What do you mean they're here because of me?"

"They know about the meeting you arranged with the women."

"And?"

"They think you are here to ask the women to make a public declaration to end FGC."

"That's ridiculous," Molly said.

"I know that, but they're convinced that is why you've come, and they're very angry. Please, don't go out there."

From where she stood, Molly could see just how extensive the crowd outside was. "But they need to understand that they're wrong," she pleaded. "There's been no talk of a public declaration of any kind. We're just here to speak to the women about their experiences."

Just then, one of the men from the crowd entered the hotel lobby and quickly approached Molly. "You and your friends should not leave this hotel," he said. "If you come outside, you'll be sorry."

"Is this a threat?" she asked.

"Take it any way you want. But you shouldn't be here. You shouldn't be talking to our women. We can assure you of one thing. There will be no declaration in Ourossogui."

Despite the sinking disappointment she felt, Molly decided, for the safety of her guests, to abandon the meeting with Mère Habi and the other women, and they left Ourossogui right away.

Back in Thiès a few days later, she discussed with the Tostan staff and UNICEF officers whether they should remain or leave the region. Had the threat of violence and of being run out of town made the work there too dangerous? Were they bringing more harm than good to the women? Molly knew that the Tostan program in the Fouta had reached a critical point, and the organization now had a very important, and difficult, decision to make. They could either pull out, as many other NGOs had done, or they could continue to believe that change was possible.

"I was unwilling to give up on the area," Molly remembers. "There was so much momentum in other areas of Senegal. By this time, 392 villages had publicly pledged to end FGC in their communities, and we chose to trust that despite the hardships, the same thing could happen here. This made the next decision a lot easier. We weren't going away. We were going to create an even greater presence in the Fouta."

MOLLY'S FIRST ORDER OF business was to find a skilled and experienced staff member to lead the efforts in the Fouta. She knew exactly the right person for the job. A tall, intelligent man with a serious composure, Khalidou Sy was born in the region of Kolda. When he was five years old, his grandfather requested he come live with him and his wives in the Fouta, where he could properly study the Koran. His parents agreed, but when Khalidou arrived at his grandfather's home, he soon discovered that the story had been a ruse. He wasn't going to Koranic school; he was being put to work. From the age of five, he worked every day as a shepherd, responsible for his grandfather's large herd of cows. At home, he was treated differently than the other grandchildren— made to do the hard work, always feeling marginalized. Whenever his mother sent him clothes or shoes, his grandfather's wives would confiscate them and give them to the other children of the house.

One day, not far from a field where he took the cows to pasture, Khalidou came across the public schoolhouse. He snuck over to the window of a schoolroom and peered in at the students. He was mesmerized by the sight—boys his own age, with open books on their laps, learning to read letters and numbers written on a large board in the front of the room. Desperate to join them, Khalidou began to spend his days standing at the window watching the students, often leaving the cows for so long he'd later have to chase after them. Before long, the director of the school took pity on Khalidou watching them from outside the window and invited him to join them inside the classroom. Sitting with his long, thin legs scrunched up against the small table, Khalidou was hooked. He arrived at the school early each morning, knowing it would take him hours to gather the herd afterward.

In time, his family heard news of his antics. They showed up at the schoolhouse and caught him in the act. That night he was whipped, as he often was, with knotted ropes or branches from a tree and forbidden from returning to the school. Frustrated and angry, he began to get into many fights with other children.

When Khalidou was about ten years old, an aunt from Kolda came to check on him and to see how he was faring at Koranic school. She was livid to find that for all these years he'd been kept from school and made to work, and to see how unhappy and unruly he'd become. She packed up his few belongings and immediately brought him back to his parents in Kolda. Khalidou was very happy to return home, hoping this was his opportunity to have a more stable life and, most of all, to enroll in school. But to his dismay, his father was impressed with the idea that Khalidou had been trained as a shepherd, and he was immediately put back to work, taking care of his family's cows.

Khalidou refused to abandon his hopes of being educated. Not long after returning to Kolda, he discovered that the director of the local school lived near his parents' house. Taking a chance, he walked to the director's house one evening, daring to explain why he had come.

"I want very badly to go to school like everyone else," he said. "It saddens me to see other children my age walking back from school every day. Whenever I can, I ask them to tell me what they studied that day. I no longer want to hear about the lessons from them. I want to go to your school."

A few days later, the director arrived at Khalidou's house and asked to speak to his father. He explained his belief that his son might have a special gift for learning, and he convinced him to allow Khalidou to give up his work as a shepherd for a few years and enroll in school. At the age of ten, Khalidou entered his first official year of school, where he was placed in a classroom alongside six-year-olds. He proved to be very smart, and he advanced quickly through the grades, skipping several entirely. In the evenings, he cultivated his own field, selling the vegetables to earn money for school supplies. Eventually transferring to a private school, paying for the tuition himself with money he earned cultivating his field, he paid his way through the eighth grade. He passed his exams two years later, and in 1982, at the age of twenty, he received his diploma. Within three years he had earned his baccalaureate degree, much like a junior college degree, and soon after graduating he took a job as a village facilitator with Tostan. He quickly moved up in the organization, promoted from facilitator to supervisor to regional coordinator, and then to national program officer.

Molly had always respected Khalidou's work ethic and attitude, and she knew that with his experience living in the Fouta as a child, and his quiet intelligence and confidence, he was the right person for the difficult work that lay ahead.

Within weeks, Khalidou moved the existing Tostan office to Ourossogui, to the heart of the opposition. He hired additional staff, brought in office equipment, and hung a large Tostan sign out front. In the weeks since the protest, Molly had come to believe that part of the resistance the organization faced might be due, in large part, to a misunderstanding about what Tostan did and what the classes were out to accomplish.

"It was clear that the religious leaders and others believed Tostan had come to impose their own ideas on the residents of the Fouta, the women in particular, forcing them into decisions they did not want to make, encouraging them to move away from their long-held traditions," Molly says. To counter these stereotypes, Khalidou established a weekly radio program on local stations and began to issue open invitations to public meetings about the Tostan program and its mission. He was always sure to invite the local religious leaders. At these meetings, he or a facilitator would explain exactly what Tostan was: a development organization established to bring education to rural communities. They were not, he made plain, out to destroy any traditions against the will of the people. Khalidou also made it known that the content of the modules had been approved by religious leaders such as Thierno Amadou Bah.

Despite these efforts, the local attitude toward Tostan did not quickly change. Just a few weeks after establishing a greater presence in Ouros-sogui, Molly received news that a group of religious leaders had become even more determined to shut down the Tostan classes across the Fouta, and insinuations were made that if facilitators did not leave the villages where they had come to live, they would be killed. As the threats became more serious, Molly and Khalidou decided to ask the women if they wanted to continue, given the obstacles they were facing.

Khalidou met with more than thirty women in the courtyard behind Mère Habi's modest home. He told them of Molly's fears for their safety, explaining that the women of Malicounda Bambara had once faced serious resistance themselves. "Molly is concerned you may be subject to the same hostility . . . perhaps worse," he said. "We would understand if you no longer want us to mention ending FGC in this region."

"We appreciate the concern," Mère Habi responded, "but we can no longer sit back and allow others to fight for us. We have learned that along with human rights come responsibilities. If we want change, we must have the courage to stand up for what we know to be right."

Mère Habi went on to organize a meeting of the coordinators of Tostan's Community Management Committees from several villages, and after much discussion, they requested a meeting with the association of religious leaders and the préfet, the local government official whose authority in the area was second only to the governor. A few weeks later, in June 2002, twenty women arrived at the office of the préfet, a man named Mar Lo, and found a group of stern-looking religious leaders waiting for them. Mère Habi was chosen to speak on behalf of the women, and once inside his office, she wasted no time.

"Why do you not like Tostan?" she asked the religious leaders.

They were clearly uncomfortable with her directness. "Well," one began, "we have all heard what you do."

"I don't understand. What do we do?"

He glanced uncomfortably at the other men and then at the préfet. "I know that in your class you ask the women to take off their clothes. And then you show each other your genitals."

The gasp in the room was audible, the anger evident in Mère Habi's voice. "How could you ever imagine such a thing as this?" she exclaimed. "It is not true, and you have greatly insulted us. We are all women of Islam. Many of us here have made the pilgrimage to Mecca." She paused to compose herself. "We must all face the facts that, like it or not, Senegal is a nation where people have human rights. If you *marabouts* do not want your children to be educated, fine. That is your choice. But you do not have the right to try to prevent entire communities from becoming educated and moving forward."

"This is very dangerous, what you are doing," another religious leader responded.

"Perhaps. Or perhaps you are misinformed. Either way, we will not allow people's threats and intimidation to hold us back, regardless of how powerful those people may be." She glanced around the room. "We now know that we have the right to pursue education, and we will not be intimidated. We are not here to cause problems. But neither will we stop our Tostan classes or give up this opportunity for an education. If you think that you've heard the last from us, you're wrong."

In the weeks that followed, the situation became more serious. Tostan staff members began to receive more frequent death threats and were accused of wanting to destroy African traditions. Notices were hung around town warning residents not to become involved with Tostan. A few times staff members found their vehicles vandalized, and the military was called in to protect the office. Rumors flew that, under the leadership of the religious leaders, men were discussing the possibility of going from house to house to harm the members of the Tostan class and run the facilitators out of town.

"What I came to understand," Molly says, "is that there was something more at play than FGC. Yes, the religious leaders were reluctant to consider abandoning such a deeply entrenched and important tradition, but I knew that at the heart of their opposition was something even greater: a serious resistance to the idea that women were gaining a voice, embracing the idea of their own human rights, that Tostan was bringing democracy to this hierarchical society." For the very first time in perhaps the history of this region, women were speaking out, firmly asserting their own views, voicing their opposition to anything that brought harm to the community. Here, in a society where an ancient caste system still held sway, even the women of the lower caste were taking on roles that were previously denied to them under the old system. Molly learned that in a village called Seedo Abbas a woman named Kummba Tokola, born into a lower caste, was elected coordinator of the Community Management Committee, something that would not have happened without human rights education.

It was clear to Molly and Khalidou that despite the threats and the tension, the women had no intention of backing down. Before long, the women announced they were ending the assistance they had long provided to the men in organizing important yearly events to celebrate and memorialize their relatives who had died. Typically, women played an important role in these events, arranging food for the men and pooling their household money to help pay for expenses.

"We've decided we are not going to help arrange these events anymore," Mère Habi told Molly one day. "If the men are not going to support our efforts to become educated, we're not going to support them either."

THIS WAS JUST THE beginning of the change about to come to the Fouta. Not long after, Molly received a call from Fatime Diop, the coordinator of the Community Management Committee in a town called Podor, located in the Fouta on the banks of the Senegal River. Fatime explained that the women of the surrounding villages had been hard at work, and she invited Molly to come to Podor to speak with them.

"We need to talk to you in person," Fatime said. "We think you need to hear what has been taking place here." Molly was eager to go, but a few days before her scheduled trip she received a call from a government official in Podor, telling her not to come.

"It's too dangerous," he said. "We cannot guarantee your safety, especially if you hold a meeting with the women. I am worried about the reaction of certain religious leaders."

Molly called Fatime to tell her of the warning. "You pay no attention to those threats," she insisted. "We hear them all the time. You are coming. The women of Podor will be here to protect you."

During the drive to Podor a few days later, Molly felt uneasy. She expected that when she arrived there would be problems, and she hoped that things would not get out of control as they had in Ourossogui. It took eight hours to get to Podor, and when she finally pulled into town, she saw that a crowd had gathered in the main square. As she drew closer, Molly felt the breath catch in her throat. The crowd was as large as two thousand people, most of them women, all dressed in their best jewelry and colorful *boubous*.

Spotting her car approaching, they began to clap and sing. Molly stepped out of the car and was greeted by thunderous cheers. Trying to hold back her tears, Molly reached for Fatime's hand as the women swelled around them. Fatime led Molly down to the banks of the Senegal River and more women were there, on the water, rowing in unison in five pirogues painted in intricate, colorful designs. Molly had seen events like this before, but always the boats had been filled with men. As each went by where Molly stood, the women inside the pirogues stood and waved triumphantly as the crowd on the banks cheered.

Fatime then invited Molly to her home, where about fifty women from surrounding communities had gathered to meet her. With the door closed tightly, they shared with Molly what they had learned about human rights and the practice of female genital cutting.

Fatime then spoke. "Despite the hardships we've faced, the intimidation and the threats, we are not going to let anyone stop us from what we need to do."

"I'm not sure I understand," Molly said. "What is it you want to do?"

"It has taken us six years, much trouble, and a lot of hard work," Fatime said. "But we have learned from our sisters in the many other villages, who have courageously stood up and pledged an end to this tradition. We are going to plan a public declaration and join the movement."

SEVERAL MONTHS LATER, MOLLY received the call from Khalidou, telling her that it had finally happened: the first public declaration in the Fouta had been arranged, scheduled to take place on November 13, 2005, in the town of Seedo Abbas. In a near state of disbelief, Molly invited the coordinators from all regions of Senegal to come and witness this historic declaration. When she arrived in Seedo Abbas on the morning of the declaration, nearly 1,500 people had already gathered. Ourèye was among them, basking in the moment—one she could have never imagined as a child.

"You see, Molly, when you chose Tostan as the name of the organization, you probably had no idea just how far this would spread." She smiled. "I am one of the chicks and the hens who have led to the breakthrough. And of that I am very proud."

The declaration represented 70 villages, and by late morning, the crowd had grown to more than 2,000 people, some of whom had traveled from as far away as 300 kilometers. It was one of the largest public declarations organized to date, and the tents set up to offer protection from the harsh sun and sandy desert wind overflowed with people. When it was time for the proceedings to begin, the crowd fell silent. Village women and village chiefs from around the region stood to express their deep commitment to the health, education, and human rights of women and girls. They spoke about the changes that had come to the villages through Tostan: that year, more than 13,000 children had been vaccinated for polio and other diseases; 2,300 children had been registered at birth; 1,350 children had been enrolled in formal schooling; nearly 2,000 trees had been planted, and more than 1,000 wood-saving stoves had been built. Several villages, where there was no state school before, managed to lobby successfully to get schools. Kummba Tokola spoke to the crowd. "Today's ceremony is for women and for the liberation of our children," she said. "Women were only surviving before, but through Tostan, we have learned, we have understood, and now we have united for change."

At the end of the event, a young girl and an older woman stood to read the declaration in both Pulaar and French as 70 men, women, and children came forward, each with a sign indicating the name of the village they represented. Throughout the declaration, Molly had a hard time keeping her eyes off one girl in particular, Khadidia Bade Diallo. At eleven years old, she was the president of the adolescent association formed as a result of the Tostan classes. As she'd told Molly earlier that day, "FGC ought to be ended once and for all. It must never return. That's what we stand up for here." And then she looked at Molly and smiled. "And I've also decided that when I get older, I'm going to become a doctor."

Molly thought back to the social evolution that had taken place in the Fouta in just a few years' time, allowing Khadidia to envision a new path forward for herself, to escape a future where she would soon have been married, likely giving birth to many children, and struggled to survive. But with these words, with these actions, Molly knew that Khadidia's future, and the future of so many girls, was forever changed.

23

Fajar gi (Dawn of a New Day)

By the time of the declaration in Seedo Abbas in November 2005, a total of 1,486 other villages had made public declarations announcing their abandonment of the practice of FGC. Unlike the first declaration in Malicounda Bambara eight years earlier, when thirty-five women solemnly declared an end to the custom, these declarations were large, celebratory events attended by hundreds, often thousands, of people from large and small villages across Senegal, and from the neighboring countries of Mali, Guinea-Bissau, The Gambia, and Mauritania. Affecting thousands of Senegalese girls, as well as future generations who would never come to know the practice, it was nothing less than a human rights revolution that showed no signs of abating.

One of these declarations was held on April 7, 2000, with hundreds of residents arriving from twenty-six islands located throughout the Sine-Saloum river delta in the Fatick region of Senegal. The event was largely the result of the efforts of one Tostan facilitator and two women from the Serer Niominka ethnic group who canoed from island to island to hold public discussions with their relatives on what they had learned about human rights and health, emphasizing the topic of FGC.

On June 5, 2002, the largest declaration yet took place when 285 Mandinka and Pulaar communities gathered in the village of Karcia, in the southern region of Kolda, under a large banner reading RESPECT THE HUMAN RIGHTS OF TODAY'S GIRLS AND TOMORROW'S WOMEN. "Today we are giving birth to a new baby, and we are naming her Abandoning FGC," said Njoba Jingary, the coordinator of the Community Management Committee in the Senegalese village of Dar es Salaam. "We are asking you, the greater community, to help us develop and raise this child."

At a declaration on December 7, 2003, before a crowd of thousands gathered in the village of Oulampane, in the region of Ziguinchor, a woman named Terema Diedhiou bravely spoke for the first time about the deaths of her daughter and niece to FGC, both at the age of twelve.

And on December 12, 2004, more than 1,500 people representing 160 villages listened intently in the village of Sinthiou Malème as the public declaration was read aloud in two national languages, Pulaar and Mandinka. "The people of these 160 communities will no longer cut our daughters," said a woman named Aminata Bah, the determination evident in her voice. "It is finished."

That year, the Frontiers in Reproductive Health project of the Population Council published a controlled study conducted from 2000 to 2003 to evaluate the success of Tostan's nonformal education program in twenty villages in which it had been implemented. The researchers found that, in terms of knowledge, attitudes, and behavior regarding reproductive health, human rights, and FGC abandonment, Tostan's results were "substantial."

"This external evaluation did what we hoped. It boosted our confidence and confirmed that we were on the right path," Molly says. "It was a great relief."

Nonetheless, Molly and her staff understood that these declarations did not always mean 100-percent abandonment of the practice in the communities represented. "We've never claimed that everyone is on board," she says. "Was it possible that a girl from Malicounda Bambara was cut after 1997? Of course that could have happened. But that doesn't mean that Tostan's approach wasn't working. What is most important is that hundreds of village activists in all regions were reaching out to their family networks, determined to end this practice. Their efforts were building a critical mass at the grassroots level that we believed would lead to a tipping point."

WITHIN TOSTAN AND ITS participating communities, the excitement was palpable: they had created a dynamic social movement to abandon FGC.

But it didn't stop there. Participants across Senegal began to call for the end of other acts of discrimination against girls and women, particularly the custom of child marriage. Common in many villages of Senegal, as well as throughout Africa, Asia, Latin America, and the Caribbean, Molly knew that child marriage could be physically and emotionally devastating. Often pushed to bear children before their bodies are ready, girls younger than fifteen are five times more likely to die during childbirth or pregnancy than older women. In fact, pregnancy-related deaths are the leading cause of death for girls aged fifteen to nineteen worldwide. And as Molly had witnessed through her work in hundreds of villages, girls who survive childbirth at such an early age can suffer from fistula, a debilitating condition that causes chronic incontinence.

Many of the women in Tostan classes had themselves been married very young, and as they came to understand the adverse consequences of child marriage, they began to advocate for an end to this once commonly accepted practice. For example, in the village of Seme in northeastern Senegal, fathers often arranged the marriage of their daughters when they were as young as ten. But after discussing the topic of child marriage in their Tostan class, and hearing that a thirteen-year-old girl named Khady was scheduled to be married in just a few days' time, the women of Seme organized to stop it. Khady's father worked in Gabon and had contacted a local family to arrange for Khady's marriage. At his request, the father's representative arrived at the local school where Khady was a student in the seventh grade and pulled her from class, explaining she was going to be married the next day. Like most child brides, her education would be terminated. Her mother, a Tostan participant, became desperate to prevent Khady's marriage, and that very evening she requested a special meeting with the Tostan facilitator, the Community Management Committee, and the director of the elementary school. Their discussion lasted long into the night, and the next morning, alongside dozens of other community members and students from the school, they marched to the home of the father's representative, who was to perform the marriage at the local mosque. Carrying handmade signs stating KEEP GIRLS IN SCHOOL and WE DON'T ACCEPT CHILD MARRIAGE, the group convinced him not to go through with the marriage. Khady was allowed to remain in school, and the women contacted Khady's father, explaining that the practice of child marriage was no longer acceptable in their community.

Similar efforts were organized around domestic violence, also a common occurrence in many communities. In Dialakoto, a village in southeastern Senegal, class participants responded to a case of spouse abuse by organizing a peaceful march against violence. Dozens of women invited members of the local media to join them in their march through the village, during which they banged pots and pans and sang songs they had composed in their Tostan class, making it publicly known that domestic violence would no longer be accepted. Even rape and incest—issues that were previously never discussed publicly—were being addressed. In the past, women felt pressure to remain silent if a family member was known to have raped a girl; they were too afraid to risk trouble within the family. But throughout the villages of Senegal, Tostan participants declared that rape and incest were not only against the law, but that there would no longer be any "family arrangements" in order to keep the peace. The social norm of maintaining silence was over. Should any man be found engaging in these violent acts, the women vowed they would alert local authorities and take every measure to ensure punishment.

"With every instance I heard of—and there were so many—I began to think differently about what was going on as a result of the human rights curriculum," Molly says. "We were witnessing something so significant— the act of people coming together to collectively reflect on their deepest values, to question if current attitudes and behaviors were, in fact, violating those values. This, among all else, felt so powerful to me, because for the first time I began to understand the possibility that our approach to ending FGC might be applied far beyond this one practice."

TOSTAN FINALLY BEGAN TO receive the recognition it deserved. In 1999, Molly was awarded a University of Illinois Alumni Humanitarian Award, and three years later, the Sargent Shriver Award for Distinguished Humanitarian Service, which honors a Peace Corps volunteer's continued work on humanitarian causes. The following year, the World Health Organization chose the Tostan Community Empowerment Program as a model of best practice for ending FGC, calling for its extension into other African nations, and in 2005, Tostan was bestowed Sweden's Anna Lindh Foundation Award for its work in human rights.

The success pulled Molly further into her work, adding to the already seemingly endless hours she spent at the office. In fact, Molly now lived at work, literally. In 1999, she had moved to Dakar, where she'd established a regional Tostan office, and since 2003, Molly had been living in a small room on the upper floor of that office. It was sparsely furnished with a bed, a table, and a hot plate where she'd sometimes cook meals for herself. When Zoé came home to visit—she was attending Concordia College in Montréal by this time—she'd sleep in a small room in the Tostan building.

"It didn't seem that strange to me at the time," says Zoé. "My mom would just say, what was the point of wasting money on renting a house when she was always at the office anyway."

While managing a staff of fifty-five full-time employees, nearly five hundred facilitators, and a budget of more than $2 million, Molly accepted as many invitations as she could manage in order to share the work of Tostan and what was happening across Senegal. The greater Tostan's success, the more uncomfortable Molly became with taking the credit herself; she was adamant that the achievements were due only to the efforts of villagers. As her friend Carrie Dailey says, "She had built an empire though a series of selfless acts. She never takes the credit for what she does. She never brags." Rather, she would insist on bringing along at least one Tostan village participant to international forums to speak of their experience, and she traveled frequently with both Demba and Ourèye. While they had once rarely traveled beyond their own villages, now they were accompanying Molly to places like Germany, Sweden, Malaysia, Egypt, the United Nations, London, Atlanta, and Washington, DC. Christian Schneider, the director of the German National Committee for UNICEF, recalls one visit in particular. "Molly and Ourèye came to speak before the German Press Club. It was the first time any of their speakers stood before the room and danced at the end of their presentation. It was unforgettable."

It was also at about this time that Tostan began responding to requests to extend its program into what would come to include six other African nations. In 2002, Tostan began to prepare to implement classes in Guinea, a resource-rich but extremely impoverished nation to the south of Senegal that had been under a dictatorship for twenty years. With this expansion, Molly took the opportunity to re-evaluate the program, revising it to make democracy and human rights the foundation of the Community Empowerment Program. "Prior to this," Molly says, "we had introduced human rights later in the curriculum, but we'd learned that in order for people to feel confident in their right to make changes, they had to first understand that they had a choice and a voice.

Once that is established, there is potential to take up whatever problems they choose."

Perhaps the most significant breakthrough at this time was the support from the UNICEF international headquarters in New York, helping to bring Tostan's work to the world stage. While Tostan had been collaborating with the UNICEF country office in Senegal since 1991, Molly had long tried to get the attention of senior staff in the New York headquarters of UNICEF. That attention finally came with the creation of the position in 2002 of Project Officer on Gender and Harmful Traditional Practices and the hiring of a brilliant and deeply committed woman named Maria Gabriella De Vita, who had previously held the position of country representative of the UNICEF office in Mongolia. By the time Gabriella, as she was known, discovered Tostan's work in 2004, she had spent two years investigating strategies to end the practice of FGC in places around the world. "When Tostan's accomplishments in this area were brought to my attention by a colleague in Kenya, I knew I had to go and see this for myself," Gabriella says.

She arrived in Senegal in May 2004 to join Molly at a public declaration—the fifteenth of its kind to date—organized by ninety-six communities and held in the village of Medina Samba Kande in Kolda, a conservative region of Senegal where FGC was practiced by 94 percent of the population. They were joined by three others: Neil Ford, the UNICEF regional director of communications in East Africa; Gerry Mackie, who was working at this time as an assistant professor of political science at the University of Notre Dame; and Gannon Gillespie, Molly's nephew, who had recently begun to volunteer with Tostan. The team spent three days in Kolda, joining thousands of villagers who arrived piled in the back of large trucks and packed in local transport vans. Many walked for miles to witness the historic celebration. Lively traditional musicians, singers, and dancers from the Pulaar ethnic group performed throughout the night as one by one women ran into the middle of an enormous circle pounding their feet, flinging their arms, and chanting to the rhythm of the drums. A mood of community and purpose permeated the air, and after speaking with many villagers and visitors who had come to witness the event, Molly and her colleagues left feeling electrified.

"After taking part in the declaration, I understood that everything I had been reading about Tostan was real and important," recalls Gabriella. "It was a novel model whose elements might be applied in other parts of the world where the practice was in place. And I wanted to understand more." The team retreated to a small hotel in Kolda, and they talked continuously for three days. Gerry Mackie presented his theory on social norms. As Mackie explained, understanding why and how communities were abandoning the practice—and to get at the core of Tostan's success—first required an understanding of the factors that perpetuated the custom and how those factors interacted with processes of social change. At the time, particularly when it came to efforts to improve the health of people in developing nations, the big thrust was so-called messaging campaigns—ads, posters, and social marketing efforts designed to tell people to stop what they were doing and do something else. However, the messaging strategy would certainly not work when attempting to change deeply entrenched social norms like FGC, held in place by the expectations of an entire group of people who believed the practice to be necessary.

Mackie's theory, on the other hand, emphasized the idea that to encourage people of the same group to stop a behavior, one needed to understand and appreciate the complex factors behind their decision to practice it. As he explained to the group in Kolda, crammed into a small hotel room, families carry out FGC to ensure the marriageability and status of their daughters within their intra-marrying group. For marriage and for status, what one family chooses to do depends on what other families in that community choose to do. Therefore, no one family can abandon the practice on its own; to change the social norm, it is necessary to coordinate abandonment by the intra-marrying community *as a whole*. Only if the decision is widespread within the practicing community can that decision be sustained, thus bringing into place a new social norm that ensures the marriageability of daughters and the social status of families that do not cut their girls.

That is why public declarations are so critical, he argued. Only if the decision to abandon is collective and explicit can each family be confident that others are also abandoning the practice, alleviating the fear that no single girl or family would be disadvantaged by their decision.

Another important element of the social norm theory was what Mackie referred to as "organized diffusion"—meaning that communities that are abandoning the practice engage others to do the same, thereby increasing the sustainability of a new social norm that rejects female genital cutting, even creating sanctions against those who continue to practice it. It was exactly what was happening in Senegal with people like Demba and Ourèye, who to that day continued their efforts of spreading the news of declarations to hundreds of additional villages across Senegal. And their efforts led to similar efforts by others. Villagers had even started traveling to surrounding African countries to reach their families, and increasingly people from villages in nearby Mali, Guinea-Bissau, Guinea, and The Gambia were crossing the border to take part in public declarations. "I heard so many stories of people willing to make the great effort to travel because they were excited to be part of a positive movement for health and human dignity that included them in the decision-making process," Molly says.

Mackie's concept of organized diffusion also confirmed Molly's belief that what mattered most was not ensuring that every person in every village abandoned the practice immediately, but rather that a growing core group of activists was committed to and making a change with those who mattered most in their networks, at a regional, national, and even international level. "At the outset of the movement, whether in foot-binding or FGC, you don't suddenly find 100 percent abandonment across a country or region," Mackie says. "Rather, abandonment proceeds through clusters in social networks and often follows very predictable patterns. It is then, at the end of the process—when most people know that others are ending a practice—that you find more comprehensive abandonment. That is how the neighborhood-to-neighborhood model worked in China and why you see declarations leading to other

declarations in Senegal and beyond; for the host village it is an end, but
for some of the invited guests it means their work has just begun."

At the end of the three days, the team could not help but focus on
one specific point that Mackie had returned to again and again: what
was happening in Senegal could very well be like the change that led to
the abandonment of foot-binding in China within a single generation. If
things continued as they were going, Molly thought, and the theory was
truly accurate, perhaps they would see similar results in Senegal. Perhaps it really was possible to end the practice of female genital cutting in
Senegal in one generation.

IN 2005, MOLLY WAS invited to a meeting at UNICEF's Innocenti
Research Centre in Florence, Italy, to discuss the Tostan approach to
ending FGC with UNICEF staff throughout Africa—a far cry from the
days when the organization was overlooked in the field. After she finished her presentation, she was approached by Wendy Carson, the child
protection officer for UNICEF in Somalia, a highly impoverished and
volatile nation located on the Horn of Africa.

"I really believe your program would be successful in Somalia,"
Wendy said.

"Somalia?" Molly said. "That's a million miles from Senegal."

"A disadvantage, perhaps," Wendy said. "But with Tostan's respectful
and nonjudgmental approach, I think you could have results similar to
what you're seeing in Senegal. People will welcome this program. So
many women have never had the opportunity to go to school, and as you
may know, they practice female genital cutting at an astounding rate."

Molly was aware of just how dire the situation was for Somali women.
With more than 98 percent of women having undergone the procedure,
Somalia has one of the highest prevalence rates of FGC in Africa. Most
girls are cut before the age of ten, enduring the most invasive and dangerous type, referred to locally as pharaonic infibulation and defined by

the World Health Organization as Type III, meaning that after the removal of the external genitalia, the vaginal lips are sewn shut. This type of cutting is extremely painful and dangerous, often bringing a lifetime of physical suffering. Plus, babies born to mothers who have undergone this procedure have a significantly higher chance of dying at birth. Yet the custom is so widely accepted and the obligation for young girls to have it done so entrenched in Somalia, that even many NGOs advocating for women's health were not promoting an absolute end to the practice but rather a switch to Type I, the *sunna,* meaning the cutting of the clitoris without cutting the labia or sewing shut the lips.

"I honestly believe that people will respond to the way you work," Wendy said. "I feel it in my bones."

"I'm not sure," Molly said. "I know so little about the culture. It would be very difficult."

"How about this?" Wendy said. "Come to Somalia for a few weeks and allow me to set up workshops with the local NGOs. You can explain how you work, and we'll see if they agree with me that this can bring about great change. Please, Molly. Come share your program with Somalia."

DESPITE WENDY'S ENTHUSIASM AND persistence, Molly was hesitant about working in Somalia, knowing it would come with a host of challenges. In the early 1990s, the country was ravaged by a devastating famine, which had killed nearly three hundred thousand people, and a brutal civil war, which had brought an end to the central government and resulted in the creation of three separate zones within Somalia: Northwest Zone, or Somaliland, a territory once under British control and not currently recognized by any nation or international organization; Northeast Zone, or Puntland, once an Italian protectorate but now considered an autonomous state; and South Central Zone, where the city of Mogadishu is located. Violent conflicts between warring factions were frequent, particularly in South Central Zone, including the use of heavy artillery. By 2005, fourteen peace conferences—each an attempt to reestablish some sort of central authority—had all failed.

After giving it a lot of thought, Molly agreed to travel to Somalia for two weeks. "I remained very unsure about bringing the program to a country like Somalia—so far away from Senegal, so different—but I agreed to make this trip," she says. "At the time, I didn't really understand the realities of Somalia. I knew there were turmoil and problems and had read about the security concerns, but when I made the decision to travel there, I didn't truly understand what that meant. When I asked UNICEF staff if it was safe to go, they assured me it would be fine."

It was only later, after she left for her first trip to Somalia on February 6, 2005, that she came to a realization: UNICEF staff members were so convinced that the Tostan approach would work, they weren't telling her exactly what she was getting into.

24

Bàyyil Dex gi Daw
(Let the River Flow)

Molly left for Somalia with Jeremy Hopkins, one of the child protection officers for UNICEF Somalia who would be accompanying her to the seminars. When Molly saw the small, eight-seat plane they would be taking to their first stop in Bossaso, a port city located on the southern coast of the Gulf of Aden in Puntland, her heart sank. While she had traveled a great deal by this point, she'd never grown comfortable flying in small planes.

"How long is the flight?" she asked Jeremy.

"I'm not quite sure," he said as they walked across the windy tarmac to board the plane. "But don't worry. It shouldn't be too long."

Molly slid into a seat behind the cockpit, trying to steady her nerves. Two hours later, she turned to Jeremy. "How much longer?"

"Six hours, perhaps?" he said.

"*Six hours?*"

"We just have a few stops to make."

"You didn't say anything about stops."

"Well, we must refuel at K50 airport and then a quick stop in Somaliland before we arrive in Bossaso," Jeremy said. The K50 airport, he explained, had been put into use after the Aden Adde International Airport in Mogadishu was shut down due to the ongoing war in Somalia.

The UNICEF representative for Somalia, who was also traveling on the small plane, turned around. "Actually, K50 was also recently closed. It reopened just two days ago."

"Why was it shut down?" Molly asked.

"Lots of fighting going on," he said nonchalantly. "But luckily we'll only be there for an hour or so to refuel."

The news did nothing to calm Molly's nerves, nor did the fact that she had begun to notice the two pilots checking and rechecking what seemed to be a map book, which seemed strange. *How silly to be concerned,* she thought. *Certainly they've made this flight many times.*

"I'm sure you've made this flight many times before, right?" she eventually leaned forward to ask over the deafening noise of the engine.

"Not quite," one of the pilots yelled back. "This is our first time to Somalia. We're trying to figure out where we're going."

Before long, Molly noticed the plane descending, and one of the pilots alerted them that they'd finally arrived at K50. From her window, Molly spotted what she guessed was the terminal—a crude wooden shack near a dirt path, which had been cut through what seemed to be the absolute middle of nowhere: a vast expanse of dry land dotted only with a few scraggly shrubs and a herd of about a hundred camels strolling lazily along the makeshift landing strip.

They climbed from the small plane into the hot, dusty air. A few minutes later, the pilot came over to the UNICEF representative. "Looks like we won't be leaving anytime soon," he said.

"What? Why not?" the UNICEF representative asked. "We have important meetings in Bossaso and can't afford to be delayed."

"There's no fuel here."

"What do you mean?"

"We'd been told they'd have fuel waiting for us, but there isn't any. I'm sorry, sir."

Noticing the look of concern on Molly's face, the pilot turned to her and pointed at the nearby shed. "Why don't you wait inside the terminal in the executive lounge," he joked. "Maybe get a cappuccino."

Molly managed a shallow laugh as she looked around the airfield where civilian men loitered about, machine guns strapped to their thin bodies. Walking to the shack, she took the wide piece of cloth she was using as a head cover and laid it on the sandy ground. As she sat in the dry African air, fighting her fear and panic, a memory came to mind. As a young girl, she had often found solace during afternoons spent at the Spring Hill Cemetery a few blocks from her house in Danville. The cemetery was a large and bucolic setting, and she sometimes spent time sitting at what she found to be the most unusual grave, that of a woman named Minnehaha, who Molly guessed was Native American and had died in 1913. Minnehaha had been buried next to her husband, a man named Vernan H. Stark, and as a ten-year-old girl, Molly loved envisioning how this woman might have spent her days in the then-sleepy village of Danville, Illinois. Sitting on the soft earth near Minnehaha's grave, she would try to picture what her own life would be as an adult, wondering if she'd get the chance to find the adventure she craved even at such a young age.

Looking around her, she never could have imagined this. Remembering the serenity she'd felt as a child, she tried to manage the fear that threatened to seize her. She was not accustomed to feeling this way. "Not once in all of my years in Africa had I ever felt unsafe," she says. "But that afternoon, sitting on the hot packed earth at that desolate airstrip, so far away from anything I had experienced in Senegal or any other African country I had visited, knowing that I was going to a place considered very dangerous—I understood that this was an important and decisive moment for me. Would I give in to this fear and beg to go home, or could I just accept the idea that whatever was going to happen would happen?" The voice of her father, Al, came back to her, offering a bit of advice he liked to share: "Don't build dams in your river, Molly. Allow the water to flow and go where it takes you. If you do, you will be okay."

"I decided to take my father's advice," she says. "If I was going to face new challenges on this trip—even if I was going to die here—so be it."

Another plane arrived a few hours later, and they eventually made it to Bossaso by evening. The descent into Bossaso was stunning. The fading sun bathed the rugged mountains and turquoise sea in golden light. The landing strip itself stopped just short of a small beach, and the airport building was a refreshingly solid structure after the wooden shack at K50.

Molly and the others were met by a few drivers. As soon as they disembarked from the plane and had their passports stamped at a small shed near the airstrip, they were told to hurry to the waiting cars.

"Why the rush?" Molly asked Jeremy as she ran behind the others.

"We're staying at the UNICEF compound, and there's a strict 6:00 P.M. curfew," he said. "For safety reasons, we aren't allowed on the streets after 6:00, and the doors to the compound are locked then. If we don't make it there in time, we won't get in."

A nondescript rental car waited for them. Climbing inside, Molly noticed a piece of thick fur lining the dashboard and plastic flowers hung throughout. It was quite a contrast from the shiny white UNICEF Land Cruisers she'd grown accustomed to during trips to other African countries. Jeremy explained that UNICEF staff in Somalia never use official UNICEF vehicles, because the chance was too great they'd be hijacked. "It's best to stay under the radar," he said.

Molly took a deep breath and concentrated on the view from her window. Women covered from head to toe walked along the dusty street, with only their eyes peeking out from behind their dark coverings. They drove down the dusty streets of Bossaso, lined with colorful shops selling all manner of goods, from tinned tuna to a dazzling array of mobile phones. On street corners, money changers sat beside make-shift tables piled high with bundles of Somali currency. Traffic was light, and donkeys loitered at the side of the road waiting to take their next load to another dusty destination.

The UNICEF compound was simple but comfortable, with rooms where personnel slept and a dining room where they took their meals. Molly had grown to greatly admire the UNICEF staff working under such conditions, knowing the monotony they endured having to remain in the compound each evening, unable to enjoy evening strolls through the city and living with constant concerns about security. On her third night in Bossaso, over a dinner of spaghetti, she watched CNN, where it was reported that earlier that day a thirty-nine-year-old senior producer for the BBC named Kate Peyton had been shot and killed by members of an extremist group outside her hotel in Mogadishu, the capital of Somalia.

The news of Kate Peyton's death shook Molly deeply. Over the next two weeks, during her travels to the cities of Hargeisa in Somaliland and then to Jowhar in South Central Zone, just fifty-five miles from Moga-dishu, she had to remember her decision to remain unafraid. It wasn't always easy.

While in Bossaso, Molly came down with a cold and needed to go to a local pharmacy for medicine. She was brought to a large market with an array of stalls filling a dusty square, each with a ramshackle shade structure providing some respite from the harsh sun. Crowds of people in search of a bargain picked through the piles of new and secondhand clothes next to vendors selling luggage, cooking pots, and sneakers. Inside the pharmacy, Molly noticed everyone looked at her. Children stopped and pointed, and as she walked back toward the car after making her purchase, stopping to admire a table covered with the beau-tiful, bright cloth worn by Somali women, she was followed by a woman who started yelling a word Molly didn't understand: "Gaal! Gaal!"

"Oh, hello!" Molly said, wanting to be polite.

Jeremy came and took Molly's elbow. "Time to go," he said.

"What's going on?"

"Just get in the car," he said. "Hurry."

"I thought perhaps they hadn't seen an American for some time," Molly recalls, "and I think I also must have looked quite strange to them in my Senegalese *boubou*. It was only once we were back in the safety of the UNICEF compound that Jeremy admitted that *gaal* is the word for infidel. Though it's used frequently for tourists, Jeremy hadn't felt comfortable. It's probably better he hadn't told me that on the spot."

Each evening everyone made certain that Molly was back at the UNICEF offices where she was staying. At the UNICEF compound in Jowhar, Jeremy announced that a well-known warlord would be coming to the city the next day and stopping at the compound next door. Molly couldn't resist. The next morning, she stood at the gate, hoping to catch a glimpse. She finally spotted the long procession of trucks arriving. On the back of each pickup truck was a man holding a machine gun. (Some months later, the warlord would return to occupy the UNICEF compound and force the staff to leave at gunpoint.)

But all the danger and fear was forgotten when it came to the people Molly met in the three seminars and the villages she visited. During the seminars, representatives from local NGOs expressed their interest in the Tostan model and their eagerness for it to come to Somalia. After speaking about the number of villages in Senegal that had declared an end to FGC, she was often pulled aside by women. They wanted her to understand what, exactly, it meant to be a woman here. They spoke specifically about their experience with FGC.

"We understand that the way it is done here is far more dangerous and has many worse consequences than how they do it in Senegal," one woman said. "After they cut us, the wound is sometimes sewn shut with thorns pulled from the acacia bush. It is so painful. I suffered so much and then had to watch my daughters go through this same procedure."

Another woman shyly told Molly that her daughter had been living in great pain since her procedure; it had gotten so bad, a doctor had recommended she be defibulated—cut open and cleaned out. Afraid she would be rejected by the community and not be considered for marriage, the girl had refused the procedure and continued to suffer. "You cannot imagine how desperate I feel, knowing that my daughter is always in pain," her mother said.

Molly hoped to hear more from the women, but she knew better than to bring up the subject during her visits to villages. Instead, she remained focused on assessing the interest in education and how the Tostan model might be applied. In every village, she was met with great enthusiasm. In one, Molly sat in a shaded circle near the banks of a river. UNICEF had been implementing a health and nutrition program here. As she listened to the villagers talk of their experiences, she asked, "How many villages are in this area?"

"About forty."

"And with how many would you consult if you were going to make a decision about an important family issue?" Molly asked. Everyone started talking at once, naming several villages where their relatives lived.

"We would never think of doing anything of consequence without including our families in our discussions. Any decisions we made without them would not be followed."

Molly felt Demba Diawara's presence as she connected the threads of the pattern; identifying the extended social network and including its members in discussions was just as important here as it was in Senegal.

After two weeks in Somalia, Molly prepared to return home to Dakar. On the plane ride back, she replayed the women's stories in her head. Her hesitation about working in Somalia remained, but then she would think about one experience in particular that had left her deeply touched. At the end of one of the seminars, a woman from a local NGO had approached her.

"We really need Tostan here," she said.

"To be honest, I'm not sure," Molly admitted. "It will be very difficult for us to come here."

"What do you mean?"

"It's so far. It will come with logistical challenges we've never faced before."

The woman looked at Molly with a stern expression. "Sorry, did I hear you right? We get our genitals chopped off and have spent a life of suffering. The same thing is happening to thousands of girls here each year. And you're telling me you are not going to come to Somalia and help us because it's too far away from you? Because it's inconvenient?"

25

Pas-pas (Perseverance)

In 2007, Tostan was awarded the Conrad N. Hilton Humanitarian Prize. With a cash award of $1.5 million, it is the largest humanitarian prize in the world. By this time, 2,643 villages, affecting approximately 2.1 million people, had publicly declared an end to FGC, and the Tostan staff had grown to 108 full-time employees.

Judy Miller, the director of the Conrad N. Hilton Foundation, which bestows the prize, came to Senegal to observe the Tostan program. "I was blown away," she says of her time spent in the villages, where she spoke with residents and observed crowds of girls holding pictures depicting the numerous human rights they now knew they had. "I didn't believe you could teach someone in a remote village who had never gone to school that just because their country had signed a paper, it could change their lives. But I kept seeing it. It was real."

In one village, a young woman explained her new understanding of her right to be free from violence. "I shared this with my husband, and he no longer beats me," she said. Judy was skeptical, and she asked to speak to the woman's husband.

"What she tells you is true," he said. "My father beat my mother, and

I thought that was what I was supposed to do. But now that my wife has learned about her rights, I don't do that anymore."

"But what made you change your mind? How did you come to accept the idea that you needed to change?"

The man thought awhile before responding. "Well, along with her rights, she also learned about her responsibilities. She now also works to keep the peace. Together, we have made a happy life for ourselves at home."

It was perhaps Judy's visits to villages where Tostan classes had *not* been established that helped her truly understand Tostan's impact. Here, the women remained in the background. When Judy tried to speak to them, most were silent, far too uncomfortable to look her in the eye or answer her questions. The opposite was true in the Tostan villages. She met dynamic women willing to share details of their lives, to speak their minds. In many, a large chalkboard had been erected, outlining the projects currently under way: establishing a health clinic, village cleanup days, creating income-generating projects to support the local women. "I've traveled all over Africa," Judy says. "What I observed in Senegal, in the Tostan villages, it was extraordinary."

The humanitarian award was bestowed at a private dinner ceremony at the Waldorf Astoria Hotel in New York City, and Molly had invited Ourèye Sall to accompany her. Before accepting the award from United Nations Secretary General Ban Ki-moon, Molly invited Ourèye to speak. "I am sixty years old now and had my first child at fifteen," Ourèye told the crowd, pulling her scarf more securely over her head. "I have cut many more girls than I can count. It is only when I got into the Tostan classes and started studying the women's health module that I began to question this tradition. . . . I was insulted and ridiculed in the beginning, but things have become easier." She went on to speak about the number of years she had been working, of her continued efforts, to that day, to travel throughout Senegal to convince more villages to join the movement.

After she had finished, Molly spoke. "People often ask me, 'How is it possible that such ancient traditional practices are ended in such a relatively short amount of time? What is the secret?' The secret is that in our extended family we are united not by what makes us all obviously different—black, white, American, European—but by the essence of what we all have in common: members of the same human family with a deep awareness of our common responsibility for our fellow human beings. . . . Together we dare to hope, to love, and to care. And together we are all, along with you, creating a better world for tomorrow."

When Molly finished speaking, she and Ourèye did not walk off the stage. They danced.

"It was unforgettable," Judy Miller says. "Listening to this, I kept thinking about a comment made by the Nobel Peace Prize winner Muhammad Yunus, who had served on the jury that chose Tostan. 'If this work is as it seems and can spread beyond Senegal to countries that are more difficult to work in, this could change Africa.' "

MOLLY HAS REMAINED DETERMINED to make this true.

In 2005, a few months after her first trip to Somalia, she returned to Nairobi to create, in partnership with UNICEF, a pilot project entitled Ending FGC in Somalia, through which Tostan classes were established in forty-two communities in the three zones of Somalia over a three-year period. Over two thousand villagers eventually enrolled in the program, and more than thirty thousand people were reached through the process of organized diffusion.

In October 2008, Molly returned to Hargeisa, her fifth trip to Somalia in two years. She was eager to see for herself the transformations that had taken place, and as she'd hoped, she heard stories of remarkable change already taking place in many of the communities where Tostan classes had been established. The facilitators reported new dialogue occurring between men and women around issues never before discussed, and women were now actively participating in, and even organizing, community discussions. In a village called Araf, the Tostan Community Management Committee helped facilitate a series of intergenerational discussions between teenagers and the adults of the community to promote ending child marriage. "We knew that being promised in marriage so young was not good for young women," a teen boy named Moustapha told Molly during a visit to his village, "but we were lacking the courage and the occasion to discuss the subject. Now we are able to talk about it without risk." In Ayah, a neighborhood in the city of Hargeisa, the women of the Tostan class organized a movement to encourage systematic child vaccination. In Dongoroyo in Puntland, the entire village, wearing Tostan T-shirts, organized a massive cleanup of the town square and surrounding streets.

Molly was most heartened to hear that women in the Tostan communities were coming to a greater understanding of their human rights. One facilitator from the South Central Zone reported an unbelievable occurrence: A man in his small town had previously imposed himself as the mayor in the community. But after participating in the class, the mayor himself called for new elections and a woman had been elected, marking the first time that a woman had held any position of responsibility in the community.

"Is she doing a good job as mayor?" Molly asked.

"Of course," he replied. "Everyone has always known that she was the most competent person for this role in the community, but it took participation in the Tostan class to allow them to be able to understand that it was now acceptable to elect her."

On her third day back in Somalia, Molly went to visit a small village called Arabsiyo, located about an hour from the Tostan office in Hargeisa. She was accompanied by supervisors and the ever-present armed guard. Along the way, one of the supervisors looked out the window and pointed.

"See those hills? We think that's where members of al Qaeda live."

Molly wasn't sure if he was kidding.

"Don't worry," he said, noticing her look of concern. "They're only looking for Americans."

"But I'm an American."

"Oh, of course. I keep forgetting you're not Senegalese."

Upon her arrival in the community, every member of the class was there to meet her, singing beautiful Somali songs they had written, and eager to talk about the changes in their village and their new participation in the activities of the community. Four women explained they were running for office in the national assembly in the upcoming elections.

"This is because of our Tostan classes," one said. "Previously we didn't even realize we had the right to vote. Now we are candidates. It was not so long ago that I wouldn't have spoken in a group. Now I am campaigning, promising that I will work to promote health and education in our community."

What surprised Molly the most was how many women were eager to speak about their work to bring an end to the practice of FGC. One woman named Shamis, a grandmother from the village of Arabsiyo, spoke with passion about the great suffering women undergo not only during the cutting, but also on their wedding night. As she explained, the traditional cutter must come and cut open the new bride, who is often so traumatized by what awaits her that she must be held down. Despite her pain afterward, she is expected to consummate the marriage that night.

Shamis was in tears while relaying the story. But she quickly wiped them away. "We have finally found a way to end this practice," she said. "And it is because of Tostan. Many of us women are now spending our days traveling to the surrounding villages. With many of my friends, we are always talking, talking, talking!"

"What do you say?" Molly asked.

"We explain our human rights and the health consequences of the practice," Shamis said.

"Are people responding well?"

"Not always," Shamis said. "But we will not stop. We are determined to do what they have done in your country. We are determined to convince our people to end this practice in Somaliland."

MOLLY'S WORK IN SOMALIA would continue to come with great risks. Two weeks into this trip, she was invited to the presidential palace in Hargeisa to meet with the wife of the president of Somaliland, who told Molly how much she supported the program and appreciated the Tostan approach, promising further involvement and a vow to visit classes in the communities.

The next day, Molly was meant to go into town for a meeting with the Ministry of the Family, but she received a call from an American reporter who was researching an article on FGC. While on the call, Molly heard a loud explosion from outside. The facilitators came running down the stairs from their training session, confused about what had happened. In the distance, they heard another explosion.

"Wait just a minute," Molly said into the phone. "I think there might be *bombs* exploding outside."

"Just one more quick thing—"

Molly hung up the phone just as a third explosion went off. From the window, she saw clouds of smoke billowing in the morning air.

Guillaume Debar, a young French volunteer who worked in the Dakar office and had come to assist with the training, appeared behind her.

"What is happening?" he asked.

"I have no idea. But move away from the window."

A few minutes later, her cell phone rang. It was her contact at the Ministry of the Family telling her to stay put. The explosions she'd heard were a series of three suicide car bombs detonated at three different locations—the president's palace, where Molly had been the day before; the Ethiopian Embassy; and the United Nations Development Program (UNDP) office, in charge of all security for the United Nations.

"It's very serious," her contact said. "Many people have been killed or seriously injured. Remain inside."

The Tostan team remained locked in the office for several hours, too afraid to venture outside for more news. Many of the staff from South Central Zone were particularly concerned they might be in danger, as it was being rumored that people from the south were responsible for the bombs. That evening, Molly received a call from a UNICEF security agent in Hargeisa.

"I don't want to have to tell you this, but I think you and Guillaume Debar should leave the Tostan office immediately," he said.

"How come?"

He hesitated. "As white people, we think you create a real risk for the Africans in the room. It's best for everyone if you leave." He suggested they somehow find their way to the nearby Mansour Hotel, where staff from the UN and other international NGOs had gathered.

Molly hung up the phone and quietly explained the situation to Guillaume. As evening fell over Hargeisa, she and Guillaume slipped as quietly as they could to the mostly deserted street below, flagging down the first taxi they saw. They climbed into the car and slid down to the floor of the backseat. Molly took her wide scarf and covered them both as much as she could.

"Keep it over your head," she said to Guillaume.

Shaken, they arrived at the Mansour Hotel. Dozens of UN staff had gathered in a large conference room, where it was being announced that plans were in place to evacuate all UN personnel to Kenya the next day.

Molly approached the speaker. "We need to get out as well," she said. "Can we be included on the plane?"

"I'm sorry," he said. "We only have room for UN personnel."

Molly felt desperate. "Can you please make an exception? Can you find room for one more?"

"One more?"

"Yes. I'm with a young man who is only twenty-one years old. Please. I want him to get home."

"It's doubtful, Molly."

"Please," she begged. "See what you can do."

The next morning, after a sleepless night, Molly and Guillaume were taken with the UN staff to the Ambassador Hotel nearer the airport. The plane for Kenya was scheduled to leave that afternoon at four o'clock. A staff member arrived to read the names of the people allowed on the flight, and Molly's heart sank when Guillaume's was not on the list. She spoke to anyone who would listen to her pleas to find a spot for Guillaume. Eventually her persistence paid off. Guillaume was given passage out.

"What are you going to do?" he asked her before walking out to meet the UN bus to the airport.

"I'm not sure," Molly said. "I'll stay at the hotel until I find another way out." Someone had brought her bags from the UNICEF compound where they'd been staying, and she took them inside the hotel. Unsure how she would eventually find her way back to Senegal, she booked a room, telling the clerk that it could be several days, maybe even weeks, that she'd need to stay. She then walked outside and took a seat on the hot steps in a garden overlooking the city of Hargeisa.

It's okay, she thought. *This is the work I chose to do, and I will find a way to cope.* She thought about her meeting at the presidential palace the previous day, just twenty-four hours before the bomb had exploded there. Everyone who had been outside waiting to enter had been killed. She shook her head in sadness and wished she could call her daughter. *Zoé, I do hope you will one day understand if anything happens to me,* she thought. *I'm so grateful to have had you and your love in my life.*

She saw the bus preparing to leave and walked over to say her goodbyes. She was about to head back into the hotel when she heard a woman calling her name from the bus.

"Molly, Molly! You can come, Molly!" she yelled. "We found another seat on the plane. Hurry! Get your bags. We have to go."

26

Jant bi Dina Fenk
(The Sun Will Rise)

The sun rose over Dakar as Molly walked the path along the beach, taking in the vast views of the Atlantic. She and Zoé, who had returned to Senegal after graduating from Concordia College and now lived with Molly, typically walked this path together each morning, hoping for an hour or so of exercise. But today, Zoé had wanted to sleep in and Molly was alone. Enjoying the calm of the morning and the salty air, she stopped to appreciate the view—the very same view she'd first encountered thirty-five years ago at the age of twenty-four—and tried to absorb the news she'd just received from a staff member in Hargeisa.

Two public declarations were going to take place in Somaliland and Puntland. The first was scheduled in a few weeks' time, on October 6, 2009; the second, just a few weeks later.

Molly's cell phone rang, startling her. It was her sister, Diane. She was preparing to come to Senegal and was calling to see what Molly wanted her to bring from the United States. Diane was working in the interdisciplinary arts and sciences program at the University of Washington Bothell, and she and her husband, Michael, came to Senegal every other year—not just to visit Molly and Zoé, but also to volunteer for Tostan. Two years earlier, Diane had spent her sabbatical in Dakar, writing about Tostan's work on human rights education and had continued to publish articles on the topic.

Molly interrupted her sister. "Diane, it happened."

"What are you talking about? What happened?"

"In Somaliland. They're doing it. They're having a public declaration. Thousands of people are ending the practice."

"Molly. Are you kidding?"

"No, I just got the call." Molly felt the breath catch in her throat. "They did it. The women there . . . they did it."

"You had something to do with it too, of course," Diane said. "How did it happen?"

How *did* it happen? Looking at the ocean, Molly thought back to the mornings, thirty-five years earlier, when she had stood at this same spot, wondering what to make of her six months in Africa. Since then, she had gone on to travel the world. She'd met presidents, first ladies, famous artists, and thinkers. She had won many awards and received great recognition. But most of all, she'd had the great opportunity of doing this work.

When she'd started, all she knew was that she desperately wanted to bring education to people from whom it had been kept, to hopefully change the lives of the 300 villagers of Saam Njaay. She never could have imagined it would become what it did. Nearly 3,500 villages in Senegal had declared an end to FGC. So had 58 villages in The Gambia, 43 in Guinea-Bissau, 332 in Guinea, 7 in Mali, and now 34 villages in Somalia.

She had made many mistakes. She had, at times, considered giving up. It was too difficult to be the female director of an NGO working in Africa. She had often doubted her abilities and felt deep frustration trying to balance her life as both the director of Tostan and a mother to Zoé. And yet she had persevered.

Why? It wasn't only a belief in herself; it was a belief in education. During her last trip to Somaliland a facilitator named Abdi had asked Molly what it was that she wanted to be remembered for a hundred years from now. Molly thought hard about her answer.

"I want to be remembered most for having made empowering education—particularly knowledge of human rights and responsibilities—accessible to millions of people at the grassroots level, helping them achieve their full potential."

"From where does your commitment to education come?" Abdi asked.

Molly didn't hesitate. "My mother."

Ann had died two years earlier, after a long battle with Alzheimer's. In the months leading up to her death, Molly frequently spoke with her on the phone, although Ann often hadn't any idea who Molly was. Even so, Molly took the opportunity to thank Ann for all she'd done for her as a mother. As she told Abdi, she knew that she was led to this work because of what Ann had instilled in her—a deep belief in education, unwavering persistence, and an unceasing willingness to create something better for herself and others.

"I'm crying," Diane said, when Molly shared this story with her.

"I know," Molly replied. "So am I."

"You know, but I'm having this thought right now . . ."

Molly knew what it was. She was thinking the same thing.

"Mom would be so proud."

EPILOGUE

New York
January 2013

As of this writing, over five thousand Senegalese villages have declared an end to the practice of female genital cutting in their communities. Drawing on this momentum, in February 2010, the government of Senegal announced a national action plan to end FGC by 2015, adopting a strategy based on the community-led, human rights approach developed by Tostan. It's fair to say that the end of FGC in Senegal is now in sight. Similar efforts are currently under way in the seven other countries where the Tostan program is in place. And on December 20, 2012, the same day that forty communities in the West African nation of Guinea-Bissau publicly declared their commitment to respect all human rights, including an end to FGC, the UN General Assembly passed an international resolution that calls for intensified global efforts to end the practice worldwide.

But this historic grassroots movement to end FGC in Africa is not the end of the Tostan story. Rather, it may be just the beginning.

During my visits to Senegal while writing this book, I knew that I was witnessing an unfolding tale on the power of human rights education. As I traveled throughout the country, I spoke with villagers who are using what they have learned through the Tostan program to address many other issues critical to the well-being of their communities. I saw community facilitators using an innovative program developed through Tostan to teach literacy through SMS texting. I met African grandmothers who, with Tostan's support, had left their villages for the first time to travel to the Barefoot College in India to learn to construct and install solar panels, bringing power and light to their remote communities. I met a Tostan team bringing together extended family networks across borders to work on promoting peace and security throughout West Africa. And I spoke with members of Community Management Committees who, after completing the Tostan program, officially registered as their own independent organizations and are now successfully running their own projects.

Molly's current obsession is something new entirely, the results of which may bring about a change as extraordinary as the end of FGC.

In 2009, in eleven regions of Senegal, a study was conducted on the reading levels of children who had attended three years of formal school. The results were highly disheartening: only 7 percent of girls and 11 percent of boys evaluated were found capable of reading at a minimum level.

Many attempts have been made over the past decades to improve the Senegalese school system—including reforming the school curriculum, constructing new school buildings, and increasing teacher training. But as the study showed, these attempts have not been working, and Molly has set out to understand if something that is essential to helping children learn better is being overlooked.

Through her experience, she knew that children enter school at the age of six with many disadvantages. A majority of rural Senegalese children have never been exposed to written letters or words in their village environment. Few have ever seen or held a book, and fewer still speak a word of French, the language in which classes are taught. Furthermore, since most parents in Senegal have extremely limited education themselves, they often feel inadequate in helping their children with schoolwork.

In 2010, Molly enlisted the help of a creative emeritus professor from Tufts University, Dr. Marian Zeitlin, who had spent more than forty years researching best practices for supporting early childhood development in Africa. With Dr. Zeitlin's help, Molly came to understand that another significant, though highly underreported, phenomenon is at play—a belief system prevalent in some parts of West Africa that discourages parents from actively engaging with their infants and young children through speech. Doing so, it is believed, can be dangerous to a child. Through interviews with parents and other caretakers, Molly, Dr. Zeitlin, and a team of Tostan staff found that mothers who talked frequently to their infants were often ridiculed for doing so. They were called crazy for speaking to "nobody," and some expressed fears that speech could summon evil spirits wishing to steal a baby or cause him or her harm. When mothers were encouraged to increase the amount they speak to their children, especially to children from birth to three years, when the brain develops most rapidly, some said they were afraid to do so, citing a belief that a child who talks before it walks will develop poorly. They also expressed concern that speaking freely or frequently to children under eight years of age may cause them to become "too intelligent," cunning, or dishonest.

Armed with this new understanding, and knowing that change would not come about by simply telling parents to speak more frequently to their children, Molly became committed to finding a way to apply social norm theory to help parents more clearly understand the importance of cognitive stimulation for children, beginning at birth. For the majority of the past two years, she has spent time researching this issue and meeting with authorities on neuroscience and cognitive development to better understand—and be able to explain—how talking to children will help them become stronger learners.

The result is a new five-month module that Molly and her team have developed with support from the William and Flora Hewlett Foundation. It is designed to help newly literate parents who have been through the Tostan program introduce their infants to learning with colorfully illustrated and engaging children's books in national languages, much like those she had developed at the Démb ak Tey children's center so many years earlier. The books will not only reinforce Tostan participants' reading skills and help children understand what reading is and how enjoyable it can be, but will also serve as a tool to encourage adults' interactions with young children. Included in the module is the latest information on brain development, allowing for in-depth dialogue on how to change the social norms that discourage speaking with children. The module will be implemented in 232 communities that have completed the three-year Tostan program, reaching 11,500 parents and adolescents and improving the learner outcomes of approximately 30,000 children. The program will reach thousands more through Tostan's organized diffusion model.

I was with Molly when she presented this new module to staff during a retreat held at the Tostan Training Center outside Thiès. The information was enthusiastically received by staff members—many of whom admitted that they had avoided talking too much to their babies on the advice of their own parents. That evening, as we left the seminar and drove to the beach house, I asked Molly what she expects will come of this new module. She was silent for a while, eventually pulling to a stop in front of a local bakery. She'd been there earlier that morning to buy bread but had forgotten to bring her wallet, and she ran in to pay. When she returned to the car, she was serious.

"I truly believe this new module has the potential to spark a revolution in learning for young children in Senegal," she said.

There's no shortage of people who agree that Tostan's efforts can continue to have a significant and lasting impact on African communities, bringing about generational change in just a few years. As Jim Greenbaum, a longtime Tostan supporter and board member, told me, "Tostan is the only organization I've found that can do it all. Want to end FGC? Tostan can do that. Want to stop war? Tostan can do that too. It may sound strange to say, but if Tostan is remembered in the history books only for the end of FGC, it will be a tragedy. If we were to get the support needed to take this model to thousands more communities, this is a model that can transform Africa."

WHEN I MET MOLLY, I didn't know just how personal this work would become, but while writing this book, I discovered I was pregnant, with a girl. While I know that my daughter will, thankfully, never have to face many of the hardships women in rural Africa confront on a day-to-day basis, I also know that Molly's work is making a better world for girls everywhere. During a visit to Los Angeles, I accompanied Molly to a talk she gave before a women's group. After Molly's presentation, a woman raised her hand with a question. "This sounds crazy," she said, "but can you bring the Tostan program here? Women in America—and our girls, especially—could really benefit from what you have done in Senegal. I know that you get a lot of attention for helping to end FGC, but what you've really done is help women realize their full potential. We could use some of that here."

I thought about this during my last trip to Senegal, at twenty-eight weeks pregnant. Molly and I spent the day in the village of Malicounda Bambara, and I was introduced to a girl of fourteen. Her mother was pregnant with her in 1997, when the women of her village declared an end to FGC in their community, and she was the first girl born into a world where cutting was no longer expected.

"What's your name?" I asked the girl, after she shyly approached to shake my hand.

"Aminata Sañ-Sañ," she said.

Molly smiled. "Sañ-Sañ is the word for human rights," she said. "They named her Aminata human rights."

Later that afternoon, as we drove out of the village and back toward Molly's beach house, Molly popped in the Sam Cooke CD we'd been listening to incessantly the past few days. The song "A Change Is Gonna Come" began—a song released in 1964 that became an anthem of sorts for the civil rights movement in the United States. Just as she had done every other time this song played, Molly stopped talking, turned up the volume nearly as high as it could go, and sang along.

It's been a long, a long time coming

But I know a change is gonna come. Oh yes it will.

Listening to these words, I thought of Aminata Sañ-Sañ and of the future of my own daughter, knowing that despite the fact that they would never meet and that they would grow up with very different experiences, both their lives would benefit from what Molly has accomplished, from her contributions to the world. Molly turned the car down the main road that led to the Atlantic Ocean. In front of us the sun was setting, nearly equal with the horizon, and for a moment, it seemed as if she were steering us straight into the sun.

ACKNOWLEDGMENTS

I am indebted to many people for their help with this book, but none more than Molly. She took time away from running Tostan to spend weeks talking to me, traveling with me, introducing me to the people and culture of Senegal, answering my questions, and serving as a wonderful host—all while being a true inspiration and real joy. I'll always feel particularly grateful for the fact that she trusted me with her story.

I'd also like to thank Jeff Skoll, Mark Tauber, Sally Osberg, and Sandy Herz for trusting me to be a part of the first book published in partnership with HarperCollins and the Skoll Foundation. My editor, Jeanette Perez, helped make this book as good as the story behind it and was always a calm, supportive, and discerning voice. Thanks to my agent, Kris Dahl at ICM, for continuing to support me in this work.

Very special thanks to Diane Gillespie. She spent countless hours providing background information, expert editing, and wonderful insight every step of the way. For their help with reading the manuscript, and the time they put into this project, I'd like to thank Gail Kaneb and Gannon Gillespie. Anna Zoé Williams was not only a great translator, but she's just so lovely and a real joy to be around.

Demba Diawara spent many hours with me, and it was a true privilege to get to know a man like him. Ourèye Sall and the women of the Malicounda Bambara Tostan class were such an inspiration to me, and I'd like to particularly thank Kerthio Diawara and her mother, Maimouna Traore, who passed away during the writing of this book.

Thanks to all the members of the Tostan staff and family, especially Khalidou Sy, Dame Guéye, Ibrahima Giroux, Jennifer Balde, Marième Diop, Baye Samba Diop, and Cheikh Seydil Moctar Mbacké.

Jim Greenbaum helped me put the story into context and was a wonderful, charming host on many occasions. Gerry Mackie provided valuable insight and background material. Caty Gordon was an astute and skilled researcher, and Hayley Downs and Lisa Selin Davis were kind enough to lend their editing expertise and overall support. Thanks to Judy Miller for answering my questions, sending me boxes of information, and providing a home in Los Angeles. Special thanks to Tess Ulrich. Thanks also to Ndeye Soukeye Guéye, Anne Charlotte Ringquist, Nafissatou Diop, Francesca Moneti, Mike Gillespie, Ann Veneman, Maria Gabriella De Vita, Samir Sobhy, Jeremy Hopkins, Christian Schneider, Claudia Berger, Duusu Konaté, Cheikh Diop, Michael Carolan, Carrie Dailey, Connie Jean Amirah, and Lois MacKinney.

Giving birth to a child three months prior to finishing a book is not easy and wouldn't have been possible without the help of Team Noelle, especially John and Judy Molloy and Sharanah Drakes, who occupied my daughter while I wrote in the other room. Extra special thanks to my parents, Bob and Moira Krum, Mark and Megan Molloy, Chris Ryan, Bill Ryan, and Jeanne Lightfoot for their general support. And of course, none of this would be possible or worthwhile if it weren't for my husband, Mark Ryan—my constant support, closest friend, and most trusted adviser, who manages to make everything so much better. And finally, to our daughter, Noelle Molloy Ryan, who reminds me each day why it's so important to tell stories like this one and who was kind enough to sleep through most nights so that her mom could write.